HOMES
OF NON-LEAGUE
FOOTBALL

HOMES
OF NON-LEAGUE
FOOTBALL

Peter Miles

TEMPUS

First published 2002

Tempus Publishing Limited
The Mill, Brimscombe Port,
Stroud, Gloucestershire, GL5 2QG

British Library Cataloguing in Publication Data.
A catalogue record for this book is available from the British Library.

ISBN 0 7524 2723 7

Typesetting and origination by Tempus Publishing Limited
Printed in Great Britain by Midway Colour Print, Wiltshire

ACKNOWLEDGEMENTS

Although all the photos contained within are mine, I wish to place on record the influence of such esteemed ground photographers as Mike Floate, Kerry Miller, Gavin Ellis, Jon Weaver, Vince Taylor, Paul Claydon, Dave Twydell, Colin Peel and perhaps the originator of the genre, Bob Lilliman. They have all done so much to promote grounds photography not only as a social record but also as an art form. I would also like to thank my wife, Cathy, for her much appreciated typing skills and for putting up with numerous unscheduled detours over the years when my inbuilt football-ground radar has begun to twitch. Finally, I would like to thank James Howarth and all the staff at Tempus for taking this project on and not dismissing it as the ramblings of a madman!

COVER ILLUSTRATIONS

Front cover (left to right from the top): Bishop Auckland, Exmouth, Falmouth, Stockbridge, March Town, Marlow, Garforth Town, Gainsborough Trinity, Sutton Coldfield.

Rear cover (top to bottom): Stourbridge, Windsor & Eton, Guiseley.

STATISTICAL NOTE

The leagues quoted are competitions competed in during the 2002/03 season. During research for this book I have found that several record attendances quoted in contemporary reference books have been exceeded or indeed exaggerated. Figures quoted here are believed to be as near as possible to the correct figures.

INTRODUCTION

Over the last 20 years this country has seen its footballing heritage disappear at an alarming rate. Nowhere has this erosion been felt greater than outside of the elite 92 Football League clubs. Non-League football grounds have been swallowed up by supermarkets, retail parks and multiplex cinemas. The resident clubs, lacking the financial clout to resist, have been forced to relocate to bland, characterless, modern out-of-town venues. While these new venues are undoubtedly more than adequate, the clubs have, in many ways, been divested of their history and identity. Similarly, in a bid to conform to the game's hierarchy, most modern stadia are built to strict ground-grading criteria and, as a result, are virtual carbon copies of each other.

The last two decades has seen us lose such historic and architecturally important venues as Champion Hill (Dulwich Hamlet), The Bull Ground (Sittingbourne), Grundy Hill (Horwich RMI) and Canal Street (Runcorn), to name but a few. In the near future more will be added to the already extensive list such as Kingsway (Bishop Auckland), Sandy Lane (Tooting & Mitcham United) and the world's oldest senior football ground – Northwich Victoria's Drill Field. All are to be razed to the ground to be replaced by brand new venues.

For many years now I have been photographing non-League grounds and my extensive collection has become almost a social history of the nation's favourite sport. James Howarth and his staff at Tempus have given me the opportunity to present my collection in book form, which also catalogues my footballing travels over the last two decades. For this opportunity, I thank him immensely.

To give this book some structure, I have included all 221 clubs from the upper two levels of the non-League 'Pyramid'. From the numerous regional and county leagues that feed into the lowest levels of the second tier, I have chosen historically interesting or particularly photogenic grounds, as well as my own particular favourite venues. It is not a complete guide to all non-League grounds, for this would require a volume many times the size of this one, but it is my sole intention to encourage people disillusioned with prohibitively expensive Premiership and Football League matches to try something new. For those who already enjoy football at the lower levels, readily available for just a few pounds, this book should act as a reminder of past visits and whet the appetite for those yet to come.

Soon the non-League pyramid will be changed forever as the newly-formed National Game Board will restructure the semi-professional game completely. This book marks the juncture at which the non-League game finds itself at the dawn of this exciting and important new era. Whatever these changes may bring, the non-League game will remain firmly within the reach of the working class man (and woman). Just as it was always meant to be.

ABINGDON TOWN

GROUND: Culham Road, Abingdon, Oxfordshire
CURRENT CAPACITY: 3,000
RECORD ATTENDANCE: 1,400 v. Oxford City (FA Cup) 27/09/60
YEAR BUILT/OPENED: 1899
CURRENT LEAGUE: Ryman (Isthmian) League Division Two
CLUB FOUNDED: 1870
PREVIOUS GROUNDS: Numerous pitches

Culham Road has just passed its centenary, although the current ground is substantially different to its original incarnation. The first pitch was rotated 90 degrees from its initial orientation and a variety of stands have been erected, burnt down and demolished. The current main stand was built in 1991 and equipped with plastic seats acquired from Wembley Stadium. The adjacent covered terrace was built in 1950 and was slightly longer in its original form. The clock in one corner was salvaged from Oxford City's much-missed White House ground. Culham Road has developed into a lovely modern ground that belies its great age as a footballing venue.

ACCRINGTON STANLEY

GROUND: Crown Ground, Livingstone Road, Accrington, Lancashire
CURRENT CAPACITY: 4,000
RECORD ATTENDANCE: 2,465 v. Farsley Celtic (Unibond League) 06/05/01
YEAR BUILT/OPENED: 1968
CURRENT LEAGUE: Unibond (Northern Premier) League Premier Division
CLUB FOUNDED: 1968
PREVIOUS GROUNDS: None

Culham Road, Abingdon Town

Recreation Ground, Aldershot Town

Of course this club is not related to the former Football League club of the same name that disbanded in financial ruin in 1962. Their former Peel Park ground is long gone, save for a steep grassy bank that was the ground's former Kop. The new club was formed in 1968 and has steadily built up the Crown Ground, which was already in use as a park pitch by a works team called Ewbanks. The ground has a large section of covered terrace on one side and on the dressing-room side there is another large covered terrace and the main stand, built in 1989, that unusually lies slightly at an angle to the touchline. This stand was extended in the spring of 2001 to increase the seating to 1,000, which brings the Crown Ground up to Conference standard. This new club with an ancient name has come a long way in a short time. I am sure the original club's founding fathers would have been proud.

ALDERSHOT TOWN
GROUND: Recreation Ground, High Street, Aldershot, Hampshire
CURRENT CAPACITY: 7,500
RECORD ATTENDANCE: 7,500 v. Brighton & Hove Albion (FA Cup) 18/11/00
YEAR BUILT/OPENED: 1927
CURRENT LEAGUE: Ryman (Isthmian) League Premier Division
CLUB FOUNDED: 1992
PREVIOUS GROUNDS: None

When Aldershot FC failed to complete the 1991/92 Football League Division Three campaign, the unusual Recreation Ground was temporarily left without a resident club. In commendably efficient time, Aldershot Town were formed out of their ashes, but were placed on the lowest rung of the Isthmian League – Division Three – five levels below the Football League place the town had been used to.

However, the town's fans have not deserted the club and in working their way back up the divisions have become the best-supported club outside the Conference. Ironically, the Recreation Ground started life as a non-League ground, as Aldershot did not attain League status until 1930 when the Railway Stand was erected. The rest of the ground was built in the immediate post-war years and, apart from a modern office block and club-house, the ground has been untouched ever since. The ground was at bursting point when a remarkable 19,138 squeezed in to watch the Shots lose an FA Cup fourth round replay to Carlisle United. In modern times the capacity has been restricted to a more sensible, although still sizeable, 7,500. The Recreation Ground's location within a public park is unique and it is a great credit to the populace of the Hampshire town that it lived to fight another day following the traumatic times of the early 1990s.

ALFRETON TOWN
GROUND: Town Ground, North Street, Alfreton, Derbyshire
CURRENT CAPACITY: 5,000
RECORD ATTENDANCE: 5,023 v. Matlock Town (Central Alliance) 1960
YEAR BUILT/OPENED: 1959
CURRENT LEAGUE: Unibond (Northern Premier League) Division One
CLUB FOUNDED: 1959
PREVIOUS GROUNDS: None

A previous incarnation of Alfreton Town used the Welfare Ground adjacent to the Town Ground that the modern club lease from Amber Valley Borough Council. Since the 1960s, the ground has been steadily built up with the current main stand being the third structure on that side of the ground. It replaced a poorly constructed stand, itself only 15 years old, in 1994. The early 1990s saw general upgrading of the ground as the club

Town Ground, Alfreton Town

Moss Lane, Altrincham

climbed to the Northern Premier League. The ground was used for Rugby League for a couple of seasons when the fledgling Mansfield Marksmen sub-let the Town Ground. Alfreton Town regained their Northern Premier League status in 2002 after suffering relegation in 1999.

ALTRINCHAM

GROUND: Moss Lane, Altrincham, Cheshire
CURRENT CAPACITY: 6,085
RECORD ATTENDANCE: 10,275 Altrincham Boys v. Sunderland Boys 28/02/25
YEAR BUILT/OPENED: 1910
CURRENT LEAGUE: Unibond (Northern Premier) League Premier Division
CLUB FOUNDED: 1903
PREVIOUS GROUNDS: Pollitt's Field (1903–10)

Moss Lane could have been a Football League venue had Altrincham not failed, by a single vote, in their 1980 election bid, with Rochdale surviving by the seat of their pants. Moss Lane was a basic venue when it opened it 1910 but has been steadily developed over many years. The cavernous main stand was built in the mid-1960s, with the rest of the ground having substantial covered and uncovered terracing. The sizeable East Terrace was erected in time for the club's election as founder members of the Alliance Premier League (Conference) in 1979. The club were champions of the new pre-mier non-League competition for its first two seasons and in total the club applied unsuccessfully for Football League status on four occasions. The Robins fell from their perch in the late 1990s, losing their Conference place in 1997. This was the same year that Cheshire rivals Macclesfield Town slipped into the

Ampthill Park, Ampthill

Football League by virtue of the automatic promotion that Altrincham had vocally championed for many years.

AMPTHILL TOWN
GROUND: Ampthill Park, Woburn Road, Ampthill, Bedfordshire
CURRENT CAPACITY: 1,500
RECORD ATTENDANCE: Not Known
YEAR BUILT/OPENED: 1946
CURRENT LEAGUE: Minerva Spartan South Midlands League Division One
CLUB FOUNDED: 1888
PREVIOUS GROUNDS: Numerous pitches

Ampthill have battled away for more than 100 years without ever really achieving anything of real note. Their leafy Ampthill Park home is a pretty little venue with an unusual raised covered terrace, which is sufficiently high to prevent spectator's vision being hampered by activities on the two benches. Builders of dug-outs in front of stands at the likes of Sidlesham and Needham Market, among many others, take note.

ANDOVER
GROUND: Portway Stadium, West Portway Ind. Estate, Andover, Hampshire
CURRENT CAPACITY: 3,000
RECORD ATTENDANCE: 1,100 v. Leicester City (Ground Opening) November 1989
YEAR BUILT/OPENED: 1989
CURRENT LEAGUE: Jewson Wessex League
CLUB FOUNDED: 1883
PREVIOUS GROUNDS: Stride's Field (1883–1894); The Walled Meadow (1894–1989)

Although not a huge ground, as the record gate of 3,500 testifies, Andover's

Portway Stadium, Andover

Walled Meadow ground was a sad loss for the football world. The ancient and revered venue was deemed unsuitable for their Southern League status in 1989 and the club relocated to the out-of-town Portway Stadium. It complies with everything required in the eyes of the ground-grading committees, but has no individuality, being a virtual carbon copy of Arlesey, Letchworth, or any other new stadium of that ilk built in the last 15 years. Andover, having acquired a stadium deemed suitable for Southern League football, voluntarily surrendered their place in that competition in 1993. How's that for irony?

ARLESEY TOWN
GROUND: New Lamb Meadow, Hitchin Road, Arlesey, Bedfordshire
CURRENT CAPACITY: 2,100
RECORD ATTENDANCE: 336 v. Westfield (FA Vase) 23/01/01
YEAR BUILT/OPENED: 1999
CURRENT LEAGUE: Ryman (Isthmian) League Division One (North)
CLUB FOUNDED: 1891
PREVIOUS GROUNDS: Papworth's Field; Long Meadow; The Common; Bury Meadow; Lamb Meadow

Arlesey's considerable ambition was made obvious to the football world when they relocated to a brand new facility on the edge of town in 1999. Although the New Lamb Meadow is very much in the mould of numerous other new stadia it fitted all the relevant criteria for 2000/01. Their former venue, Lamb Meadow, now under a housing development, was purchased from a brewery by the supporters club. The team had, in fact, played there much earlier in their history until 1912. The Lamb Meadow was an eclectic mix of buildings from different eras – from the post-war years to as recently as 1991 when the main stand was replaced. Now with their new ground still polished and shiny, the Bedfordshire club face a very bright future.

New Lamb Meadow, Arlesey Town

ARUNDEL
GROUND: Mill Road, Arundel, West
Sussex
CURRENT CAPACITY: 2,000
RECORD ATTENDANCE: 2,200 v.
Chichester (West Sussex League) 1967
YEAR BUILT/OPENED: 1930s
CURRENT LEAGUE: Sussex County
League Division One
CLUB FOUNDED: 1889

PREVIOUS GROUNDS: Castle Park;
Station Road

Some ostensibly ordinary-looking
grounds can be set off a treat in a photograph by their surroundings and there are
few more stunning backdrops than that
enjoyed by Arundel's Mill Road ground,
standing as it does under the vast omnipo-
tent presence of Arundel Castle. The

Mill Road, Arundel

The Homelands, Ashford Town

current stand was built in 1971, replacing a much older wooden stand. Since then Mill Road has been gradually updated to become a very pleasant, leafy county-level venue. Ironically, its close proximity to the castle will mean any large-scale development of the ground will inevitably fall foul of the planning committees.

ASHFORD TOWN (KENT)
GROUND: The Homelands, Ashford Road, Kingsworth, Ashford, Kent
CURRENT CAPACITY: 3,200
RECORD ATTENDANCE: 3,363 v. Fulham (FA Cup) 12/11/94
YEAR BUILT/OPENED: 1987
CURRENT LEAGUE: Dr Marten's (Southern) League Eastern Division
CLUB FOUNDED: 1930
PREVIOUS GROUNDS: Essella Park (1930–1987); Folkestone Town FC (1987)

Although the passing of old football grounds is often mourned, the death knell for Ashford Town's old and decidedly decrepit Essella Park did not reverberate to any great degree. It was a cramped venue penned in by housing and the old stand was decidedly the worse for wear. The club had bought the site and when land prices soared in the mid-1980s, Ashford cashed in and relocated to an out-of-town venue at Kingsworth. However, the move was not without complications as the new venue was a green-field site, and lengthy delays saw the club play several games at Folkestone before Homelands was officially declared open. In many ways it is a perfectly modern venue with a substantial main stand and excellent social facilities, but in other ways it is totally devoid of character.

ASHFORD TOWN (MIDDX)
GROUND: Short Lane, Stanwell, Middlesex
CURRENT CAPACITY: 2,000
RECORD ATTENDANCE: 750 v. Brentford (Friendly) 29/07/98
YEAR BUILT/OPENED: 1964
CURRENT LEAGUE: Ryman (Isthmian)

League Division One (South)
CLUB FOUNDED: 1964
PREVIOUS GROUNDS: Clockhouse Lane

The club has built up this modest little ground in the last 15 years when it was previously derelict waste ground. The facility also had a separate cricket ground and the list of steady improvements have included floodlights and a new stand. The club's progress on the field matched the improving stadium and soon the club dominated the Combined Counties League, finally gaining deserved promotion to the Ryman League at the end of 1999/2000. They have built a 100-seater stand on the airport side of the ground, and the existing cover has been reterraced. Extra terracing has been built behind the Short Lane goal. Also, to comply with their increased status, Ashford have at last fully enclosed the ground.

ASHINGTON
GROUND: Portland Park, Ashington, Northumberland

CURRENT CAPACITY: 2,000
RECORD ATTENDANCE: 13,199 v. Rochdale (FA Cup) 09/12/50
YEAR BUILT/OPENED: 1909
CURRENT LEAGUE: Albany Northern League Division One
CLUB FOUNDED: 1883
PREVIOUS GROUNDS: Recreation Ground (1883–1908); Station Road (1908–09)

This elderly stadium hosted Football League football during the club's brief stint in Division Three (North) between 1921 and 1929. Originally, the ground had a huge main stand and steep terracing on all three sides, although much of this was removed to cater for the installation of a greyhound track in the immediate post-World War Two era. The main stand was gutted by fire in 1971 and was replaced by the more modest current structure. The lengthy cover opposite the main stand was condemned in 1990 when it was discovered that the roof contained asbestos. The roof was removed and replaced by a smaller section of cover.

Portland Park, Ashington

Similar to other former League venues like Workington, Gainsborough and Barrow, you cannot help but wonder what places these grounds must have been during their respective heydays.

ASHTON UNITED

GROUND: Surrey Street, Hurst Cross, Ashton-under-Lyne, Lancashire
CURRENT CAPACITY: 4,500
RECORD ATTENDANCE: 11,000 v. Halifax town (FA Cup) 25/11/52
YEAR BUILT/OPENED: 1886
CURRENT LEAGUE: Unibond (Northern Premier) League Premier Division
CLUB FOUNDED: 1878 as Hurst FC
PREVIOUS GROUNDS: Holebottom; Rose Hill; Robinson Lane

Hurst Cross is one of the oldest grounds in the country, having opened in September 1886. It had previously been an agricultural showground and in the early years was developed when finances permitted. The main stand was erected in 1912 and housed a boardroom and changing rooms. As the ground developed, the rest was extensively banked and a covered terrace went up opposite the main stand. The ground had become sufficiently well-appointed that the club applied for election to the Football League Division Three (North) in 1947, although they lost out when Southport and Halifax were re-elected. However, the club's fortunes declined and by 1990 the ground was in a doomed state of dereliction. The main stand had to be replaced before it fell down. The terracing was relaid and a new cover erected. The whole ground was given a vibrant paint job in the club's red and white colours. In recent times the club looked into the possibility of moving to a new council-built stadium at Richmond Park, which would be shared with near neighbours, Curzon Ashton. However, Ashton United have since pulled out of the proposed move, preferring to stay at their cherished long-standing home.

ATHERSTONE UNITED

GROUND: Sheepy Road, Atherstone, Warwickshire
CURRENT CAPACITY: 3,500
RECORD ATTENDANCE: 2,873 v. VS Rugby (FA Cup) 17/11/87
YEAR BUILT/OPENED: 1900
CURRENT LEAGUE: Dr Marten's (Southern) League Western Division
CLUB FOUNDED: 1979
PREVIOUS GROUNDS: None

Originally Sheepy Road played host to Atherstone Rovers, who played on a basic field adjacent to the current ground. The ground was first used in 1900 when Atherstone Town moved from Ratcliffe Road, bringing a small wooden stand with them. They used the facilities at the nearby Angel Inn until dressing rooms were erected in 1931. The present main stand was erected before World War Two and the popular side-covered terrace was erected in 1954. The ground was steadily improved throughout 1960s and '70s, including a new clubhouse and pitch surround. Disaster struck when Atherstone Town went to the wall with massive debts in 1979. However, Atherstone United were formed and took over the tenancy of Sheepy Road, working their way up to the Southern League by 1984. The new club concreted over the old railway sleeper terracing and in 1989 the club used the £50,000 transfer fee received from Manchester United for star forward

Sheepy Ground, Atherstone United

Andy Rammell to erect a new stand on the car park side of the ground, naming the new structure in Rammell's honour. The club have overcome considerable financial difficulties in recent years and Sheepy Road remains a popular venue.

AVELEY
GROUND: Mill Field, Mill Road, Aveley, Essex
CURRENT CAPACITY: 4,000
RECORD ATTENDANCE: 3,741 v. Slough (FA Amateur Cup) 27/02/71
YEAR BUILT/OPENED: 1953
CURRENT LEAGUE: Ryman (Isthmian) League Division One (North)
CLUB FOUNDED: 1927
PREVIOUS GROUNDS: Numerous pitches

Aveley's Mill Field is an impressive venue with steep terracing and two good stands. The side moved to the ground in 1953 and the main stand was erected in 1957, housing changing rooms in its bowels. The club purchased an unwanted stand, known as the Pepper Stand, from near neighbours Grays Athletic for £100. The ground had superb bankings all around, erected with the help of voluntary labour at the club. The extensive work allowed the ground to have a capacity in the 1950s of some 8,000, although it was never tested. The ground has changed little in recent times, save for additional terracing and other cosmetic touches like modern turnstiles and a new pitch surround. It is a crying shame that over the years the club has never reached the heights their excellent ground deserves.

AYLESBURY UNITED
GROUND: The Stadium, Buckingham Road, Aylesbury, Buckinghamshire
CURRENT CAPACITY: 4,000

Mill Field, Aveley

RECORD ATTENDANCE: 4,000 v. England XI (Friendly) 1988
YEAR BUILT/OPENED: 1986
CURRENT LEAGUE: Ryman (Isthmian) League Premier Division
CLUB FOUNDED: 1897 merger of Aylesbury Printing Works and Aylesbury Night School
PREVIOUS GROUNDS: Print Works Ground; Turnfurlong Lane; Tring Town FC; Flackwell Heath FC; RAF Halton

There was little wrong with Aylesbury's ground at Turnfurlong Lane, which had been their home since 1935. Like any 50-year-old ground it was a little worn out, but far from being beyond salvation. However, in February 1985 the club took a decision that was to change non-League football forever. They moved to an out-of-town site and drafted in a contractor to provide a modern, almost kit-built ground that would provide first-class facilities for players, officials and specta-tors. However, the manufactured nature of the ground meant this venue, and numerous others of the ilk that would fol-low, were carbon copies of each other. In short, while being perfectly functional, stadiums were totally devoid of character. The new ground was not without its share of developmental problems, but after 18 months of the club sharing at nearby venues, the new was ready for the start of the 1986/87 campaign. The Buckingham Road stadium has one main stand that provides all seating accommo-dation, changing rooms and social facilities. The rest of the ground is ter-raced on all three sides, with the side opposite the main stand being covered. While this stadium and its identical suc-cessors are sleek and shiny, they lack any semblance of history and soul.

AYLESFORD PAPER MILLS
GROUND: Cobdown, Ditton Corner, Station Road, Aylesford, Kent

Cobdown, Aylesford Paper Mills

CURRENT CAPACITY: 1,000
RECORD ATTENDANCE: Not Known
YEAR BUILT/OPENED: 1919
CURRENT LEAGUE: Kent County
League Division One West
CLUB FOUNDED: 1919
PREVIOUS GROUNDS: None

Aylesford Paper Mills dates back to World War One and their Cobdown ground remains an impressive venue, despite the historic pitch roof stand being out of bounds for spectators in recent years, due to safety concerns. The original club played in the Kent League between 1928 and 1951 before a four-season stint in the London League. However, the club fell into decline and disbanded in the late 1960s. The club were re-formed in 1974, rejoining the Kent County League and in the mid 1980s they briefly changed their name to Reeds International following a takeover. Reverting to their original name, the club enjoyed some success in the early 1990s, but decline set in the latter part of the decade, culminating in relegation from the Premier Division in 1999. Since then the club has teetered on the brink of folding for a second time, but struggle on doggedly. The pitch and social facilities at Cobdown are excellent and, despite the advances of prospective developers, the ground remains intact. It would be nice to think that maybe someday the lovely old stand could be restored to its former glory.

B

BAMBER BRIDGE
GROUND: Irongate, Brownedge Road, Bamber Bridge, Preston, Lancashire
CURRENT CAPACITY: 3,000
RECORD ATTENDANCE: 2,300 v. Czech Republic (Friendly) 1996

Irongate, Bamber Bridge

YEAR BUILT/OPENED: 1986
CURRENT LEAGUE: Unibond
(Northern Premier) League Division
One
CLUB FOUNDED: 1952
PREVIOUS GROUNDS: King George V
Ground (1952-86)

Bamber Bridge have come a very long
way in a short time. Until 1991 the club
were playing minor football in the
Preston and District League. Some eight
years earlier they had acquired a patch of
land wedged behind some housing and
the railways that bisect the Lancashire
town. The ground was opened with a cel-
ebratory match against near neighbours
Preston North End in August 1987, with
a crowd of 2,241 witnessing the event. In
the following years the club have erected
a quite magnificent clubhouse at the car-
park end that offers a superb view of the
pitch. There is also a covered terrace and
a modest seated stand on the railway side
of the ground.

BANBURY UNITED
GROUND: The Stadium, off Station
Road, Banbury, Oxfordshire
CURRENT CAPACITY: 6,500
RECORD ATTENDANCE: 7,160 v.
Oxford City (FA Cup) 30/10/48
YEAR BUILT/OPENED: 1933
CURRENT LEAGUE: Dr Marten's
(Southern) League Eastern Division
CLUB FOUNDED: 1965 re-formation of
a club originally formed in 1933 as
Banbury Spencer
PREVIOUS GROUNDS: None

Banbury United have been at this ground
since their formation as Banbury Spencer
in 1933. However this always-modest
venue seen has seen some very hard
times in the last couple of decades. By the
late 1980s the ground had fallen into near
total dereliction. The now-demolished
main stand had become so badly vandalized that it was condemned and closed by
the council. The covered terraces had
been severely damaged by the elements

The Stadium, Banbury United

and the local itinerants. The ground's retaining fencing was also badly damaged and was left easy to breach. The stadium was given a breath of life when the club acquired the floodlights from Oxford City's old White House stadium. Since then the club have set about the arduous task of restoring the ground. The approach road and car park remain mercilessly pot-holed and the covered stands still sport gaping holes in the roofs, but the ground is at least on the way back from oblivion. The club's renaissance was completed by their promotion back to the Dr Marten's League in 2000, 10 years after their dilapidated ground brought a 24-season stint in the Southern League to an ignominious end.

BANSTEAD ATHLETIC

GROUND: Merland Rise, Tadworth, Surrey
CURRENT CAPACITY: 3,500
RECORD ATTENDANCE: 1,400 v. Leytonstone (FA Amateur Cup) 1953
YEAR BUILT/OPENED: 1950

CURRENT LEAGUE: Ryman (Isthmian) League Division One (South)
CLUB FOUNDED: 1944 as Banstead Juniors
PREVIOUS GROUNDS: Tattenham Way Recreation Ground (1944–50)

The club formed as a junior side in 1944 and when the town's pre-war senior sides, Banstead and Banstead Hospital, decided not to re-form after the war, Banstead Juniors changed their suffix to Athletic and moved up the senior ranks. The club played at Tattenham Way Recreation Ground, which was a council-owned site with multiple pitches. In April 1950, the Banstead Urban District Council offered the fledgling club use of a patch of land off Merland Rise. The pitch was basically another park pitch with a hut for use as a combined clubhouse and changing rooms. It was still a public thoroughfare, but after a couple of seasons an adjacent field was enclosed by the council and leased to the club. A small cover was erected but the club did not develop the ground until a lengthy lease was secured in 1966. A clubhouse went up in 1969 and was joined in 1972 by a function hall. A new dressing-room block was built in 1979 to satisfy requirements for the club's election to the Athenian League. A further 25-year lease was secured in 1990 and since then the old stand has been replaced and floodlights erected. Merland Rise has slowly developed into a perfect Isthmian League venue.

BARKING & EAST HAM UNITED

GROUND: Mayesbrook Park, Lodge Avenue, Dagenham, Essex
CURRENT CAPACITY: 2,500
RECORD ATTENDANCE: 1,972 v. Aldershot (FA Cup) 16/12/78
YEAR BUILT/OPENED: 1976
CURRENT LEAGUE: Ryman (Isthmian) League Division One (North)
CLUB FOUNDED: 2001 merger of Barking (1880) and East Ham United (1890)
PREVIOUS GROUNDS: Barking: Vicarage Field (1880–1976); East Ham: Whitebarn Lane; Tillet's Farm; Ferndale Sports Ground (1946–2001)

Barking FC have been in existence in various guises since 1880 and their ground from their earliest days was the Vicarage Field. Originally it was shared with a cricket pitch, but was eventually enclosed on its own as housing encroached all around. The Vicarage Field ground had opened in 1884 and originally had a small wooden stand. In 1929 local firm Sanders and Forster were commissioned to build a new grandstand that housed dressing rooms underneath. On the railway side there was an extensive covered terrace and the ground regularly accommodated five figure crowds in the post-World War

Two years. The club replaced their ineffective floodlights in 1970, just three years before the council decided to build a bypass through the ground. Interestingly the club would have needed a lot of money to repair the grandstand that had been badly damaged by fire, so the enforced move to Mayesbrook Park was a blessing in disguise. The club were able to take their new lights with them to Mayesbrook Park, which was an open space in a densely populated area of Dagenham. Ironically the bypass never happened and the Vicarage Field ground lay derelict for many years before the current Vicarage Field shopping centre was built in its place. Mayesbrook Park has a low-roof, pitch-length covered stand on one side and this was the only covered accommodation until the clubhouse end terrace was covered in 2000. Although a relatively dull ground, Barking came out well from the deal as they would have invariably lost Vicarage Field sooner or later. The club merged with East Ham United in 2001 after the latter lost their shambolic but much-loved Ferndale Sports Ground to a housing development. The last game at the ground had a paying attendance of nil. How very sad.

BARNET

GROUND: Underhill, Barnet Lane, Barnet, Hertfordshire
CURRENT CAPACITY: 4,057
RECORD ATTENDANCE: 11,026 v. Wycombe Wanderers (FA Amateur Cup) 1952
YEAR BUILT/OPENED: 1907
CURRENT LEAGUE: Nationwide Football Conference
CLUB FOUNDED: 1888 as Barnet Alston
PREVIOUS GROUNDS: Queens Road; Totteridge Lane

Underhill, Barnet

Barnet Alston played their first match at Underhill against Crystal Palace in September 1907. The ground's first stand was not built until 1926 and this stood until 1964, when the current main stand was opened. In the next two years the ground was completely reterraced and the cavernous East Terrace was erected. Despite relative success, the 1980s nearly saw the club's demise with huge debts. Then manager, Barry Fry, bailed the club out with cash raised from a second mortgage of his house. By 1985 the club was once again saddled with crippling debts and Fry brought in Stan Flashman, who had made a fortune from ticket touting, as chairman and saviour. In a mad spell of 8 years, the pair had a strange relationship, with Fry being sacked on countless occasions. However, the club thrived and won the Conference title in 1991. Flashman left in bitter acrimony in 1993, with the team in great shape, but the ground hopelessly outdated. The South Terrace cover was condemned and pulled down in 1995, being replaced by a temporary platform with seats bolted on. It looks an awful mess. The Football League began a witch-hunt against the club for its failure to update the ground. An attempted expulsion failed, but Underhill had its capacity reduced to a meagre 3,200, by far the smallest in the League. The club still had not addressed the stadium's problems when they suffered last-day relegation in 2000/01. So a 10-season whirlwind blew out and even the club admitted that, should they regain Football League status, a ground-share at Leyton Orient would be the only option. However, recently the club have entered into negotiations with the local council with regards to rebuilding Underhill using the adjacent playing field. In hindsight perhaps this has come a decade too late.

BARROW
GROUND: Holker Street, Wilkie Road, Barrow-in-Furness, Cumbria
CURRENT CAPACITY: 4,500
RECORD ATTENDANCE: 16,854 v.

Holker Street, Barrow

Swansea Town (FA Cup) 09/01/54
YEAR BUILT/OPENED: 1909
CURRENT LEAGUE: Unibond
(Northern Premier) League Premier
Division
CLUB FOUNDED: 1901
PREVIOUS GROUNDS: Strawberry
Park; Ainslie Street; Little Park

The club was formed in 1901 and wanted to play at Cavendish Park, the local athletics ground, which had previously been used by the defunct Furness AFC. However, the athletic club and nearby rugby club colluded to force the fledgling club to look elsewhere. They settled on a ground behind the Strawberry Hotel, which was later used by Barrow RUFC. After three years there, one at a sloping ground in Ainslie Street and four spent at Little Park in Roose, the club chose to take over the vacated ground of Hindpool Athletic in Holker Street. The main stand went up in 1912 and was later extended, but suffered bomb damage in World War Two. Rather than pull the stand down, the club repaired it with marine timber salvaged from an unseaworthy

boat! The club also had large covered terraces on the other three sides. Unusually the ground was enclosed by massive concrete blocks, donated by the nearby Vickers company, who had used them for protecting machinery from enemy bombs. After several flirtations with re-elections, the remote location and lack of success saw the club bow out of the Football League in 1972 in favour of Hereford United. Since then, the club have come back from the brink of extinction on more than one occasion and in the interim have sympathetically modernized the stadium. Maybe one day the club and the Holker Street ground may return to the Football League stage.

BARTON ROVERS
GROUND: Sharpenhoe Road, Barton-le-clay, Bedfordshire
CURRENT CAPACITY: 4,000
RECORD ATTENDANCE: 1,900 v. Nuneaton Borough (FA Cup) 06/11/76
YEAR BUILT/OPENED: 1975
CURRENT LEAGUE: Ryman (Isthmian) League Division One (North)
CLUB FOUNDED: 1898

PREVIOUS GROUNDS: Church Field; Barton Cutting; Sharpenhoe Road; Barton Recreation Ground

Despite dating back to 1898, the club did not join the Luton and District League until after World War Two. The club's relatively remote location meant that until then they had to be content with matches against nearby villages. The club enjoyed considerable success in the South Midlands League during the 1970s, winning the title on eight occasions and faring very well in the FA Vase – reaching the final in 1978, before losing to Newcastle Blue Star at Wembley. The club's heyday coincided with a move to their current ground in 1975, having spent the post-war years at the town's Recreation Ground. After so much continued success, it was no surprise that the club moved to the Isthmian League in 1979. Since then Sharpenhoe Road has been developed beyond all recognition and now boasts a smart brick-built main stand on one side and a remarkable collection of no less than five separate areas of covered standing on the opposite side.

BASHLEY
GROUND: Recreation Ground, Bashley, Hampshire
CURRENT CAPACITY: 4,250
RECORD ATTENDANCE: 3,500 v. Emley (FA Vase) 1988
YEAR BUILT/OPENED: 1947
CURRENT LEAGUE: Dr Marten's (Southern) League Eastern Division
CLUB FOUNDED: 1947
PREVIOUS GROUNDS: None

When the Recreation Ground was opened in 1947, the only permanent structure at was a disused Nissen hut that the club acquired for use as a dressing room. The club had a meteoric rise in the 1980s from the sedate surroundings of the Bournemouth League. The village hall that abuts the ground in Bashley Road was extended to provide a basic clubhouse. Their promotion to the Wessex League in 1986 saw the ground completely enclosed for the first time and the first stand with wooden-bench seating was erected. The club's amazing success continued when, in 1991, they won promotion to the Southern League. A large pre-built cover was winched into place next to the existing stand and a small VIP stand was also erected at the opposite end of the main stand. Strangely the club chose to put all the dressing rooms and offices on this side of the ground, thus leaving the opposite side totally undeveloped. Although the club has enjoyed considerable success, the sympathetic development of the ground has seen the Bashley Recreation Ground's rural aspect remain relatively unsullied.

BASINGSTOKE TOWN
GROUND: The Camrose Ground, Western Way, Basingstoke, Hampshire
CURRENT CAPACITY: 6,000
RECORD ATTENDANCE: 5,085 v. Wycombe Wanderers (FA Cup) 25/11/97
YEAR BUILT/OPENED: 1945
CURRENT LEAGUE: Ryman (Isthmian) League Premier Division
CLUB FOUNDED: 1896
PREVIOUS GROUNDS: Castle Field (1896–1945)

In 1945 Basingstoke Town were offered a piece of land to develop as a new ground close to the railway station. The offer came from Lord Camrose and the site was made available on a 99-year lease. The ground was fairly basic, with a wooden stand and grass banking, until the late 1960s. The club were trying to move up from the Hampshire League to the Southern League so ground improvements were essential. The club-house was opened in 1969 and a year later the current main stand was erected. This houses dressing rooms underneath the seating area. The old grass banking was replaced with more politically-correct concrete terracing and floodlights were switched on for the first time. The hive of activity was rewarded with election to the Southern League in 1971. Later that year the ground attracted a then-record gate of 4,091 for a FA Cup tie with Northampton. The record stood until a local derby with Wycombe 26 years later. The mid-1970s saw the start of the covering of the terraces, a task that was not completed until 1996. Although the Camrose is of relatively recent vintage, its slightly hotchpotch nature lends an older appearance.

BATH CITY

GROUND: Twerton Park, Lower Bristol Road, Bath, Avon
CURRENT CAPACITY: 8,840
RECORD ATTENDANCE: 18,020 v. Brighton & Hove Albion (FA Cup) 09/1/60
YEAR BUILT/OPENED: 1932
CURRENT LEAGUE: Dr Marten's (Southern) League Premier Division
CLUB FOUNDED: 1889
PREVIOUS GROUNDS: Belvoir Ground (1889–1932)

A historic venue that played host to League football when Bristol Rovers ground-shared at Twerton Park between 1986 and 1996. Twerton Park had been purchased for £2,000 in 1932 and Bristol firm Lysaghts were commissioned to build the main stand. This stand was severely damaged by fire in 1991, but sympathetically renovated to today's excellent structure. Opposite, the covered terrace was originally much larger, but much of it was sold for a housing development to alleviate a financial crisis.

Twerton Park, Bath City

Holloway Park, Beaconsfield

The end terraces were built into the original banking, which in turn were the result of the huge earth-moving exercise needed to create a level playing surface when the site was acquired. The money earned by Rovers' lengthy ground-share has been used wisely and this lovely Georgian town boasts a truly first-class football venue.

BEACONSFIELD S Y C O B
GROUND: Holloway Park, Slough Road, Beaconsfield, Buckinghamshire
CURRENT CAPACITY: 3,000
RECORD ATTENDANCE: 300
Beaconsfield United v. Chesham United 1985
YEAR BUILT/OPENED: 1971
CURRENT LEAGUE: Minerva Spartan South Midlands League Premier Division
CLUB FOUNDED: 1994 merger of Beaconsfield United and Slough Youth Club Old Boys
PREVIOUS GROUNDS: None

The original Beaconsfield club played at White Hart Meadow, but after the war played at another ground called Holloway Park. It was at this ground that they moved up from the Maidenhead League to the Spartan League in 1979. Senior status was attained two years later and the Spartan League Championship was won in 1983 when they shared the title with Collier Row. In the mid-1980s the ground was required by the Highways Agency for the extension to the M40. The club were re-housed at a new site on Slough Road, handily placed just off junction 2 of the M40. The Slough Youth Centre team started in 1938 and worked their way up to the Chiltonian League in 1992. However, they were unable to develop their ground so a merger was the only option. Version two of Holloway Park has a large stand and some terracing. In 2000 the club harboured ambitions of promotion to the Ryman League and built an extension to their stand that

College Meadow, Beccles Town

doubled the seating capacity. However, local council jobsworths decided that, because the new extension could now be seen from the Slough Road, the club would have to return the stand to its former size. The club's oversight in seeking planning permission, and the subsequent legal wrangle, cost the club an ill-afforded £40,000. The extension was duly demolished and the club have tried to recoup their losses by hiring their pitch to the Chelsea Ladies team.

BECCLES TOWN

GROUND: College Meadow, Station Road, Beccles, Suffolk
CURRENT CAPACITY: 1,500
RECORD ATTENDANCE: 2,732 Bungay v. Lowestoft (Suffolk Premier Cup) 10/03/56
YEAR BUILT/OPENED: 1920s
CURRENT LEAGUE: Lovewell Blake Anglian Combination Premier Division
CLUB FOUNDED: Not Recorded
PREVIOUS GROUNDS: None

One of East Anglia's hidden gems, College Meadow is a welcome rarity in the sleepy football backwater of North Suffolk. Located behind the railway station in this ancient border market town, College Meadow has been Beccles Town's home since the late 1920s. The ground's crowning glory is a wonderfully evocative low-roofed covered stand that is immaculately kept and resplendent in the club's black and white colours. The Black Dogs' heyday was in the late 1940s and '50s when four-figure crowds were commonplace at Crown Meadow. Ironically, the largest attendance at the ground was for a match that did not involve Beccles. The ground staged the semi-final of the Suffolk Premier Cup in March 1956 when nearly 3,000 watched near-neighbours Bungay Town take on Lowestoft Town. To the delight of any ground addict, in an area with hardly a surfeit of stands to admire, the adjacent ground of Beccles Caxton also sports a covered stand. Admittedly it is not a patch on its elderly neighbour, but welcome nonetheless.

BEDFORD TOWN

GROUND: The New Eyrie, Meadow Lane, Cardington, Bedfordshire
CURRENT CAPACITY: 3,000
RECORD ATTENDANCE: 3,000 v. Peterborough United (Ground opening) 06/08/93
YEAR BUILT/OPENED: 1993
CURRENT LEAGUE: Ryman (Isthmian) League Premier Division
CLUB FOUNDED: 1989 re-formation of a club originally formed in 1908
PREVIOUS GROUNDS: London Road; Gasworks Ground; Queen's Park; The Eyrie; Allen Park

Of the many large non-League grounds lost to redevelopment in the last two decades, Bedford Town's superb Eyrie ground's demise has been one of the hardest to stomach. The Eyrie ground was a massive venue next to the Charles Wells brewery in Ford End Road and had been home to Bedford Town since 1923. Until World War Two the ground had a small seated stand but huge banks of wooden terracing. The post-war years saw big changes with the huge wooden grandstand, which was to become renowned throughout non-League football, opened. There was also a vast covered terrace at the Brewery End. The concreting of the old wooden terraces enabled Town to attract huge crowds in the 1950s and '60s. The record gate came in 1966 when 18,407 watched a FA Cup tie with Everton. In 1971 the ground was adapted to cater for greyhound racing, which was successful for a time. However, the ground's lease with the brewery was coming to an end by the late 1970s and the club entered into negotiations with the council regarding their relocation. By 1982 negotiations broke down and the brewery reclaimed the ground for their own expansion programme. The club were forced to disband, leaving Bedford as the largest town in England without a senior football club. The club relaunched in 1989, playing at a modest level on a public pitch at Allen Park. In 1993 the club opened a ground on the outskirts of Cardington. It has steadily been built up to an excellent

The New Eyrie, Bedford Town

venue. A nice touch is the statues of eagles that guard the entrance from the dressing rooms to the pitch. Although the Eyrie is sorely missed it is a testament to the enthusiasm of a few loyal club men that the club has survived at all.

BEDWORTH UNITED
GROUND: The Oval, Coventry Road, Bedworth, Warwickshire
CURRENT CAPACITY: 7,000
RECORD ATTENDANCE: 5,127 v. Nuneaton Borough (Southern League) 23/02/82
YEAR BUILT/OPENED: 1946
CURRENT LEAGUE: Dr Marten's (Southern) League Western Division
CLUB FOUNDED: 1896 as Bedworth Town
PREVIOUS GROUNDS: British Queen Ground; Miners Welfare Ground

There were several incarnations of Bedworth Town (1895-1900, 1905-22, 1925-40), all of which lead to the current club forming in 1947, when they joined the semi-professional Birmingham Combination. The ground in Coventry Road has been used by at least two of the Bedworth Town clubs, and was also used as a local miners' welfare ground. A venue called the British Queen Ground was also used at various times. The Oval in its current state began to take shape in the immediate post-war years. It has steadily been built up to a thoroughly modern venue with the requisite seated stand and clubhouse, yet has managed to maintain its leafy, rural outlook. The Oval has certainly come a long way since its early days when it was a recreation ground known locally as The Knob! Thank goodness, it was renamed.

BELPER TOWN
GROUND: Christchurch Meadow, Bridge Street, Belper, Derbyshire
CURRENT CAPACITY: 2,640
RECORD ATTENDANCE: 3,200 v. Ilkeston Town 1955

The Oval, Bedworth United

Christchurch Meadow, Belper Town

YEAR BUILT/OPENED: 1951
CURRENT LEAGUE: Unibond (Northern Premier) League Division One
CLUB FOUNDED: 1883
PREVIOUS GROUNDS: Acorn Ground

Although centrally located in this very pleasant part of Derbyshire, Christchurch Meadow and the adjacent cricket ground, tennis courts and bowling green have a surprisingly rural aspect. This is partly due to the ground being on the flood-plain of the River Derwent, which hampers the construction of anything with deep foundations. The club have been at the ground since their re-formation in 1951, although Christchurch Meadow was already in use for football by a junior side, Field Head. The first structure on the ground was the original main stand on the mill side of the ground. This had a short life as it was demolished when just over 10 years old, to make way for an extension to the mill. The timber was put to good use for the construction of the current main stand on the opposite side. This was curiously built from the halfway line down to the corner flag, rather than the usual position of straddling the halfway line. The clubhouse and changing rooms date from the mid-1960s and floodlighting arrived for the first time in 1980. Christchurch Meadow remains a remarkably unspoilt ground with trees, fields and the river on three sides. The omnipresent hulking mass of the mill shadows the Bridge Street side of the ground.

BERKHAMSTED TOWN
GROUND: Broadwater, Lower Kings Road, Berkhamsted, Hertfordshire
CURRENT CAPACITY: 2,500
RECORD ATTENDANCE: 1,732 v. Bedlington Terriers (FA Vase) 24/03/01
YEAR BUILT/OPENED: 1983
CURRENT LEAGUE: Ryman (Isthmian) League Division One (North)
CLUB FOUNDED: 1895

Broadwater, Berkhamsted

PREVIOUS GROUNDS: Sunnyside Enclosure; Berkhamsted Cricket Club

The original Berkhamsted Town club were formed in 1895. It lasted 11 seasons before spending a period in abeyance until the town's war veterans re-formed the club in 1919 as Berkhamsted Comrades. The club played at Berkhamsted Cricket Club on Lower Kings Road further down the road from the club's current home at Broadwater. The old Lower Kings Road pitch had its own stand and clubhouse but being so close to the road and the Grand Union canal, there was little scope for expansion. By 1983 the club were in the Spartan League and were eyeing a return to the higher-standing Athenian League. The club arranged for their existing ground to be sold for housing and they also took over the cricket club's clubhouse. A new pitch was laid on the other side of the clubhouse, a main stand and covered ter-

race also followed as the club progressed through the Isthmian League divisions following the demise of the Athenian League. Originally the main stand had wooden-bench seating but this was replaced with the current modern plastic seating. In the early 1990s terracing was laid around the ground, and an all-weather training surface was also built. The West Herts club will never be a well-supported outfit, as Broadwater's record gate testifies, but the casual visitor will be pleasantly surprised by the facilities on offer.

BEXHILL UNITED
GROUND: The Polegrove, Brockley Road, Bexhill-on-Sea, East Sussex
CURRENT CAPACITY: 2,000
RECORD ATTENDANCE: Not Known
YEAR BUILT/OPENED: 1926
CURRENT LEAGUE: Sussex County League Division
CLUB FOUNDED: 1926
PREVIOUS GROUNDS: None

Bexhill Town have only ever played at The Polegrove since their formation in 1926. The superb brick-and-timber built grandstand went up soon after their arrival. The spectacular stand houses the teams' changing rooms and a smaller referees' room. Adjacent to the stand on the seafront side of the ground is the clubhouse that was completed in 1987. The club has spent recent years in the lower reaches of the Sussex County League, but are rightly proud of their grandstand, one of the most attractive in the county. During summer 2002, Bexhill Town merged with the local East Sussex League outfit, Bexhill Amateur Athletic Club, and have adopted a new suffix to reflect the combined clubs.

BIDEFORD
GROUND: The Sports Ground, Kingsley Road, Bideford, Devon
CURRENT CAPACITY: 6,000
RECORD ATTENDANCE: 5,750 v. Gloucester City (FA Cup) 12/11/49

YEAR BUILT/OPENED: 1946
CURRENT LEAGUE: Screwfix Direct Western League Premier Division
CLUB FOUNDED: 1946
PREVIOUS GROUNDS: Hansen Ground 1952

The Sports Ground in Bideford is an increasingly rare commodity these days, being a large town centre ground. The ground was originally shared with the town's rugby union club, but in 1952 the football club moved across the town to a new venue called the Hansen Ground. Unfortunately the supporters did not follow and after one season the football club returned, having struck a deal with the rugby outfit who took up residency, as they still do, at the Hansen Ground. The neat grandstand dates from 1990, its predecessor having fallen victim to the Safety of Sports Grounds Act constituted after the Bradford City fire disaster. The other covered terrace was funded by the club, who rent the ground at a not inconsider-

The Sports Ground, Bideford

The Fairfield, Biggleswade Town

able fee from Bideford Council. The only drawback for supporters is the presence of an athletics track, which inevitably increases the viewing distance from the stands to the pitch.

BIGGLESWADE TOWN
GROUND: The Fairfield, Fairfield Road, Biggleswade, Bedfordshire
CURRENT CAPACITY: 2,400
RECORD ATTENDANCE: Not Known
YEAR BUILT/OPENED: c1914
CURRENT LEAGUE: Minerva Spartan South Midlands League Premier Division
CLUB FOUNDED: 1874
PREVIOUS GROUNDS: Numerous pitches

The Fairfield area of this pleasant Bedfordshire town has a substantial amount of space dedicated to sport and recreation. There is a cricket club, hockey club and two football clubs. The neighbouring Biggleswade United ground, called Second Meadow, is a modern development that has been built up to a good standard in recent years. The Biggleswade Town ground is far more elderly, having been used for more than a century. The original clubhouse burned down in 1948 and was replaced six years later – a plaque recording the fact that the new building was donated by a local brewery, Wells & Winch. There is an ancient-looking wooden main stand, which until recently was flanked by two corrugated-iron-covered stands that looked suspiciously like converted Nissen huts. However, these were recently dismantled due to safety concerns. Floodlights went up at Fairfield in 1989 when the Waders successfully acquired the old set from the Valley after Charlton Athletic were forced to abandon their home for many years.

BILLERICAY TOWN
GROUND: New Lodge, Blunts Wall Road, Billericay, Essex
CURRENT CAPACITY: 3,500

RECORD ATTENDANCE: 3,841 v. West Ham United (Floodlight Opening) 1977
YEAR BUILT/OPENED: 1971
CURRENT LEAGUE: Ryman (Isthmian) League Premier Division
CLUB FOUNDED: 1880
PREVIOUS GROUNDS: Archer Ground

Billericay's move from the Archer Ground on the Laindon Road in 1971 coincided with a decade of extraordinary success for the club, which included three FA Vase triumphs and three Essex Senior League titles. They joined the Athenian League in 1977 and on that competition's demise, the Isthmian League two years later. The New Lodge ground was an open field with two football pitches and a cricket square and was previously home to Outwell Common FC. The ground was so basic that the club brought the old dressing-room hut from the Archer Ground and it was erected at the north end of the ground – where it still serves as a refreshment kiosk. The clubhouse was opened in 1972, although the brick-built viewing gallery was a later extension. The club often borrowed wooden bleachers from Essex County Cricket Club for accommodating the large crowds of the 1970s. The main stand, with an awkwardly large roof, was opened in 1980, but has a limited amount of seats. The only other stand for many years was a supporters-club-erected wooden stand on the west side. In recent years the club have collected an extraordinary number of stands. The first was a covered terrace next to the main stand, which was later extended. In the mid-1990s the club acquired two pre-cast-iron stands from the defunct Newbury Town. These were equipped with plastic seating and originally sited behind each goal. The Ryman League's edict that member clubs provide at least 200 seats in one stand saw these two stands re-sited and joined together on the west side of the ground. The old supporters' club stand was replaced in 1999 with a larger stand. In

New Lodge, Billericay

Central Avenue, Billingham Sythonia

recent months the club have announced plans to replace the original main stand and adjacent terrace with a new 1,000-seater stand. We await with bated breath. There is also talk of the club relocating to a new Conference-standard ground next to the existing Gloucester Park athletics stadium in Basildon. There would be some irony and no little controversy if this plan comes off, as Town's old rivals from their Essex Senior League days, Basildon United, tried and failed to get planning permission for a ground at the same site some years ago.

BILLINGHAM SYNTHONIA

GROUND: Central Avenue, Billingham, Cleveland
CURRENT CAPACITY: 1,970
RECORD ATTENDANCE: 4,200 v. Bishop Auckland (Northern League) 06/09/58
YEAR BUILT/OPENED: 1958
CURRENT LEAGUE: Albany Northern League Division One
CLUB FOUNDED: 1923 as Billingham Synthonia Recreation

PREVIOUS GROUNDS: ICI Ground; Belasis Lane

The club are irrevocably linked to the chemical company ICI and all three of their grounds were built on land owned by the company. Indeed their unique suffix is a pleasingly poetic corruption of the company's leading product – synthetic ammonia. The Central Avenue ground was built over a rugby pitch and was a magnificent venue. The ground was fully enclosed and had steep banking, a cinder athletics track and a huge 2,000-seater grandstand. In 1958 the ground had the honour of staging an England 'B' international, such was the high standard of the venue. In more recent years the powers-that-be at the local council have deemed the grandstand unsafe. Originally many of the seats were removed to satisfy the council, the club then returned the wings of the stand to terracing, only for the council to deem them too steep! Surprisingly the ground's largest gathering is only a shade over 4,000, which congregated for the opening match at the ground against Bishop Auckland. Sizeable crowds only gather at Central Avenue nowadays when the ground is used by the overpaid prima donnas of Middlesbrough's reserve team.

BILLINGHAM TOWN
GROUND: Bedford Terrace, Billingham, Cleveland
CURRENT CAPACITY: 3,000
RECORD ATTENDANCE: 1,500 v. Manchester City (FA Youth Cup) 1985
YEAR BUILT/OPENED: 1974
CURRENT LEAGUE: Albany Northern League Division One
CLUB FOUNDED: 1967 as Billingham Social Club
PREVIOUS GROUNDS: Mill Lane (1967–74)

Billingham Town's only real claim to fame is that Bedford Terrace was an early stomping ground for Middlesbrough, Manchester United and England centre-back Gary Pallister. The club progressed from the Stockton District League to the Teeside League, and originally played at a modest ground in Mill Lane. This ground had such a lateral slope that at its crest, the corner flag was level in height to the crossbar! The club eventually moved to a new ground in 1974, to an area of derelict land called Bedford Terrace. Over the years much fundraising was done and the £100,000 produced a perfectly acceptable stadium with a smart cantilevered-roof main stand. By 1982 the ground had been built up to a sufficient standard to gain election as founder members of the new Northern League Division Two. Bedford Terrace has a healthy capacity of 3,000, yet to be fully tested, and in many ways is more suitable to their level than its more famous neighbour at Central Avenue.

BILSTON TOWN
GROUND: Queen Street, Bilston, West Midlands
CURRENT CAPACITY: 4,000
RECORD ATTENDANCE: 7,500 v. Wolves (Floodlight Opening) 1953
YEAR BUILT/OPENED: 1919
CURRENT LEAGUE: West Midlands Regional League Division One North
CLUB FOUNDED: 1895 as Bilston United
PREVIOUS GROUNDS: Prouds Lane; Willenhall Road

Bedford Terrace, Billingham Town

A classic Black Country ground, Queen Street opened in September 1919. Soon after the club erected the main stand. This remains at the ground although it has undergone substantial renovation in the intervening years. A small covered terrace went up at the Trinity Road end. This stood until 1987, when it was condemned and replaced some eight years later. The clubhouse was opened in 1958 and extended in 1972 at a cost of £3,000 (funds received from the sale of Ronnie Pountney to Southend United). The ground has twice accommodated crowds of 7,000. The first was the floodlight inauguration against near-neighbours Wolverhampton Wanderers in 1953 and again in 1968 when Halifax Town contested a FA Cup tie. The club's election to the Southern League in 1985 saw the ground regenerated with extensive terracing being laid on the old grass banking. The late 1980s saw the construction of the Black Country Route that now zips past the southern side of the ground. The problem of stray balls on a busy road has been overcome with the erection of huge mesh fences painted in the club's tangerine colours. Despite the loss of the cover and banking on the south side, the regeneration of the Queen Street ground has seen it mature into one of the West Midlands' top venues. However, the 2001/02 campaign was a harrowing one off the field and the club resigned from the Dr Marten's League. They have decided to regroup further down the pyramid. Hopefully reduced expenditure will ensure the survival of the club and its splendid ground.

BISHOP AUCKLAND
GROUND: Shildon FC, Dean Street, Shildon, County Durham

CURRENT CAPACITY: 4,000
RECORD ATTENDANCE: 17,000 v. Coventry City (FA Cup) 06/12/52
YEAR BUILT/OPENED: 1886
CURRENT LEAGUE: Unibond (Northern Premier) League Division One
CLUB FOUNDED: 1886
PREVIOUS GROUNDS: Kingsway (1886-2002)

Without doubt, Bishop Auckland were the most famous and successful amateur club of all time, winning the FA Amateur Cup on a record 10 occasions and taking the Northern League title in no less than 19 seasons – also a record. The club was formed by theological undergraduates from Oxford and Cambridge Universities who studied at nearby Auckland Castle, and adopted the famous colours of both universities. Kingsway, the Two Blues' home since their formation, is a ground truly befitting the kings of amateur football. The ground was opened in 1886 when the football club and cricket club obtained a joint 999-year lease from the Church Commissioners. The ground is superb. The main stand was built in 1919 with its elevated extensions, known as Harold's Lugs, being added in 1955. The steep terracing on this side and at either end is hugely impressive and offers superb views of this three-sided ground. There was another small stand and a clubhouse at one time, but these were gutted by fire in 1961 with the clubhouse taking five years to rebuild. Despite the great history attached to the Kingsway ground, the club are actively searching for a suitable site to build a new ground, with a site off Tindale Crescent the current favourite. Although amateurism was officially abolished in 1973, the move from this classic ground has somehow severed

Kingsway, Bishop Auckland

the last vestige of amateurism in this country. The club will ground-share at Northern League Shildon until the new ground is ready. However, this arrangement saw them demoted from their Northern Premier League Premier Division place as the Dean Street ground is not up to the necessary ground-grading criteria.

BISHOPS STORTFORD
GROUND: Woodside Park, Dunmow Road, Bishop's Stortford, Hertfordshire
CURRENT CAPACITY: 4,000
RECORD ATTENDANCE: 918 v. Norwich City (Ground Opening) 20/07/99
YEAR BUILT/OPENED: 1999
CURRENT LEAGUE: Ryman (Isthmian) League Premier Division
CLUB FOUNDED: 1874
PREVIOUS GROUNDS: Silver Leys; Hadham Rd; South Mill; Laundry Field; Rhodes Avenue

Stortford enjoyed many great moments at the Town Ground in Rhodes Avenue (renamed the George Wilson Stadium in 1970), most notably capacity crowds of 6,000 for epic FA Cup ties against Peterborough in 1972 and Middlesbrough in 1983. The later tie was said, unofficially, to have a true attendance in excess of 9,000. The club moved into Rhodes Avenue in 1919 and acquired the polo pavilion from their first ground at Silver Leys. The club purchased the ground in 1927 with £300 raised by the supporters' club. A small stand was erected in 1930 but was replaced by a much larger grandstand in 1962 at a cost of £13,282. The covered terrace dated from the mid-1950s, although the Thorley End was not covered until 1967. The next development came in the late 1970s when a glazed viewing area was installed to allow an excellent view of proceedings from the comfort of the clubhouse. Maybe the future of the ground was settled in the summer of 1988 when the club sold off much of the car park for housing. Nine years later the club was approached by Crest Homes who wanted the site to build 45 new houses. The club's perilous financial position meant that the proposition was accepted and work on their new venue in Dunmow Road started in November 1997. However, money troubles and numerous other unanticipated problems meant that the new stadium was not ready until the start of 1999/2000, when Norwich City did the opening-match honours. Many great memories went as the old ground was dismantled, but it was an offer that the club could ill afford to turn down.

BLIDWORTH WELFARE
GROUND: Welfare Ground, Mansfield Road, Blidworth, Nottinghamshire
CURRENT CAPACITY: 2,000
RECORD ATTENDANCE: Not Known
YEAR BUILT/OPENED: 1989

CURRENT LEAGUE: Central Midland League Premier Division
CLUB FOUNDED: 1980 as Folk House Old Boys
PREVIOUS GROUNDS: Chesterfield Road (1980–89)

Blidworth Welfare's current incarnation dates from 1980 and suffered a torrid time in the early 1980s with the miners' strike. The colliery never recovered and eventually closed in 1989. In that year the football club erected a handsome cover on a bank behind the Welfare Club end. The Welfare Club itself closed in 1990, the same year the ground inaugurated its new floodlights. To cope with the loss of both the colliery and the Welfare Club, a separate committee was elected to ensure the football club's survival. Since then the club have gone from strength to strength and the now somewhat inappropriately named Welfare Ground is a tidy, well-maintained venue. The vast emptiness of the old Welfare building is a stark reminder of the decline of British industry.

Welfare Ground, Blidworth Welfare

BLYTH SPARTANS

GROUND: Croft Park, Blyth, Northumberland
CURRENT CAPACITY: 6,000
RECORD ATTENDANCE: 10,000 v. Hartlepools United (FA Cup) 02/12/56
YEAR BUILT/OPENED: 1909
CURRENT LEAGUE: Unibond (Northern Premier) League Premier Division
CLUB FOUNDED: 1899
PREVIOUS GROUNDS: Percy's Gardens; The Spion Kop Ground; Thoroton Cottages

Croft Park was opened in September 1909 with a friendly against Newcastle United. The ground had a fine wooden grandstand that stood until it was destroyed by fire in 1971. Spartans eventually purchased the ground in 1921, but were forced into selling it to the council 23 years later to alleviate debts. The cavernous West Stand covered terrace was opened in the 1920s, but has been re-clad in recent years. The current cantilevered main stand was opened in 1972 with the £15,000 cost being met by the local council. The club moved from the disbanded semi-professional North Eastern League to the strictly amateur Northern League in 1964, a league Spartans would win on no less than 10 occasions. The club became renowned FA Cup giant-killers, reaching the first round on 47 occasions, most notably excelling themselves in the 1977/78 season, when a controversial injury-time equalizer denied them a fifth-round triumph over Wrexham. The replay in front of 42,000 people at St James' Park saw a narrow defeat for the Spartans. The epic Cup run generated sufficient funds for the rest of the ground to be fully terraced in the summer of 1978. In 1994 the club took a well-deserved step up to the Northern Premier League, where they have performed well ever since. Croft Park has been brought up to modern standards that belie its near-100 years of existence.

BODMIN TOWN

GROUND: Priory Park, Bodmin, Cornwall
CURRENT CAPACITY: 3,000
RECORD ATTENDANCE: Not Known
YEAR BUILT/OPENED: c1948
CURRENT LEAGUE: Carlsberg South-Western League
CLUB FOUNDED: 1889
PREVIOUS GROUNDS: Coldharbour; Barn Lane; West Heath

As you arrive in Bodmin on the A389, the huge site that is Priory Park lies in the shallow valley to the left and its photogenic stand looks great from the roadside. Adjacent to the ground is Athelston House and behind it the valley banks up sharply and the superb vista is completed by the distant focal point of Gilbert's Monument. The stunning pitched roof stand was opened in September 1958, some 10 years after the club started leasing the site from Bodmin Council. At the time the stand cost some £2,500 to construct but was worth every penny as it remains one of the best in the area. However, the club have lofty aspirations and in 2000 announced redevelopment plans that would see this great stand demolished in favour of a more modern and promotion-friendly structure. For stadium purists these plans are sacrilegious.

BOGNOR REGIS TOWN

GROUND: Nyewood Lane, Bognor Regis, West Sussex

Priory Park, Bodmin Town

CURRENT CAPACITY: 6,000
RECORD ATTENDANCE: 3,642 v.
Swansea City (FA Cup) 21/11/84
YEAR BUILT/OPENED: 1916
CURRENT LEAGUE: Ryman (Isthmian)
League Division One (South)
CLUB FOUNDED: 1893 as Bognor
PREVIOUS GROUNDS: Numerous
pitches

Bognor Regis Town have suffered from their geographically remote location and have incurred hefty travelling expenses in their spells in the Southern and Isthmian Leagues since rising from the Sussex County League in 1972. The club moved to Nyewood Lane during World War One and after football recommenced after hostilities ceased, the club set about developing the ground. A small stand with wooden benching was opened and changing rooms erected. The pitch was fenced off with a post and rope surround. The club changed its name in 1935 when the town incorporated Regis into its

name following King George V's convalescence in the town for several months. The club's first set of floodlights had excellent provenance, being the original set at Wembley Stadium. These were mounted on telegraph poles and did excellent service until replaced in 1985. Two huts were bought from the RAF in 1970 and converted into a clubhouse. This was re-clad in 1990 and given a new lease of life. The club's rise in status has seen the seated stand joined by three areas of covered terrace and ample open terracing. The club claim a capacity of 6,000, although this has never truly been tested. A fine ground in a harshly maligned seaside town.

BOREHAM WOOD
GROUND: Meadow Park, Broughinge Road, Borehamwood, Hertfordshire
CURRENT CAPACITY: 4,500
RECORD ATTENDANCE: 4,030 v.
Arsenal (Friendly) 13/07/01
YEAR BUILT/OPENED: 1946

CURRENT LEAGUE: Ryman (Isthmian) League Premier Division
CLUB FOUNDED: 1948 merger of Boreham Rovers and Royal Retournez
PREVIOUS GROUNDS: Eldon Avenue (1948–63)

Boreham Wood strangely spell the club's name as two words, although the town spells the name as one. The club played at Eldon Avenue until 1963, when they moved to a patch of land off Broughinge Road. The ground has been developed in separate spells. The old main stand went up shortly after the move, but this odd-looking stand, with a huge sloping roof minimizing viewing height, was replaced in 1999. The original covered terrace has also been revamped in recent years. In the 1980s the club built a physiotherapy room and completely refurbished their popular clubhouse. An all-weather five-a-side surface was also opened behind the main stand. In 1990 the boardroom and office facilities were also renovated. The gradual upgrading of all facilities over the last 15 years now see Meadow Park right up to date and compliant with ground-grading criteria.

BOURNE TOWN
GROUND: Abbey Lawn, Abbey Road, Bourne, Lincolnshire
CURRENT CAPACITY: 3,000
RECORD ATTENDANCE: 3,000 v. Chelmsford City (FA Trophy) 1970
YEAR BUILT/OPENED: 1947
CURRENT LEAGUE: Eagle Bitter United Counties League Premier Division
CLUB FOUNDED: 1883
PREVIOUS GROUNDS: Cricket Field

Rejoicing in the unusual and seemingly inexplicable nickname of 'The Wakes', Bourne Town have led an interesting life since their formation in 1883. They have always played in the confines of the Recreation Ground on Abbey Road. Originally they played on the outfield of the cricket pitch but moved east in 1947 when their own pitch was made available. It was dubbed Abbey Lawn and has an

Abbey Lawn, Bourne Town

Larges Lane, Bracknell Town

interesting melange of three stands on the Abbey Road side of the ground. Each has a different roof level to add to the ground's eccentric appearance. The two nearest to the entrance are modest covered shelters with gently lilting, rather than pitched, roofs. The furthest structure is a more modern brick-built stand that provides the ground's only seated accommodation. This is a thoroughly pleasing venue that makes the long drive to this isolated part of fenland Lincolnshire well worthwhile.

BRACKNELL TOWN
GROUND: Larges Lane, Bracknell, Berkshire
CURRENT CAPACITY: 2,500
RECORD ATTENDANCE: 2,500 v. Newquay (FA Amateur Cup) 1971
YEAR BUILT/OPENED: 1933
CURRENT LEAGUE: Ryman (Isthmian) League Division One (South)
CLUB FOUNDED: 1896 as Bracknell Wanderers

PREVIOUS GROUNDS: Devonshire Arms; Station Field

Always a modest ground, Larges Lane has an eclectic mix of stands and buildings. The club moved to the ground in 1933 and at first had to put up with a pronounced latitudinal slope. However, the massive housing boom of the post-war years supplied enough material to level the pitch to a more agreeable rake. The ground was relatively undeveloped until 1962 when the club was bequeathed a large amount of money from respected townsman, Sir Raymond Brown. A clubhouse, function hall and new changing rooms sprang up as well as a small cover for spectators. Another cover went up in 1988 together with a seated stand on the clubhouse side of the ground. Six years later a further small covered terrace went up behind a goal to comply with Isthmian League requirements. It is a perfectly functional venue that will never pretend to be more than an adequate lower-level stadium.

BRADFORD PARK AVENUE

GROUND: Horsfall Stadium, Cemetery Road, Bradford, West Yorkshire
CURRENT CAPACITY: 5,000
RECORD ATTENDANCE: 1,007 v. Bradford City (Centenary Match)
YEAR BUILT/OPENED: Not Known
CURRENT LEAGUE: Unibond (Northern Premier) League Premier Division
CLUB FOUNDED: 1988 re-formation of club that existed between 1907–1974
PREVIOUS GROUNDS: Park Avenue (1907–73); Valley Parade (1973–74); Manningham Mills(1988–89); Bramley RLFC (1989–93); Batley RLFC (1993–96)

Much has been written about the rise and fall of Bradford Park Avenue and their Football League career, which lasted 62 years between 1908 and 1970. They grew out of Bradford Rugby Club and adopted professionalism in 1907 before being denied a place in the Football League. They then controversially 'bought' a place in the Southern League Division One in 1907/08, bypassing Division Two and denying a promotion place for Division Two champions, Southend United. They spent only one season in the Southern League, finishing 13th of 20 clubs. Despite their modest playing record, they joined their neighbours, Bradford City, in the Football League for the 1908/09 campaign. They rose to Division One in 1913 and stayed for eight years before a dramatic collapse began, which culminated in four successive re-election applications between 1966 and 1970. Their luck ran out in 1969/70 when finishing bottom for the third straight season saw Avenue booted out of the League in favour of Cambridge United. Within three years financial problems meant they had lost their cherished and unusual Park Avenue ground, affectionately known as the 'Dolls House' due to its striking pavilion. They shared at Valley Parade for one last season before disbanding in 1974. The great old name was revived in 1988 when the club joined the West Riding County Amateur League, playing at the modest ground of Manningham Mills. Between 1989 and 1993 Park Avenue played at two rugby League grounds, Bramley's McLaren Field and Batley's Mount Pleasant before returning to the city boundaries at an existing athletics stadium. It is great to see such an evocative old name back in the limelight. Long may it continue.

BRAINTREE TOWN

GROUND: Cressing Road Stadium, Clockhouse Way, Braintree, Essex
CURRENT CAPACITY: 4,000
RECORD ATTENDANCE: 4,000 v. Tottenham Hotspur (Charity Match) 08/05/52
YEAR BUILT/OPENED: 1923
CURRENT LEAGUE: Ryman (Isthmian) League Premier Division
CLUB FOUNDED: 1898 as Manor Works
PREVIOUS GROUNDS: Fairfield (1898–1903); Spalding's Meadow (1903–23)

John Weaver's excellent history of this stadium does far more justice to it than I can do in a few hundred words, but I will relate the essential facts. The club were originally the works team of window company called Crittal Manufacturing. That firm provided a brand-new and hugely impressive venue for the team in 1923. The new venue had a first-class athletics track and a year later a smart 800-seater wooden grandstand was erected, which stood until destroyed in a

Cressing Road, Braintree Town

severe gale in 1974. In 1932 a small stand was built on the cricket ground side of the ground. However, 15 years later this was dismantled and added onto the existing main stand to lengthen it at both ends. By 1973 one of main-stand extensions was demolished. Following the devastating gale the roof was removed and the bench seating was left as uncovered seating. By the late 1970s the ground had become quite rundown, but a renaissance started with the opening of the new clubhouse in 1982. A new covered terrace, the Chicken Run Stand, was opened in 1986. Further development came in the late 1980s when the clubhouse was extended and a new grandstand erected in the summer of 1989 by Tiami Developments. In December 1993 the infamous Quag End, so called as it often resembled a quagmire, was covered and a year later the Sportsman's Stand was opened opposite the main stand. This stand was extended during the summer of 2002. The regeneration of this historic venue has seen it returned to being a first-class venue.

BRIMSCOMBE & THRUPP

GROUND: The Meadow, London Road, Brimscombe, Gloucestershire
CURRENT CAPACITY: 1,000
RECORD ATTENDANCE: Not Known
YEAR BUILT/OPENED: 1946
CURRENT LEAGUE: Gloucestershire Northern Senior League Division Two
CLUB FOUNDED: Not Recorded
PREVIOUS GROUNDS: None

One of the many picture-postcard grounds that grace the Gloucestershire countryside. The Meadow was levelled off to form a useable playing surface and much of the earth was compacted to form a sizeable bank on the London Road side of the ground. A wooden cover was erected into a cutting in the bank and, although appearing somewhat precarious, provides a marvellous view of the match. The pitch is set off by a smart white post and rail fence. Looking past the stand and bank, the overall picture is complete by extensive woodland rising sharply in the distance. Brimscombe and Thrupp is a modest club with a pretty little home.

The Meadow, Brimscombe & Thrupp

BROMLEY

GROUND: Hayes Lane, Bromley, Kent
CURRENT CAPACITY: 5,000
RECORD ATTENDANCE: 10,789 v.
Nigeria National XI (Friendly) 24/09/49
YEAR BUILT/OPENED: 1938
CURRENT LEAGUE: Ryman (Isthmian)
League Division One (South)
CLUB FOUNDED: 1892
PREVIOUS GROUNDS: Queensmead;
Glebe Road; Plaistow Cricket Ground

Since Bromley moved to their second ground in Glebe Road, the club have played at a further three grounds, all within 500 yards of each other. Glebe Road was home until 1900, when that side of the road was needed for a housing development. The club relocated to a nearby site that had been used for many years by the defunct Plaistow Cricket Club. This move lasted for a mere four years before this ground was seized for more housing. The next ground was less than 100 yards away in Hayes Lane but was little more than an open field. The new ground lasted until 1938, when a new smarter site in the same road was made available. The cricket club that had followed the football club in its moves was relocated on the other side of town. This time the club came up trumps, the ground boasted a huge wooden grandstand with seating for 2,000 and was officially opened by Stanley Rous. A record crowd gathered in 1949 when a touring XI of allegedly bare-footed Nigerian players created a huge interest around the country. The ground remained superbly untouched until October 1992, when the beautiful grandstand was gutted by fire. It was nearly a year until its bland replacement was ready for action. The ground now has one modern side with the old wooden covers and extensive terracing, still doing admirable service, being a wonderful relic of times past.

BROMSGROVE ROVERS

GROUND: Victoria Ground,
Birmingham Road, Bromsgrove,
Worcestershire
CURRENT CAPACITY: 4,900

RECORD ATTENDANCE: 7,839 v.
Worcester City 1957
YEAR BUILT/OPENED: 1910
CURRENT LEAGUE: Dr Marten's
(Southern) League Western Division
CLUB FOUNDED: 1885
PREVIOUS GROUNDS: Old Station
Road; Recreation Ground; Churchfields;
Well Lane

The club's promotion from the Midland
Alliance as runners-up to Stourbridge in
the 2001/02 season halted a dramatic
slide in the club's fortunes. Rovers were
a Conference club between 1992 and
1997 but relegation from that league and
subsequent drops through the divisions
of the Dr Marten's League were a devastating blow to the club. Relegation to the
Midland Alliance saw the club at its lowest level for many years. They had
previously graced the powerful
Birmingham Combination and the West
Midlands League before their initial spell
in the Southern League, which started in
1973. The club moved into the Victoria
Ground in 1910, although it only really
took shape in the immediate post-World
War Two years. The present 350-seater
main stand was opened around then and
replaced an old wooden stand erected in
1924. The original dressing rooms were
built in 1953 and later extended to
include clubhouse facilities. Floodlights
also arrived in this year although they
would be replaced in 1971. The ground
was extensively terraced and a covered
stand went up opposite the main stand.
One end of the ground had a cover
erected in readiness for the club's elevation to the Football Conference. The
most recent change at the Victoria
Ground has been the provision of new
changing rooms, a referee's room and a
modern physio's room under the main
stand. After a period of great trauma
when the club's very existence was in
some doubt, it is pleasing to see
Bromgsrove on the way back up.

BUGLE
GROUND: Molinnis Park, Molinnis
Road, Bugle, Cornwall
CURRENT CAPACITY: 3,000
RECORD ATTENDANCE: Not Known
YEAR BUILT/OPENED: c1933
CURRENT LEAGUE: Club not currently
active
CLUB FOUNDED: Not Recorded
PREVIOUS GROUNDS: None

The unusual stand at Molinnis is a carbon
copy of one that stood at Helston's former Beacon Parc ground. This was due
to the fact that Bugle's board borrowed
the plans that Helston had commissioned for their own stand. It is pretty
impressive, mainly due to its height, but
reflects the club's former status as a
respected South-Western League side.
However the 1990s has seen the club
drop out of that league, straight through
the East Cornwall League, and due to
lack of volunteers and support, the club
are currently in a state of limbo, with no
team to compete at any level. It is hoped
that this once-proud club can regroup
and ensure that Molinnis Park is restored
to its former glory. It remains, even in its
advanced state of decay, one of the many
treasured grounds of the Cornish China
Clay Hills area.

BUNGAY TOWN
GROUND: Maltings Meadow, Pirnhaw
Road, Ditchingham, Norfolk
CURRENT CAPACITY: 1,500
RECORD ATTENDANCE: 2,001 v. Ilford

Molinnis Park, Bugle

(FA Amateur Cup) 25/01/58
YEAR BUILT/OPENED: 1953
CURRENT LEAGUE: Lovewell Blake
Anglian Combination Division One
CLUB FOUNDED: 1925
PREVIOUS GROUNDS: Recreation
Ground (1925–53); Outney Common;
Honeypot Meadow

Ironically both of Bungay's permanent grounds have been over the border in Norfolk, the Suffolk town being separated from the neighbouring county by the River Waveney. Their Recreation Ground was on the flood plain of the Earsham Down and was frequently reduced to a quagmire. On such occasions the club staged matches at Outney Common or Honeypot Meadow, with, ironically, both temporary venues being in Suffolk! Honeypot Meadow was off Bardolph Road and now lies under Bungay Police Station. A record gate at

the Recreation Ground of 2,498 was recorded for the visit in January 1950 of Wycombe Wanderers. By this time the club had decided the flooding meant their future was best served by a move to a more suitable venue. After protracted negotiations the new venue at Maltings Meadow in Ditchingham was opened in August 1953. In the best tradition of non-League grounds, the material for the new stand was cannibalized from the old race-track stand at Outney Common. The new changing rooms were part funded by the generous donation of £1,200 from the mother of a Town player killed during World War Two. The town has suffered from smaller crowds at Maltings Meadow, but have proudly maintained senior status throughout, which is not bad for a town with a population of just over 5,000. In May 1987 the stand was badly damaged by fire, but the club have repaired it admirably, although some-

Maltings Meadow, Bungay Town

what reduced in size and capacity. The Black Dogs' ground, however, remains a very pleasant venue in a picturesque part of East Anglia.

BURNHAM
GROUND: The Gore, Wymers Wood Road, Burnham, Slough, Buckinghamshire
CURRENT CAPACITY: 2,500
RECORD ATTENDANCE: 2,380 v Halesowen Town (FA Vase) 02/04/83
YEAR BUILT/OPENED: 1920
CURRENT LEAGUE: Dr Marten's (Southern) League Eastern Division
CLUB FOUNDED: 1878
PREVIOUS GROUNDS: Baldwin's Meadow (1878-1920)

Burnham were formed in 1878, which makes them Buckinghamshire's second-oldest club behind Marlow. The club originally played at Baldwin Meadow, which was off the High Street, the club's headquarters being at the nearby George Hotel. The club moved to the Gore Recreation Ground in the early 1920s and have shared with the cricket club ever since. The small stand was erected in 1948 and the club moved up to the Hellenic League, in which they remained until 1985. In that year the club took the bold move to merge with the financially struggling Southern League club, Hillingdon. That club had lost its Leas Stadium to a housing development and the newly merged club became Burnham and Hillingdon. However, as often happens following mergers the club dropped the joint name after only two seasons, reverting to plain Burnham FC. Surprisingly, Burnham managed to hold onto their Southern League place until 1995 when they returned to the Hellenic League. Following four seasons of regrouping and carrying out ground improvements to The Gore, the club regained Southern League status for the 1999/2000 campaign. The Gore remains a pleasant venue, although how long a three-sided ground will be allowed in the Southern League will be interesting to see.

BURNHAM RAMBLERS

GROUND: Leslie Field, Springfield Road, Burnham-on-Crouch, Essex
CURRENT CAPACITY: 2,000
RECORD ATTENDANCE: 1,500 v. Arsenal (Grandstand Opening) 1987
YEAR BUILT/OPENED: 1987
CURRENT LEAGUE: Foresters Essex Senior League
CLUB FOUNDED: 1900
PREVIOUS GROUNDS: Millfields; Saltcourts; Wick Road

The club was formed in 1900, playing matches on four different pitches including those at Millfields and Saltcourts. They played in the North Essex and later the Mid-Essex League. They joined the Intermediate Olympian League in the 1960s and had considerable success. However their Wick Road ground, their permanent home since 1927, was never going to be a senior ground. So the club entered into protracted negotiations for a new site at the edge of town. The plans came to fruition when the Leslie Field was opened in 1987 with a celebration match against Arsenal. The club's long-standing chairman, Gordon Brasted, had joined the Highbury club from Burnham in 1953 so the first opponent was an appropriate choice. The Leslie Field has the main stadium, a training pitch as well as two other full-size pitches to cater for Ramblers many youth and junior sides. The social facilities are first class, with a two-storey clubhouse, lounge bar and function suite. It provides the club with a reliable source of income. The grandstand is up to Isthmian League standard and a simple corrugated-iron cover provides accommodation on the far side. The Leslie Field is without doubt the perfect, modern small-town venue.

BURSCOUGH

GROUND: Victoria Park, Hart Lane, Burscough, Lancashire
CURRENT CAPACITY: 2,500
RECORD ATTENDANCE: 4,798 v. Wigan Athletic (FA Cup) 28/10/50
YEAR BUILT/OPENED: 1901

Leslie Field, Burnham Ramblers

CURRENT LEAGUE: Unibond (Northern Premier) League Premier Division
CLUB FOUNDED: 1946
PREVIOUS GROUNDS: None

Originally Victoria Park was used for cricket but soon Burscough Rangers began playing football matches there. During World War One, the pitch was dug up and used for crop growing to aid the war effort. On resumption of football in 1919, Rangers played at Travis's Field before Victoria Park was returfed and ready for football. In 1928 the club secured the purchase of the Stanley Road grandstand from Everton FC. The stand was shipped to Victoria Park by rail and steam-driven pantechnicon. Club volunteers painstakingly re-erected the grandstand, which was to stand at the Hart Lane ground for almost 60 years. However by the early 1930s, Rangers were in financial trouble and sold the stand to the local council. Simultaneously the council also purchased the ground from its owners James Martland Ltd. Unfortunately the sale did not cure Rangers' troubles and they went bust in 1935. After World War Two the town's footballers formed a new club, Burscough FC, and signed a lease at Victoria Park. In 1951 the club ran a subscription fund to raise the £400 required to buy the site from the council. The club immediately started ground improvements by covering the Crabtree Lane end. The ground was developed steadily over the next 30 years when the club were hit with a fearful blow. In the wake of the Bradford fire disaster, the old Goodison Park stand was closed down and estimates for repairs topped £100,000. The old stand was sadly pulled down and replaced with a smart modern structure,

officially opened by a visit from a strong Liverpool side.

BURTON ALBION
GROUND: Eton Park, Princess Way, Burton-on-Trent, Staffordshire
CURRENT CAPACITY: 4,500
RECORD ATTENDANCE: 5,860 v. Weymouth (Southern League Cup Final) 1964
YEAR BUILT/OPENED: 1957
CURRENT LEAGUE: Nationwide Football Conference
CLUB FOUNDED: 1950
PREVIOUS GROUNDS: Wellington Street (1950–57)

This Staffordshire town has a long history in football and, amazingly, had three clubs representing the town in the early years of the Football League. Burton Swifts (1892-1901), Burton Wanderers (1894-97) and Burton United (1901-7) have all long since bitten the dust and the town's sole senior club is now Burton Albion, formed as recently as 1950. Albion's first ground in Wellington Street was owned by Lloyds Foundry, but when a large piece of land at the existing Sports Ground became available, the Burton Albion Supporter's Club met the £2,000 asking price. The ground was opened in September 1957, when 5,527 watched a FA Cup tie with Nuneaton. The Eton Park ground was built up steadily, covered terracing complementing the main stand (itself costing a not inconsiderable £6,000), and a second-hand set of floodlights were purchased from Bristol City. The supporter's club came to the club's aid in the 1960s when they parted with £2,000 to buy a piece of land to erect a clubhouse. The club remained a considerable force in the 1960s and '70s, but in

Ram Meadow, Bury Town

more recent times Albion have suffered severe financial problems. In 1995 monetary trouble was so grave that the club considered offers for the ground. Fortunately, Eton Park survived to fight another day and remains a comfortable and attractive Northern League venue.

BURY TOWN
GROUND: Ram Meadow, Cotton Lane, Bury St.Edmunds, Suffolk
CURRENT CAPACITY: 3,500
RECORD ATTENDANCE: 2,500 v. Enfield (FA Cup) 11/10/86
YEAR BUILT/OPENED: 1977
CURRENT LEAGUE: Jewson Eastern Counties League Premier Division
CLUB FOUNDED: 1872
PREVIOUS GROUNDS: King Road (1873–76), Hardwick Heath (1976–77)

Bury Town played at the splendid stadium in Kings Road for 103 years until the district council decided the town needed a bypass and the chosen site would bisect the football ground. The road was duly built and the remaining land was turned into a car park, although plans are afoot to turn this into a cinema complex. The old ground saw many historic matches and was held in great affection by supporters. The record gate at Kings Road was set in 1958 when the visit of Kings Lynn attracted 4,710 spectators. The club had been compensated for the inconvenience of the move to the tune of £15,000 and were offered a site across town on a derelict site occupied previously by a public house called The Ram. Although many of the supporters were sceptical of the move, and the out-of-town location has undoubtedly affected attendances, Ram Meadow has proved to be an excellent venue in its own right. However the new ground was not ready until the summer of 1977, which meant the 1976/77 campaign was spent playing on an unenclosed site at Hardwick Heath. Therefore the club were unable to charge admission for that season, relying solely on donations. Ram Meadow's first game saw a pre-season friendly against Harwich & Parkestone in July 1977, with the stadium record attendance coming nine years later in a FA Cup tie against Enfield. The ground's most eye-catching feature is the main stand with its unusual roof, elevated at an improbable angle. So unusual is its construction that it sees the beams of the roof carcass at its lowest point causing a severe threat to any spectator of reasonable height. Caution is advised.

BUXTON

GROUND: The Silverlands, Silverlands, Buxton, Derbyshire
CURRENT CAPACITY: 4,000
RECORD ATTENDANCE: 6,000 v. Barrow (FA Cup) 03/11/62
YEAR BUILT/OPENED: 1884
CURRENT LEAGUE: Northern Counties East League Premier Division
CLUB FOUNDED: 1877
PREVIOUS GROUNDS: The Park; Wyelands; Macclesfield Road; Cote Heath

Buxton is an ancient spa town in a beautiful area of the Peak District and one of the highest towns above sea level. Buxton claim to have the most elevated ground in the country, although the good folk of Tow Law Town would be willing to cross altimeters. The club played their first match at Silverlands in November 1884, when it was little more than an unenclosed field. The first covered accommodation was erected in 1890, primarily 'to encourage lady supporters to the ground'. Soon after a grandstand was opened and stood until it was replaced by the current main stand in 1965. In 1980 the dressing rooms were replaced with new facilities under the main stand. The club invested in a new drainage system in 1979 and the move has paid dividends, with waterlogging in this area of copious precipitation being a rare event. In the early 1990s the terracing was relaid and the old covers replaced. A visit to this ancient sports ground and delightful town is a must for any stadium buff.

The Silverlands, Buxton

C

CADBURY ATHLETIC

GROUND: Bourneville Recreation Ground, Bourneville Lane, Bourneville, Birmingham
CURRENT CAPACITY: 1,500
RECORD ATTENDANCE: Not Known
YEAR BUILT/OPENED: 1897
CURRENT LEAGUE: Midland Combination Division One
CLUB FOUNDED: 1994
PREVIOUS GROUNDS: None

This is a magnificent venue, although it lacks a stand of any description. The ground is adjacent to the famous chocolate factory and was opened in 1897. The superb pavilion, built in mock-Tudor style with a tall tower, was built five years later and has therefore just reached its centenary. The ground does have extensive terracing cut into the grass banking, which affords the spectator a superb view of the proceedings. The bank and playing surface are immaculately trimmed and the venue even boasts a spectacular ornamental waterfall, complete with a harp-wielding water nymph gazing skyward. The Recreation Ground is just a beautiful sporting venue and an essential part of this country's footballing heritage.

CAMBRIDGE CITY

GROUND: City Ground, Milton Road, Cambridge, Cambridgeshire
CURRENT CAPACITY: 5,000
RECORD ATTENDANCE: 2,325 v. Hereford United (FA Cup) 14/11/93
YEAR BUILT/OPENED: 1985
CURRENT LEAGUE: Dr Marten's (Southern) League Premier Division
CLUB FOUNDED: 1908
PREVIOUS GROUNDS: 11 grounds before the Town Ground, Milton Road (1922–84)

Bourneville Recreation Ground, Cadbury United

City Ground, Cambridge City

Having played on many grounds in their first 16 years of existence, Cambridge Town (as they were then) moved into their new ground in Milton Road in April 1922. The ground boasted a grandstand and extensive banking and cost the club the not-inconsiderable sum of £2,769. In 1931 a new stand with 750 seats was erected and was later joined by extensive terracing around the ground. The club progressed to the Southern League and became a major force in the non-League game. A record gate of 12,078 attended an Amateur Cup tie against Leytonstone in 1950. Two more five-figure crowds were recorded in the same decade for the FA Cup visit of Cambridge United in 1953 and for a visit of West Ham United to inaugurate the ground's new floodlights in 1959. The club progressed well and applied for Football League membership on four occasions between 1959 and 1967, only to see their near neighbours given the nod in 1970 when Bradford Park Avenue lost their League status. That must have been a severe blow to the club as they were always the more senior side in the town. A further application was made in 1974, but the chances of a second League place being given to the same city was remote in the extreme, and the club's application received no votes of support. The club's fortunes declined, support dwindled and by 1985 the club accepted a bid from a property developer for the ground. Finance received meant the club could build a modern new stadium on the site of the former training ground, at right angles to the old stadium. The facility is first class and has recently seen its main stand extended westwards by 100 seats, although disappointingly the level of the new roof is lower than the existing stand, somewhat spoiling the aesthetics. In the summer of 2002 Milton Road became the new headquarters of the Cambridgeshire Football Association.

Krooner Park, Camberley Town

CAMBERLEY TOWN
GROUND: Krooner Park, Krooner Road, Camberley, Surrey
CURRENT CAPACITY: 3,000
RECORD ATTENDANCE: 3,146 v. Crystal Palace (Friendly) 14/10/74
YEAR BUILT/OPENED: 1922
CURRENT LEAGUE: Ryman (Isthmian) League Division Two
CLUB FOUNDED: 1896 as Camberley & Yorktown
PREVIOUS GROUNDS: Recreation Ground (1898–1905,1910–22); Southwell Park (1905-09); Martin's Meadow (1909-10)

Tragedy struck Krooner Park in August 1990 when a devastating fire wrecked the 63-year-old main stand. The classically designed wooden stand was burned beyond salvation and the heat from the fire was so intense that part of the pitch was badly scorched. Camberley moved to Krooner Park in 1922 and five years later, following a collection, the wooden stand was erected at a cost of £500. They drifted along for many years until hitting the headlines with the devastating fire. The club had to borrow grounds to stage matches, but in an amazingly quick time, by November, the ground was back in use, complete with a splendid new stand. The club have recovered well from a serious setback and although they have remained in the lower reaches of the Isthmian League, the club face a more than healthy future.

CANVEY ISLAND
GROUND: Park Lane, Leigh Beck, Canvey Island, Essex
CURRENT CAPACITY: 4,000
RECORD ATTENDANCE: 3,250 v. Brighton & Hove Albion (FA Cup) 11/11/95
YEAR BUILT/OPENED: 1962
CURRENT LEAGUE: Ryman (Isthmian)

War Memorial Sports Ground, Carshalton Athletic

League Premier Division
CLUB FOUNDED: 1926
PREVIOUS GROUNDS: Furtherwick
School; King George's Recreation
Ground; The Paddocks

I can remember attending a match at Park
Lane in the early 1980s when I was the
12th and last paying punter through the
turnstiles! However, this was before the
arrival on the scene of local businessman
Jeff King in 1991. Since then the club has
sky-rocketed up the non-League pyramid, culminating in the FA Trophy victory
at Villa Park in 2001. The ground has been
developed beyond all recognition, with
the bus shelter that provided the
ground's only cover being developed
into a main stand, which has now been
extended right down one side of the
pitch down to the sea-wall end of the
ground. The rest of the ground now has
extensive terracing, both covered and
uncovered, all round the remaining sides.
The club now have a fearsome reputation

and have become a modern-day Yeovil, in
terms of FA Cup giant-killings. Certainly
many Football League clubs will be quak-
ing in their boots when the FA Cup first
round comes around again. The club
have come a long way in the last decade
and should be proud of the way they play
the game.

CARSHALTON ATHLETIC

GROUND: War Memorial Sports
Ground, Colston Avenue, Carshalton,
Surrey
CURRENT CAPACITY: 8,000
RECORD ATTENDANCE: 8,200 v.
Tooting & Mitcham United (FA Cup)
28/10/50
YEAR BUILT/OPENED: 1921
CURRENT LEAGUE: Ryman (Isthmian)
League Division One (South)
CLUB FOUNDED: 1903 as Mill Lane
Mission
PREVIOUS GROUNDS: Wrythe
Recreation Ground (1907-14); Culvers
Park (1919–21)

The Colston Avenue site was leased from the Urban District Council in 1920 and was enclosed in time for the opening match on New Year's Day 1921. The site was named in memory of local men lost in World War One. The first covered accommodation arrived in 1926 when the club secured a disused Jockey Club stand from Epsom Racecourse. It provided admirable service until it was damaged beyond repair by severe gales in 1968. This was replaced by the present structure in 1972. The extensive terrace was laid in 1949 and extended a year later to cater for the record crowd that attended the FA Cup clash with near-neighbours Tooting & Mitcham United. The opposite side was terraced in 1953 and covered in sections, when finance permitted, giving the unusual stepped effect with uneven roof sections. In recent years a covered terrace has been erected at the turnstile end of the ground. The War Memorial ground is a super venue with ample covered accommodation, although an attempt at a new

ground record attendance would be a very tight squeeze to say the least.

CHALFONT ST PETER

GROUND: Mill Meadow, Amersham Road, Chalfont St Peter, Buckinghamshire
CURRENT CAPACITY: 4,500
RECORD ATTENDANCE: 2,500 v. Watford (Benefit Match) 1985
YEAR BUILT/OPENED: 1952
CURRENT LEAGUE: Ryman (Isthmian) League Division Two
CLUB FOUNDED: 1926
PREVIOUS GROUNDS: Gold Hill Common; Welch's Farm

It is a funny old League, the Ryman League. They are more-often-than-not accused of being pedantic and fussy in terms of enforcing ground-grading criteria to the 'n'th degree. So it is therefore baffling that one of its member clubs, Chalfont St Peter, have an extremely basic ground in a very poor state of repair. The ground's enclosing fence is either miss-

Mill Meadow, Chalfont St Peter

59

ing panels or has gaping holes. The two areas of cover behind either goal, erected as recently as 1988, have been dismantled. The main stand, erected in 1956, could not be more awkwardly sited, being blocked by all manner of obstructions. To the right the extension to the clubhouse blocks the view to the car-park end, a portakabin does the same for the opposite end. Roof supports, a floodlight pylon and dugouts make this one of the most poorly designed stands in senior football. The club have been at Mill Meadow since 1952 and, in fairness to them, they have faced considerable problems in upgrading the ground as it is on protected countryside in this leafy and posh commuter town.

CHATHAM TOWN
GROUND: Sports Ground, Maidstone Road, Chatham, Kent
CURRENT CAPACITY: 5,000
RECORD ATTENDANCE: 5,000 v. Gillingham (Friendly) 1980

YEAR BUILT/OPENED: 1890
CURRENT LEAGUE: Dr Marten's (Southern) League Eastern Division
CLUB FOUNDED: 1882 as Chatham FC
PREVIOUS GROUNDS: Great Lines (1882-89)

Chatham Town started by playing matches on Great Lines, a huge, Army-owned, open space containing several pitches. Indeed contemporary newspaper reports state crowds in excess of 20,000 congregated at that venue for FA Cup ties against West Bromwich Albion and Nottingham Forrest in 1889. In a strange twist of fate, the club were forced to return to the Great Lines area in 1997 when a new drainage system at the Maidstone Road ground saw parts of the pitch collapse, leaving it unplayable. The Kent League allowed the club to use the Garrison Ground in Kings Bastian for several matches in 1997/98. The ground boasts an attractive barrel roof stand and is in the shadow of quite possibly the

Sports Ground, Chatham Town

largest war memorial you are ever likely to see. Having cured their pitch problems, Chatham returned to Maidstone Road with renewed vigour, determined to regain their place in the Southern League. The ground has two stands on the Cemetery side and the Bourneville Avenue side. The latter was originally part covered standing and part seating, but the seating was later extended. Both stands replaced earlier wooden stands during the 1950s. In 1996 the club erected an impressive structure at the Maidstone Road end, which housed new changing rooms and offices, as well as providing some cover at that end of the ground. The club's dogged persistence was rewarded with a return to the Southern League in 2001.

CHATTERIS TOWN
GROUND: West Street, Chatteris, Cambridgeshire
CURRENT CAPACITY: 2,000
RECORD ATTENDANCE: 2,000 v. March Town United (Eastern Counties League) 1988
YEAR BUILT/OPENED: 1946
CURRENT LEAGUE: Peterborough & District League
CLUB FOUNDED: 1920
PREVIOUS GROUNDS: Chatteris Park; Chatteris Recreation Ground

Chatteris Town have struggled financially in recent years and despite finishing in a healthy fifth place in the Jewson League Division One at the end of 2000/01, the club accepted voluntary demotion to the Peterborough & District League in order to cut travelling expenses. The club have been in existence since 1920 when they started playing at Chatteris Park. They soon overtook Chatteris Engineers as the town's leading side and eventually moved home to the town's Recreation Ground. After World War Two, the club looked for a new ground, and an undeveloped site off West Street was chosen. In 1951 the two stands were built. The

West Street, Chatteris Town

main stand has wooden-bench seats with unusually steep tiers and is set off nicely by having the club's name picked out in the centre section. The second stand has shallow terracing and various forms of benches and chairs. In the early 1960s, the club needed more pitches for training purposes, as well as its youth sides, and acquired the adjacent field from the Shepherd's Society and installed several pitches. The hedge that divided the football ground from the field was removed, causing the site to be exposed to howling winds that would often blow into the fenland town. However, West Street remains a lovely venue and it can only be hoped the club can put aside their troubles of the 1990s and regroup in a lower level of the non-League pyramid.

CHELMSFORD CITY
GROUND: Billericay Town FC
CURRENT CAPACITY: 3,500

RECORD ATTENDANCE: 16,807 v. Colchester United (Southern League) 10/09/49 at New Writtle Street
YEAR BUILT/OPENED: Ground-shared since 1998
CURRENT LEAGUE: Dr Marten's (Southern) League Premier Division
CLUB FOUNDED: 1938
PREVIOUS GROUNDS: New Writtle Street (1938–97); Maldon Town FC (1997–98)

Call me morbid, but I felt I had to go New Writtle Street one more time when it was being demolished in July 1999. I photographed the wreckage, the main stand gutted, broken and twisted floodlight pylons lying like slain goliaths across the pitch. It was indeed a sorry sight. As I snapped away I realized I was not alone; an old man in his 70s was standing on the old uncovered terrace. We spoke at length and he had supported City since 1940, just two years after the professional

New Wittle Street, Chelmsford Town's former ground

club was formed, replacing the old amateur Chelmsford FC at New Writtle Street. The Stadium, as it was simply known, had been opened in 1925 and had been developed so well that the club applied for Football League membership on no less than 18 occasions. The old man reckoned the beginning of the end of New Writtle Street came in 1989 when the board took the unwise step of demolishing the pitch length covered terrace, known as The Barn, on the Central Park side of the ground. Its unusual barrelled roof, fairly common if not exactly indigenous to Essex (fine examples are to be found at Southend United and Southend Manor), marked this out as a classic stand. It was demolished in order for the pitch to be rotated through 90 degrees to allow total redevelopment of the ground to Conference standard. Unfortunately the council turned down City's planning application, the first of many such run-ins. The ground saw some memorable matches, the noise that could be generated by a full Wolseley End at a big game was something else. By the summer of 1997 the receivers had to be called in and City were booted off the ground six days after the opening League fixture of the 1997/98 campaign. So hasty and unceremonious was the exit that officials had to return to claim equipment and fittings. The club spent the rest of the season at Maldon Town, although the groundshare was to end in acrimony on both sides. The huge site was eventually sold to Countryside Commercial for a meagre £900,000 and now hosts a housing development and the vast Esporta fitness centre. I wonder how much the site is worth now. The club's meagre recompense dwindles by the week in rent while the ever-intransigent County Council

turns down planning application after planning application. As with Maidstone, in Kent, a county town now has no senior football ground, and that cannot be right. As the old man and I parted, my wish was for the councillors and property developers to see his face and the sorrow it showed. Hope, however, has surfaced with a plan to return the club to the borough by using a temporary home on field adjacent to the existing Melbourne Athletics Stadium. In the long term the club hope to gain permission for a new ground near Boreham.

CHERTSEY TOWN
GROUND: Alwyns Lane, Chertsey, Surrey
CURRENT CAPACITY: 3,000
RECORD ATTENDANCE: 2,150 v. Aldershot (Ryman League) 04/12/93
YEAR BUILT/OPENED: 1929
CURRENT LEAGUE: Ryman (Isthmian) League Division One (South)
CLUB FOUNDED: 1890
PREVIOUS GROUNDS: Willow Walk; Free Prea Road; Chilsey Green; The Grange; The Hollows

Chertsey had played on various venues around the Surrey town until 1929 when local philanthropist Sir Edward Stein left a field of suitable size to be used purely for football by the town's most senior team. An adjacent field was similarly donated to Chertsey Cricket Club. The first permanent structure at Alwyns Lane was a wooden dressing room, which meant the sides no longer had to change at the nearby pub. The superb main stand was built in 1954 solely by club volunteers. In 1960 a cover was erected at one end but lasted only three seasons when it was destroyed in a storm and never replaced. Instead a small cover went up opposite

C

the main stand in 1963 and has lasted thus far unscathed by the elements. A new dressing room block arrived in 1988 and more recently extensive terracing has been laid. With these being the only recent developments, it has always been impeccably well kept. Sir Edward Stein would certainly have approved.

CHESHAM UNITED
GROUND: The Meadow, Amy Lane, Amersham Road, Chesham, Buckinghamshire
CURRENT CAPACITY: 5,000
RECORD ATTENDANCE: 5,000 v. Cambridge United (FA Cup) 05/12/79
YEAR BUILT/OPENED: 1919
CURRENT LEAGUE: Ryman (Isthmian) League Premier Division
CLUB FOUNDED: 1886 as Chesham FC
PREVIOUS GROUNDS: Chesham Cricket Club

Chesham were formed in 1886 and became Chesham Town before merging with the powerful Chesham Generals during World War Two and becoming Chesham United. At this time the club played at Chesham Cricket Club, which is still in existence adjacent to The Meadow. United moved up to the top field in 1919, dismantling the ornate stand at the cricket club and re-erecting it at their new home. It gave sterling service at The Meadow until it was destroyed beyond economic repair in a huge blaze in 1982. This was replaced with the present main stand. Extensive covers were erected before World War Two and as the years progressed, large tracts of terracing were laid underneath them. The covers were eventually replaced, section by section, as they had fallen into disrepair. The ground was always a three-sided affair at

the cricket-ground end until 1991, when the Isthmian League insisted on fully enclosed grounds. An interesting turn of events happened in 1979 when the grass bank at one end was excavated to allow for a temporary stand for the FA Cup visit of Cambridge United. To the astonishment of club officials, the removal of the earth uncovered already existing and perfectly serviceable terracing, that had been laid in the immediate post World War Two era. This unlikely tale is typical of non-League football and it is what makes grounds like The Meadow so special.

CHESHUNT
GROUND: The Stadium, Theobalds Lane, Cheshunt, Hertfordshire
CURRENT CAPACITY: 2,500
RECORD ATTENDANCE: 6,300 v. Bromley (FA Amateur Cup) 28/01/59
YEAR BUILT/OPENED: 1949
CURRENT LEAGUE: Ryman (Isthmian) League Division Two
CLUB FOUNDED:1946
PREVIOUS GROUNDS: College Road; Brookfield Lane

There were grandiose plans for Theobalds Lane when it opened in the immediate post-war years. Plans to make it a multisport venue, to play host to cricket, athletics and cycling, never materialized. In truth, the large site covered by the ground has seen relatively little development. The Stadium opened in October 1949 with film star Christine Norden cutting the ribbon and the Cheshunt side fully played their part in a memorable day by defeating Hastings United 11-1! The cramped stand has been there since day one and has seen better days. Opposite is a large cover, built strangely off centre and well away from the touchline. This was erected in 1963, the same year floodlights came to Theobalds Lane. Cheshunt have had some lean years, but Theobalds Lane is bristling with potential, with extensive terracing and much room to expand should a change in fortunes occur.

CHESTER CITY
GROUND: Deva Stadium, Bumpers Lane, Chester, Cheshire
CURRENT CAPACITY: 6,000
RECORD ATTENDANCE: 5,638 v. Preston North End (Football League) 02/04/94
YEAR BUILT/OPENED: 1992
CURRENT LEAGUE: Nationwide Football Conference
CLUB FOUNDED: 1884
PREVIOUS GROUNDS: Faulkner Street (1885–98); Old Showground (1898–99); Whipcord Lane(1901–06); Sealand Road (1906–90); Macclesfield Town FC (1990–92)

Admittedly Chester's old Sealand Road ground was well beyond its serviceable life at the end of the 1980s, but when the club eventually relocated to a new ground a few hundred yards away, not many peo-ple would have predicted the torrid times that lay ahead. Many of the club's fans were alienated by an autocratic chairman and the club lost its Football League status at the end of 1999/2000. The Deva Stadium, so named after the Latin for Chester, was opened, much delayed, in 1992 after problems with methane-contaminated land on the originally chosen site. To all intents and purposes it provides everything the club needs for its current level of support, but really there ought to be a law against the construction of stadia this dull and uninteresting.

CHIPPENHAM TOWN
GROUND: Hardenhuish Park, Bristol Road, Chippenham, Wiltshire
CURRENT CAPACITY: 4,000
RECORD ATTENDANCE: 4,800 v. Chippenham Utd (Western League) 1951
YEAR BUILT/OPENED: 1919
CURRENT LEAGUE: Dr Marten's (Southern) League Premier Division
CLUB FOUNDED: 1873
PREVIOUS GROUNDS: Westmead; Lowden; Little George Lane; Malmesbury Road

Deva Stadium, Chester City

C

Such are the vagaries of the English language that names do not always sound as they are written. Take the small Northamptonshire town of Cogenhoe, whose inhabitants somehow contrive to pronounce their team's name as 'Cookner'. Until I visited the Wiltshire town of Chippenham and its most senior football club I had always assumed, erroneously, that their ground was pronounced as it was spelt. However the locals dispense with no less than four letters and settle for the contracted pronunciation of 'Harnish'. This ground has been home to Chippenham Town since World War One. The smart main stand, with its distinctive pitch roof, is a bit of a landmark as it can be seen from a considerable distance. The stand was joined in 1979 by the new clubhouse, which was purposely attached to the rear of the stand so a glazed area could be inserted into the stand, allowing a view of the pitch from the comfort of the clubhouse. The dressing rooms in the

bowels of the stand were updated in the mid-1980s and the following decade saw the whole stand reclad in the club's blue colours and looks better than ever. The main stand has had several companions around the ground over the years. An extensive cover on the opposite side was replaced on three occasions, most recently in 1993. Hardenhuish Park now sees its greatest-ever standard of football in the Dr Marten's League Premier Division following promotion in their first season in the Western Division. This lovingly well-kept ground looks far from being out of place.

CHORLEY
GROUND: Victory Park, Duke Street, Chorley, Lancashire
CURRENT CAPACITY: 4,000
RECORD ATTENDANCE: 9,679 v. Darwen 1931
YEAR BUILT/OPENED: 1920
CURRENT LEAGUE: Unibond (Northern Premier) League Division One

Hardenhuish Park, Chippenham Town

CLUB FOUNDED: 1883
PREVIOUS GROUNDS: Dole Lane
(1883–1901); Rangletts Park (1901–05);
St.George's Park (1905–20)

Victory Park is a quite magnificent venue. its main stand, built in 1947, is a national treasure. The roof is supported by an impossible amount of criss-crossing metalwork. It also has that rare sight nowadays of floodlight pylons that pierce the roof. Its brick base and glorious pitched roof was a revolutionary design for a non-League ground and was copied at the grounds of Chelmsford City, Cheltenham Town and Morecambe with the latter pair still providing sterling service. Both ends at Victory Park have large covered terraces, the car-park end, the elder of the two, is another design classic with a multitude of roof supports. The ground, however, has had its share of disasters with the original Pilling Lane end being blown down in a gale in 1929 and the first grandstand being reduced to a pile of smouldering ash in 1945. The side opposite the main stand has substantial grass banking and has never seen any real development. Victory Park has survived the push for modernity intact and is a welcome reminder of how grounds used to look. A truly classic venue.

CINDERFORD TOWN
GROUND: The Causeway, Hilldene, Cinderford, Gloucestershire
CURRENT CAPACITY: 2,500
RECORD ATTENDANCE: 4,850 v. Minehead (Western League) 1957
YEAR BUILT/OPENED: 1947
CURRENT LEAGUE: Dr Marten's (Southern) League Western Division
CLUB FOUNDED: 1922

PREVIOUS GROUNDS: Royal Oak
(1922–32); Mousel Barn(1932–39)

A truly picturesque ground, with fine views of the Forest of Dean, it has not suffered aesthetically from recent modernization. The Causeway Ground has been Cinderford's home since 1947, when their previous ground at Mousel Barn was sold without their knowledge after World War One. To their additional annoyance, the club's equipment that was stored in a shed at the ground had totally disappeared. The club acquired three adjacent fields for the not-inconsiderable sum of £1,000. Such was the drain on finances that the first covered accommodation at the ground was a converted tool shed! Two more stands were erected soon after, following a successful fundraising appeal. New changing rooms followed in 1952. The ground remained unchanged for more than 40 years until 1994, when the club undertook the arduous task of levelling the considerable latitudinal slope. The excess earth was formed into banking, which was terraced on their promotion to the Southern League in 1995. It was a remarkable achievement for a club that was in the Gloucestershire County League in 1989.

CIRENCESTER TOWN
GROUND: Corimium Stadium, Kingshill Lane, Cirencester, Gloucestershire
CURRENT CAPACITY: 4,000
RECORD ATTENDANCE: 2,600 v. Fareham 1969 (at Smithsfield)
YEAR BUILT/OPENED: 2002
CURRENT LEAGUE: Dr Marten's (Southern) League Western Division
CLUB FOUNDED: 1889
PREVIOUS GROUNDS: Smithsfield
(1958-2002)

Smithsfield, previous home of Cirencester Town

Cirencester Town's Smithsfield ground will soon be no more as they have chosen to move from their ground, located off a roundabout on the main Fosseway Road through the town. Their chosen site for the new venture is at Kingshill, a new residential estate on the southern edge of town. Its is a somewhat curious move, as the Smithsfield ground has been upgraded considerably since their elevation to the Dr Marten's League from the Hellenic League in 1996. The ground was first used in 1958, with the club buying the site a decade later. They sold part of the ground to the council for the construction of the current roundabout. This meant the re-orientation of the pitch to its current east/west axis. A stand was erected behind the goal to fully enclose the newly turned pitch. In the 1990s, with their aspirations of Southern League membership, floodlights went up and in 1995, a smart, shiny new main stand was opened, as was an all-weather training surface. The new facility at Kingshill will certainly offer the club more room for expansion, but the question remains, what was so wrong with Smithsfield? Cirencester's brand-new home was officially opened on 20 July 2002, with Tottenham Hotspur doing the inauguration honours.

CLAPTON

GROUND: The Old Spotted Dog, Upton Lane, Forest Gate, London E7
CURRENT CAPACITY: 2,000
RECORD ATTENDANCE: 12,000 v. Tottenham Hotspur (FA Cup) 19/11/1898
YEAR BUILT/OPENED: 1888
CURRENT LEAGUE: Ryman (Isthmian) League Division Two
CLUB FOUNDED: 1878 as Downs FC
PREVIOUS GROUNDS: Elm Farm

An ancient and well-respected club with an equally vintage ground that reached its centenary in 1988. Clapton, five time FA Amateur Cup winners, moved to a field behind The Old Spotted Dog public house in Upton Lane. Originally it also catered for cricket, but once the side started attracting healthy four-figure crowds, the ground was fully enclosed. A record gate of 12,000 turned up for a FA Cup tie with Tottenham and the club hired temporary stands to accommodate the masses. The ground only ever had two stands, both wooden, on opposite sides of the pitch. One was dismantled after being badly damaged in a storm and the other was replaced in the 1990s, with a small rather ugly-looking metal stand with a cantilever roof. Clapton's decline in recent years has been dramatic, clinging to their continuous membership of the Isthmian League. Much of 2001/02 was spent playing 'home' games on nearby grounds due to severe pitch problems. The club hold a lot of affection amongst non-League fans, but officials must look back on the crowds of their early years with no little degree of jealousy.

CLEVEDON TOWN

GROUND: Hand Stadium, Davis Lane, Clevedon, Avon
CURRENT CAPACITY: 3,650
RECORD ATTENDANCE: 1,600 v. Bristol City (Friendly) 27/07/98
YEAR BUILT/OPENED: 1991
CURRENT LEAGUE: Dr Marten's (Southern) League Western Division
CLUB FOUNDED: 1974 merger of Clevedon (1880) and Ashtonians
PREVIOUS GROUNDS: Dial Hill (1880–93); Teignmouth Road (1893–1991)

Clevedon spent nearly 100 years at Teignmouth Road when it was sold for housing in 1991. The club did rather well from the deal, having purchased the land for £450 in 1949 and selling for a cool £1.3 million. The old ground, in truth, was well past its serviceable life and within weeks of the sale the small wooden stand and clubhouse were razed to the ground with

Hand Stadium, Clevedon Town

Hazel Grove, Cockfield

almost indecent haste. The club moved to the new ground, which was handily located close to Junction 17 of the M5. The new ground has two open terraces at either end and a large full-length covered terrace on one side. The main stand houses all changing rooms, social and office facilities. The only remnant of the old ground is the floodlights that were moved across town to the new venue and erected to illuminate the training pitch.

COCKFIELD

GROUND: Hazel Grove, Cockfield, County Durham
CURRENT CAPACITY: 1,500
RECORD ATTENDANCE: Not Known
YEAR BUILT/OPENED: 1919
CURRENT LEAGUE: Auckland & District League
CLUB FOUNDED: 1985 re-formation of club formed in 1884
PREVIOUS GROUNDS: Various pitches

A renowned village club who made their own little piece of history when they reached the final of the FA Amateur Cup in 1928. They had an excellent record in that competition throughout their glory days of the 1920s, but without doubt reaching the final was a crowning achievement that made national headlines of a tiny Durham mining village. Sadly, as so often happens, the opposition in the final, Leyton, did not follow the script and triumphed 3-2 in the final in front of 12,200 spectators at Ayresome Park. The club played in several local leagues before gaining election to the prestigious Northern League in 1921. The club remained in that League until the competition ceased in for World War Two. The club later fell on hard times, especially when the colliery closed, and eventually disbanded for many years, until a revival came about in 1985. The Hazel Grove ground has been home throughout most of their history and when I visited the ground, even though I was alone, you could sense the history and atmosphere of this classic venue. The rough-hewn timber stand and its more modern tin cover opposite provide much needed shelter from the elements. The ground positively aches for a large gathering, and you can almost hear the ghosts of yesterday watching those great old Amateur Cup matches and earthy yells of: 'Play up Cockfield!'

COLWYN BAY
GROUND: Llanelian Road, Old Colwyn, Clwyd, North Wales
CURRENT CAPACITY: 2,500
RECORD ATTENDANCE: 2,000 v. Marine (Northern Premier League) August 1994
YEAR BUILT/OPENED: 1982
CURRENT LEAGUE: Unibond (Northern Premier) League Premier Division
CLUB FOUNDED: 1885
PREVIOUS GROUNDS: Eiras Park; Northwich Victoria FC; Ellesmere Port FC

Colwyn Bay have a long history and have had to endure a severe test of their resolve in the last decade. The club played on numerous pitches around this pleasant North Wales coastal town until 1930, when they gained the use of an enclosed field called Eiras Park. The ground was extensively developed after the war and was sufficiently capacious to accommodate more than 5,000 for the visit of the now long-defunct Borough United in 1964. The club were founder members of the Welsh League in 1934 and remained in that league until making the move to the English pyramid in 1983, gaining election to the North West Counties League. The move came a year after the club relocated to Llanelian Road in the old part of town. The new ground had extensive covered accommodation, but a limited amount of seating. The

move to English football and their subsequent promotion to the Northern Premier League in 1991 was to cause the club considerable trouble in the 1990s. In 1992 the Welsh FA decreed that all Welsh clubs playing in English non-League competition would have to resign and join their new League of Wales competition. Colwyn Bay and four other clubs refused and spent two seasons playing in exile at English grounds. In July 1994 the Welsh FA's court case was overruled and the Bay made a triumphant return to Llanelian Road, attracting a record gate for their first match back against Marine. Somewhat wisely, the club have made purely cosmetic adjustments to the ground since then, wary that the Welsh FA may again question the legitimacy of their continued involvement in the English game.

CONGLETON TOWN
GROUND: Booth Street Ground, Crescent Road, Congleton, Cheshire
CURRENT CAPACITY: 5,000
RECORD ATTENDANCE: 7,000 v. Macclesfield Town (Cheshire League) 1954
YEAR BUILT/OPENED: 1910
CURRENT LEAGUE: North West Counties League Division One
CLUB FOUNDED: 1901
PREVIOUS GROUNDS: Willow Street

The early history of football in Congleton is littered with unusual names such as St James North Street, Pointers Joiners Shop FC and Congleton Hornets. Congleton Town superseded all these clubs when they came onto the scene in 1901. They played at a ground in Willow Street until around 1910 when the club acquired a rough field off Booth Street,

Booth Street Ground, Congleton Town

close to the Wheatsheaf pub, which became headquarters and changing rooms in the early years. A rudimentary stand and dressing rooms were opened in the early 1920s but the ground's notorious longitudinal slope of 9ft remained a major problem. The slope remained until the 1960s despite the offer from US Servicemen to level the field during World War Two. The covered terrace opposite the main stand was erected in 1962. The ground remained virtually unchanged until the early 1990s when the old stand was dismantled and the old army hut that served as a clubhouse was demolished. A smart new cantilevered seated stand was erected in their place and later a plush new clubhouse was opened, bringing the old Booth Street ground right up to date.

CORBY TOWN
GROUND: Rockingham Triangle, Rockingham Road, Corby, Northamptonshire
CURRENT CAPACITY: 3,000

RECORD ATTENDANCE: 2,240 v. Watford (Friendly) 1986
YEAR BUILT/OPENED: 1985
CURRENT LEAGUE: Dr Marten's (Southern) League Eastern Division
CLUB FOUNDED: 1948
PREVIOUS GROUNDS: Occupation Road (1948–85)

Corby Town were formed when members of the existing Stewarts & Lloyds steel-works club split, citing lack of ambition on the committee's part. They formed their own club and decided to turn professional. They acquired land next to Stewart & Lloyd's existing ground in Occupation Road and swiftly developed a ground that was of sufficient standard to merit Corby Town applying for Football League status on no less than five occasions during the 1960s, the club's undoubted heyday. The ground was indeed sizable with a record gate of 10,239 being posted for a FA Cup tie with near-neighbours Kettering Town in 1952. The team had a huge supporters club in

Rockingham Triangle, Corby Town

the 1950s and '60s, many of whom were exiled Celtic and Rangers supporters who had moved south in search of work with local steelworks. However, the decline of that industry in the late 1970s and early 1980s was mirrored in the fortunes of the football club. Dwindling gates saw the club attempt to relaunch itself in 1985 by moving away to a newly erected athletics stadium on the outskirts of town. However, it was to prove a fatal mistake with crowds sinking to an all-time low. The Rockingham Triangle athletics stadium is the least atmospheric and most desperate place I have ever had the misfortune to watch a football match.

CORINTHIAN CASUALS
GROUND: King George's Field, Hook Rise South, Tolworth, Surrey
CURRENT CAPACITY: 1,700
RECORD ATTENDANCE: Not Known
YEAR BUILT/OPENED: 1988
CURRENT LEAGUE: Ryman (Isthmian) League Division One (South)
CLUB FOUNDED: 1939 merger of Corinthian (1882) and The Casuals (1883)
PREVIOUS GROUNDS: Kingstonian FC; Chiswick Poly; The Oval; Crystal Palace Stadium; Motspur Park; Wimbledon Park; Tooting & Mitcham FC; Molesey FC

The Corinthians and The Casuals were two great amateur clubs in the early history of the game. The Casuals were formed in 1883 and membership was limited to former pupils of Charterhouse, Eton and Westminster schools, although it was later extended to all public school and university old boys. The club wore interesting colours of chocolate and pink and, in 1905, were founder members of the Isthmian League. The Corinthians were formed a year earlier by Lane 'Pa' Jackson in an attempt to stop England's poor run of international results against Scotland. They played their first match at the Lambeth Palace Grounds and went on to become the greatest team in the land, renowned for their fair play and sportsmanship. Corinthians had their

King George's Field, Corinthian Casuals

headquarters at the old Crystal Palace and when this burnt to the ground, the clubs opted to merge in 1939, six days before the start of World War Two. The merged club played on numerous grounds, but never had a home ground of their own. In 1983 the Isthmian League outlawed ground-sharing and the club joined the Spartan League. In 1988 the club absorbed the struggling Tolworth FC and, at last, had a ground of their own. The ground is not terribly interesting, but has been sufficiently developed in recent years to allow the club to return to the Isthmian League via the Combined Counties League in 1997. It marked a triumph of old school ideals over modernism.

COWES SPORTS
GROUND: Westwood Park, Reynolds Close, Cowes, Isle of Wight
CURRENT CAPACITY: 1,700
RECORD ATTENDANCE: Not Known

YEAR BUILT/OPENED: 1912
CURRENT LEAGUE: Jewson Wessex League
CLUB FOUNDED: 1903 re-formation of a club formed in 1881
PREVIOUS GROUNDS: Brooklyn Ground

Cowes is a historically important nautical town, so it is perhaps appropriate that their football club has a ground of no little historical importance. The club moved to Westwood Park in 1912 after their Brooklyn Ground was redeveloped for housing. (It was even happening before the First World War!) The main stand was opened in 1921 with the construction being carried out by local boatwrights and chandlers in a nearby sawmill in Medina Road. There was also a smaller seated stand opposite the main stand, which stood until damaged beyond repair in the storms of 1987. By the 1990s the main stand had fallen into

Westwood Park, Cowes Sports

a considerable state of disrepair. However, to their credit, the club resisted the temptation of demolishing and starting again as their neighbours at East Cowes would do to their even older stand at Beatrice Avenue. The whole stand was reclad to give it a smart, modern appearance and the rotting timber seating was replaced. The glass screen ends, which had been broken for years, were renewed and dugouts were incorporated into the stand to complete the total regeneration of this antique edifice.

CRAWLEY TOWN
GROUND: Broadfield Stadium, Brighton Road, Crawley, West Sussex
CURRENT CAPACITY: 5,000
RECORD ATTENDANCE: 2,504 v. Aldershot (FA Cup) 30/09/00
YEAR BUILT/OPENED: 1997
CURRENT LEAGUE: Dr Marten's (Southern) League Premier Division
CLUB FOUNDED: 1896

PREVIOUS GROUNDS: Malthouse Farm(1896–1914, 1938–40); Victoria Hall(1914–29); Rectory Fields (1929–38); Town Mead (1949–53, 1954–97); Ifield Rec(1953–54)

There was little actually wrong with Crawley Town's old ground at Town Mead, save for the lack of character in the 1949-built council-owned ground. The ambitious council, however, wanted to bring Conference football to the Sussex town and the lack of space around Town Mead meant the only option was to start from scratch. The old site was sold for a nightclub and retail outlets, while the finance received was sufficient to erect a state-of-the-art 5,000-seater stadium on the southern edge of town, adjacent to the Broadfield housing estate. Ironically Town Mead had been built up steadily since its opening in 1949, including a brand-new main stand as recently as 1994. The new Broadfield Stadium

Broadfield Stadium, Crawley Town

boasts a superb cantilevered main stand with striking exposed steel roof supports. The stadium was opened in time for the start of the 1997/98 campaign and has been a tremendous success, with use of facilities being open to all sectors of the community as well as the club. Although the stadium is well up to Conference standard, the team has yet to respond and remain firmly rooted in the Dr Marten's League.

CROCKENHILL

GROUND: Wested Meadow, Eynesford Road, Crockenhill, Kent
CURRENT CAPACITY: 2,000
RECORD ATTENDANCE: 800 v. Maidstone United (Kent Amateur Cup) 1948
YEAR BUILT/OPENED: 1930s
CURRENT LEAGUE: British Energy Kent County League Premier Division
CLUB FOUNDED: 1946

PREVIOUS GROUNDS: Erith & Belvedere FC (1998–99)

Considering Wested Meadow is little more than a hearty punt of the ball from Junction 3 of the M25, it is situated in an amazingly rural location. A previous incarnation of Crockenhill had played matches at the then-undeveloped field before World War Two. When the new club were constituted in 1946, they began developing the ground. Within five years Wested boasted a covered stand, dressing rooms and offices. The stand was considerably longer than the present truncated version and sported a different, more pronounced pitched roof. An old Nissen hut was converted into a clubhouse and the club acquired an ancient turnstile from the ground of Thameside Amateurs. The turnstile certainly pre-dates the Thameside ground and is generally believed to have begun

Wested Meadow, Crockenhill

its working life, perhaps as early as 1890, at Gravesend United's old Central Avenue ground. The old stand was badly damaged in the severe storms of 1987 with a tree demolishing the roof. Originally it was intended to replace the stand, but instead the committee patched up the stand and put on a new corrugated iron roof to give the battered old structure a new lease of life. However, the Kent League's insistence on floodlights and the club's failure to obtain planning permission meant the club were forced to join the Kent County League. A similar fate befell near neighbours and rivals, Furness, at the old Alma Swanley ground.

CROOK TOWN

GROUND: Millfield, West Road, Crook, County Durham
CURRENT CAPACITY: 3,500
RECORD ATTENDANCE: 17,500 v.

Walton & Hersham (FA Amateur Cup) 24/12/52
YEAR BUILT/OPENED: 1898
CURRENT LEAGUE: Albany Northern League Division Two
CLUB FOUNDED: 1889 as Crook FC
PREVIOUS GROUNDS: Peases West Welfare Ground (1889–98)

A very famous club from the old amateur days, being five times winners of the FA Amateur Cup. The club is renowned throughout Europe and even played the mighty Barcelona no less than ten times between 1913 and 1922, losing only four times. So close were their ties with the Catalan club that they even borrowed Barca's famous goalkeeper, Ricardo Zamora for one game. Crook also went on tour to Norway in 1963 and, famously, to India in 1976 when crowds in excess of 100,000 flocked to see the side from the Northern League. In 1898 the club left their Welfare Ground at Bankfoot having purchased a new site in West Road for the princely sum of £625. The ground at Millfield expanded rapidly and the original grandstand was replaced by the current 500 seater in 1925 at a cost of £1,300. The rest of the ground was steeply banked with ash to create a massive capacity. Millfield was packed for an Amateur Cup tie against Walton & Hersham in 1952 when the official record gate of 17,500 was set. Contemporary press reports put the real crowd as being in excess of 20,000 as entrance gates were barged down. In the late 1940s and '50s the ground never saw a match with a crowd of less than 4,000, which is remarkable for such a small town with a population then of 12,000! The stand was joined on the same side in 1960 by a large section of covered terrace. The old grandstand, however, was condemned in 1989 but sympathetic renovation has seen it restored to its former glory. Although the crowds are long gone, Millfield remains a classic venue.

CROYDON

GROUND: Croydon Sports Arena, Albert Road, South Norwood, Croydon, Surrey
CURRENT CAPACITY: 8,000
RECORD ATTENDANCE: 1,450 v Wycombe Wanderers (FA Cup) 01/11/75
YEAR BUILT/OPENED: 1953
CURRENT LEAGUE: Ryman (Isthmian) League One (South)
CLUB FOUNDED: 1953 as Croydon Amateurs
PREVIOUS GROUNDS: None

There is always an argument against football grounds that double as athletics stadia, but at the likes of Croydon, the first-class facilities more than make up for the lack of atmosphere caused by the gulf between supporters in the stand and the action on the pitch. The Croydon Sports Arena was opened in 1953 and the elevated main stand has been modernized on a couple of occasions since then. The old clubhouse, often a target for local vandals, was replaced in 1981 with the

Croydon Sports Arena, Croydon

present structure. Floodlights were erected in 1970 and a new athletics track was installed in 1989. The ground also has a well-stocked club shop. When all is said and done, the Arena has everything a modern stadium needs, but what it cannot provide is a heaving, cheering crowd to support the team. In a town the size of Croydon, that is a great pity.

CROYDON ATHLETIC

GROUND: Mayfields, off Mayfield Road, Thornton Heath, Surrey
CURRENT CAPACITY: 3,000
RECORD ATTENDANCE: 550
YEAR BUILT/OPENED: 1982
CURRENT LEAGUE: Ryman (Isthmian) League Division One (South)
CLUB FOUNDED: 1986 merger of Wandsworth (1948) and Norwood (1947)
PREVIOUS GROUNDS: Wandsworth: Kimber Road; Wisley Gardens; Moorfax Sports Ground. Norwood: Wandle Park; Lloyd Park

This club, a merger of the Wandsworth

and Norwood clubs, have climbed the pyramid rapidly in recent seasons. The Mayfields ground, previously known as the NFC Sports Ground, had been used for junior football for many years until Norwood took the ground over in 1982. Since the merger in 1986, the ground has been developed beyond all recognition. It has been fully enclosed and the small corrugated iron cover has been successfully converted into a functional seated stand. Floodlights were switched on in 1990. The club, now renamed Croydon Athletic, joined the London Spartan League in order to get into a feeder league for the Ryman League. The committee's efforts in upgrading the ground were rewarded with election to the Ryman League in 1997.

Mayfields, Croydon Athletic

D

D

DAGENHAM & REDBRIDGE
GROUND: Victoria Road, Dagenham, Essex
CURRENT CAPACITY: 6,000
RECORD ATTENDANCE: 5,949 v. Ipswich Town (FA Cup) 05/01/2002
YEAR BUILT/OPENED: 1930s
CURRENT LEAGUE: Nationwide Football Conference
CLUB FOUNDED: 1992 merger of Dagenham(1949) and Redbridge Forest(1988)
PREVIOUS GROUNDS: Dagenham Arena (1949–55)

Surely there can be few towns in the country with a more complicated foot-balling history than that of Dagenham. At one time the town boasted no less than six clubs with senior status within its boundaries. Dagenham were playing at Dagenham Arena, which still exists, in reduced circumstances, within Old Dagenham Park. Dagenham Cables, Dagenham British Legion, Ford Sports, Chadwell Heath and Brigg Sports were the town's other senior sides. The latter vacated Victoria Road in 1955, eventually merging with Ford Sports and playing at a new site in Rush Green Road. The other three clubs lost senior status and eventually their grounds. Dagenham became the town's senior club and merged with Redbridge Forest, ground-sharers at Victoria Road, in 1992. Forest themselves emerged from the ashes of three great East London clubs, Walthamstow Avenue, Leytonstone and Ilford, all of whom lost

their much-loved grounds (Green Pond Road, Granleigh Road and Lynn Road respectively) in a ten-year period of financial ruin between 1979 and 1989. The merged club regained their Conference status in the late 1990s and in 2001 Victoria Road was treated to its first major development for many years when a brand new main stand was opened, replacing the old wooden stand that had stood on the clubhouse side of the ground since the late 1950s. This new structure now sits somewhat awkwardly against another reasonably modern, but considerably smaller, stand, which has been cruelly dubbed the 'Marie Celeste Stand' as few people have patronized it since its opening.

DARLASTON TOWN
GROUND: City Ground, Waverley Road, Darlaston, West Midlands
CURRENT CAPACITY: 2,000
RECORD ATTENDANCE: Not Known
YEAR BUILT/OPENED: 1899
CURRENT LEAGUE: Express & Star West Midlands League Division One (North)
CLUB FOUNDED: 1874
PREVIOUS GROUNDS: Wake Field (1890–99)

The superb City Ground in now more than 100 years old, and to the casual observer would appear to be somewhat down at heel. However, the truth is that the wonky post and rail pitch surround, the retaining fence propped up with wooden stakes and the disused turn-stiles all add to the charm of this historic Black Country ground. The ground has a long history of begging and borrowing and do-it-yourself conversions. The current dressing rooms were built as a favour by the Government, who erected

City Ground, Darlaston Town

a building on the ground during World War Two. A former youth club behind one goal still does sterling service as a clubhouse. The wonderful old stand has stood at the ground since 1932, when it is believed to have been acquired from Aggborough, the home of Kidderminster Harriers. Opposite the main stand is a small area of cover, which was once much longer but was reduced in size after being damaged in a gale. The pitch has a pronounced slope which was originally much worse before remedial levelling work in 1974. When the ground opened in 1899 the area was very rural, but in the intervening century the ground has been tightly hemmed in by housing. Fortunately the City Ground has a covenant on it protecting the site from any use other than for football. Therefore, for once, this really historic old ground has an assured future.

DARTFORD
GROUND: Gravesend & Northfleet FC
CURRENT CAPACITY: 3,300
RECORD ATTENDANCE: 11,004 v. Leyton Orient (FA Cup) 27/11/48 at Watling Steet
YEAR BUILT/OPENED: Ground-shared since 2001
CURRENT LEAGUE: Dr Marten's (Southern) League Eastern Division
CLUB FOUNDED: 1888
PREVIOUS GROUNDS: The Brent; Potter's Meadow; Engley's Meadow; Summer's Meadow; Watling Street (1921–92); Welling United FC; Cray Wanderers FC; Erith & Belvedere FC; Purfleet FC

Watling Street was always an impressive football stadium, which had been opened in 1921. The large stand and dressing rooms were gutted in a fire in 1926 and were replaced with the vast timber and steel grandstand that stood until the ground's untimely demise in May 1992. The large covered terrace opposite the main stand opened in 1930, with the whole ground being terraced between 1946 and 1949 – Dartford's first years as a professional club. The club had unsuccessfully applied for Football League membership in 1936 and it was something of surprise that the club were never tempted to apply in later years. League football did come to Watling Street in 1989 when Maidstone United joined the Football League, having lost their London Road ground a year earlier to an MFI development. Maidstone's League status seemed to overwhelm Dartford and the ground was painted in Maidstone's yellow and black colours. Maidstone resigned from the Football League in May 1992 and took Dartford and the 71-year-old Watling Street ground down with them. Maidstone folded with massive debts and Watling Street was demolished overnight and replaced with housing. Dartford started the 1992/93 season at Welling United but folded after four games. The club later reformed and ground-shared at several venues. The 2000/01 campaign saw them enter an arrangement with Gravesend and Northfleet, which at least saw the club back in their native county after several farcical seasons playing 'home' games over the Thames in Essex at Purfleet's Ship Lane ground.

DAVENTRY TOWN

GROUND: Elderstubbs, Browns Road, Daventry, Northamptonshire
CURRENT CAPACITY: 2,000
RECORD ATTENDANCE: 350 v. Ford Sports (Daventry) 1991

YEAR BUILT/OPENED: 1991
CURRENT LEAGUE: Eagle Bitter United Counties League Premier Division
CLUB FOUNDED: 1886
PREVIOUS GROUNDS: The Hollow

Daventry Town played at a relatively low level in the likes of the Rugby & District League, Northampton League and the Central Northants Combination before gaining election to the United Counties League in 1989. Their election to the senior league was conditioned on the club relocating from their basic ground at The Hollow to a new better-equipped venue. The site chosen was by the A45 bypass near the Staverton Road Sports Centre. The Elderstubbs ground has a large covered stand but its general poor facilities cost them promotion to the Premier Division in 1990. However, with the ground improvements completed, promotion was achieved a year later. The move to Elderstubbs has seen support dwindle and with it the enthusiasm of the committee members. The club accepted voluntary relegation to Division One in 1994, citing financial problems and lack of support. However the period of prolonged struggle was ended in 1999/2000 when the club won Division One on goal difference from Deeping Rangers. Elderstubbs has come through some lean times, which are best illustrated in the ground's record gate of 350 against near neighbours Ford Sports, a record that has stood for a decade.

DAWLISH TOWN

GROUND: Playing Fields, off Sandy Lane, Dawlish, Devon
CURRENT CAPACITY: 2,000
RECORD ATTENDANCE: 1,500 v. Heavitree United (Devon Premier Cup)

YEAR BUILT/OPENED: c1901
CURRENT LEAGUE: Screwfix Direct
Western League Premier Division
CLUB FOUNDED: 1899
PREVIOUS GROUNDS: Elm Grove
Road; Sandy Lane; Newberry's Field

Dawlish is a delightful coastal Devon town, standing on the mouth of the River Exe where that waterway flows into the English Channel. The town's football ground is equally charming, sitting in an area of the town that is set aside for all manner of sports. The large area of the Playing Fields devoted to recreational activities has meant the club has been unable to fully enclose the ground, using large canvas sheets on match days to prevent free viewing of the game. The ground has been brought up to date with a modern clubhouse and floodlighting, but the endearingly rickety wooden stand dates from World War Two, when the ground was commandeered for military activities.

DEAL TOWN

GROUND: Charles Sports Ground, St Leonard's Road, Deal, Kent
CURRENT CAPACITY: 2,500
RECORD ATTENDANCE: 2,495 v. Newcastle Town (FA Vase) 26/03/00 (4,000 watched a charity match 1961)
YEAR BUILT/OPENED: 1933
CURRENT LEAGUE: Go Travel Kent League
CLUB FOUNDED: 1908 as Cinque Ports FC
PREVIOUS GROUNDS: Bowling Green Lane

In 1933 the club was the beneficiary of the donation of a field, opposite their existing pitch, by local dignitary Sir Justice Charles. He bequeathed the site to the town on condition it was used for benefiting the youth of the area. The ground came equipped with a changing room block and a curiously shaped wooden stand, which remained the ground's talking point until its sad

Dawlish Town

The much-missed former main stand at Charles Sports Ground, Deal Town

demise in 1999. The club terraced the Charles Road side and Mill Road end during the 1950s, although the latter has recently been returned to flat, hard standing. In 1961 a showbiz match attracted 4,000 to the venue. They also acquired a set of floodlights from Oxford United's Manor Ground, although in recent years they were only suitable for training sessions. The strange wedge-shaped stand was truly remarkable and even at its widest part was no more than 20 ft deep. It had a multitude of roof struts and bench seating, with unusual wrought-iron supports. By the late 1990s, due to safety concerns, it had been cordoned off from the rest of the ground as if waiting sentence. The death knell for the old stand finally came in spring 2001, when it was demolished to be replaced by an ugly prefabricated stand with bolted-on seating. The club's lease on the ground ran out in 1990 and has since been bounced back and forth between Dover District Council and its trustees, the Charity Commissioners. This lack of a permanent, secure future sees this interesting old ground in considerable jeopardy.

DIDCOT TOWN
GROUND: Loop Meadow, Bowmont Water, Didcot, Oxfordshire
CURRENT CAPACITY: 5,000
RECORD ATTENDANCE: 825 v. Oxford United (Friendly) 2001
YEAR BUILT/OPENED: 2000
CURRENT LEAGUE: Cherry Red Records Hellenic League Premier Division
CLUB FOUNDED: 1907
PREVIOUS GROUNDS: Brasenose Road; Station Road

It is nice to see little clubs coming out on top just once in a while. The club sold their ground in Station Road for devel-

Loop Meadow, Didcot Town

opment and were able to secure a new site on undeveloped land at nearby Bowmont Water. Built on the well-used plans used at Arlesey, Letchworth and Bishops Stortford, the new ground offers a perfectly adequate 150-seater main stand and a well-appointed clubhouse. The most notable feature is the superb playing surface, which the club wisely allowed to bed in until the start of the 2000/01 season, although it was actually ready several months earlier. The old floodlights from Station Road were re-erected at the new ground and now provide a floodlit training surface. The club must surely now harbour ambitions for a future in a higher echelon of the pyramid.

DONCASTER ROVERS
GROUND: Belle Vue, Bawtry Road, Doncaster, South Yorkshire
CURRENT CAPACITY: 7,200

RECORD ATTENDANCE: 37,149 v. Hull City (Football League) 02/10/48
YEAR BUILT/OPENED: 1922
CURRENT LEAGUE: Nationwide Football Conference
CLUB FOUNDED: 1879
PREVIOUS GROUNDS: Intake Ground (1880–1916); Benetthorpe Ground (1920–22)

Doncaster Rovers have played at Belle Vue since 1922 when the ground was called Low Pasture. The supporters banked the ground on all four sides with ash from nearby coal tips. The old cover from Bennetthorpe was re-erected on the north bank and is the ground's finest point. Soon a new main stand was built on the Bawtry Road side. The popular side terrace was covered in 1938. The main stand was extended on both sides and unusually has two players' tunnels. The south bank was always an open terrace and unfortunately, due to safety concerns, has been considerably reduced in size in recent years. Of course much has been written about the demise of Doncaster Rovers and the loss of their Football League status in 1998. The systematic asset stripping of the Ken Richardson regime came to a head when the main stand was the subject of an arson attack, for which Richardson was jailed. Dark days indeed, but mercifully the club and stadium appear to have turned the corner. A visit to this particular corner of South Yorkshire would not be complete without a visit to the adjacent racecourse with its two fabulous grandstands, one a magnificent Georgian edifice erected in the 1790s and the other, built in 1964, which is very pleasant in its own right. Kind of ugly-beautiful, if you know what I mean.

DORCHESTER TOWN
GROUND: Avenue Stadium, Weymouth Avenue, Dorchester, Dorset
CURRENT CAPACITY: 7,210
RECORD ATTENDANCE: 4,159 v. Weymouth (Southern League) 01/1/99
YEAR BUILT/OPENED: 1990

CURRENT LEAGUE: Dr Marten's (Southern) League Eastern Division
CLUB FOUNDED: 1880
PREVIOUS GROUNDS: Recreation Ground (1880–1929); Avenue Ground (1929–90)

When Dorchester Town sold their historic Avenue Ground in 1990, the football world mourned the passing of another great, if somewhat worn out, venue. However, on moving a few hundred yards, the loss was tempered when the new Avenue Stadium was opened in August 1990. The builders, McIntyre Construction, and architects, provided a state-of-the-art stadium that had its own character and was unlike many of the almost identical new stadia built in recent years. The vast grandstand has a superb pitched roof and is crowned by that all too rare sight of a roof gable. The fact that AFC Bournemouth were able to comfortably stage its first 9 Football League fixtures of 2001/02 at the Avenue Stadium proved beyond doubt the new ground's potential. It also proves that 'modern' can be beautiful.

Avenue Stadium, Dorchester Town

Meadowbank, Dorking

DORKING
GROUND: Meadowbank, Mill Lane,
Dorking, Surrey
CURRENT CAPACITY: 3,600
RECORD ATTENDANCE: 4,500 v.
Folkestone Town (FA Cup) 24/09/55
YEAR BUILT/OPENED: 1953
CURRENT LEAGUE: Ryman (Isthmian)
League Division Two
CLUB FOUNDED: 1880
PREVIOUS GROUNDS: Pixham Lane

Although the club have slid down the divisions in recent years, their Meadowbank ground remains one of the most aesthetically pleasing in the Ryman League. The club were given the ground by the council in 1953 and the move coincided with considerable success in the Surrey Senior League, a league they had joined as founding members in 1922. The club have a long history dating back to 1880, making them the county's second-oldest club behind Reigate Priory – one of the oldest clubs in the world. The Meadowbank ground boasts a nicely 'lived-in' main stand, with a pitch roof that is set off well by the towering spire of a neighbouring church. The rest of the ground has ample terracing and a rickety cover opposite the main stand. In 1974 the club had an ill-fated merger with the homeless Guildford City, but Guildford & Dorking United lasted only three years before folding. Dorking Town emerged from the ashes in 1977 and dropped the suffix on joining the Isthmian League in 1981. The only worry for the club is the decline in interest in recent years as fortunes have waned. The ground's prime location, Mill Lane, being a narrow road leading to the High Street, and the town's apathy to its club will not have gone unnoticed by property developers.

DOVER ATHLETIC
GROUND: Crabble Athletic Ground,
Lewisham Road, River, Dover, Kent
CURRENT CAPACITY: 6,500
RECORD ATTENDANCE: 4,035 v.

Crabble Athletic Ground, Dover Athletic

Bromsgrove Rovers (Southern League)
1992
YEAR BUILT/OPENED: 1947 (Top
pitch); 1897 (Bottom pitch)
CURRENT LEAGUE: Dr Marten's
(Southern) League Premier Division
CLUB FOUNDED: 1983
PREVIOUS GROUNDS: None

The Crabble Athletic Ground is a historic
footballing venue, with the original
Dover club first playing on the lower
pitch in 1897, during their early Kent
League days. The lower pitch, with its
unusually steep banked terracing, is now
used solely for rugby and cricket, with
Kent County Cricket Club occasionally
staging festival games at the ancient
venue. The professional Dover club had
formed in 1947 and by January 1951 they
had persuaded the Dover Corporation to
fund an extension of the existing stand on
the upper pitch. The building work was
completed in three months and Dover
moved up to the top pitch for good.
Some new dressing rooms were opened
and the supporters club funded a covered terrace at the town end. However,
by the early 1980s the club had incurred
massive debts, eventually folding. In 1983
a new club, Dover Athletic, took over at
the Crabble, setting about revamping the
ground in order to attain a grading suitable for Conference football. The original
terracing was ripped up and replaced and
the old stand had modern plastic seating
installed. The club were denied promotion to the Conference in 1990 when the
ground was not prepared in time for
inspection. However, three years later
their promotion to the top flight was at
last secured when a new stand was
erected at the ground. Relegation from
the Conference was suffered after a dis-
astrous 2001/02 campaign.

DROYLESDEN
GROUND: Butchers Arms, Market

Butchers Arms, Droylesden

Street, Droylesden, Manchester
CURRENT CAPACITY: 3,500
RECORD ATTENDANCE: 4,250 v.
Grimsby Town (FA Cup) 20/11/76
YEAR BUILT/OPENED: 1892
CURRENT LEAGUE: Unibond (Northern
Premier) League Premier Division
CLUB FOUNDED: 1892
PREVIOUS GROUNDS: Moorside
Stadium (1948–51)

The ancient Butchers Arms ground has
had a turbulent history which now
stretches back over 100 years. The field
next to the public house saw its first football match in 1892, but was not properly
enclosed until 1921. Three stands were
erected between 1923 and 1933, with the
official capacity being a substantial 8,000.
The club earned some extra revenue by
hosting 'A' team games for Blackpool and
later Manchester City. After World War
Two, the stands had become severely run
down. In 1948 another club, Droylesden

United, purchased the ground from the
brewery and Droylesden FC were unceremoniously evicted, seeking refuge at
the nearby Moorside Stadium. Their
exile ended three years later when the
local council purchased the Butchers
Arms from the ailing United club. In a bid
to put Droylesden back on the footballing map, the two clubs, at one time
bitter rivals, merged and played at
Moorside while the Butchers Arms was
completely gutted. The pitch was rotated
and levelled and new stands and offices
were erected. In the early 1990s the club
had to remove terracing from behind
one stand and extend the pitch north-
wards as its length was found to be
illegally short. In more recent times the
second main stand made way for a smart
new 650-seater stand and the ground
was once again modernized. A classic old
ground with an interesting history, rang-
ing from partial dereliction to periodic
gentrification.

Creasey Park, Dunstable Town

DUNSTABLE TOWN
GROUND: Creasey Park, Brewers Hill
Road, Dunstable, Bedfordshire
CURRENT CAPACITY: 4,000
RECORD ATTENDANCE: 6,000 v.
Manchester United (Friendly) 1974
YEAR BUILT/OPENED: 1963
CURRENT LEAGUE: Minerva Spartan
South Midlands League Premier Division
CLUB FOUNDED: 1950
PREVIOUS GROUNDS: Recreation
Ground

Creasey Park has had a chequered history, even though it is barely 40 years old. The Dunstable club have folded and reformed many times, but were, in the 1960s and '70s, a powerful force under the management of Barry Fry and the controversial ownership of Keith Cheeseman. The club paid extremely high salaries and bonuses and even attracted the likes of George Best and Jeff Astle to the club. Of course it all ended in tears, with the club owing thousands in tax and VAT and Cheeseman was hauled off to jail. The ground had opened in 1963 and the stand had been erected with a covered terrace opposite. This covered terrace was beset by bad luck, being blown down and replaced no less than three times! Dunstable Town folded in 1976, being replaced by Dunstable FC who in turn collapsed in1994. Dunstable Old Boys played there for just four months before resigning from the South Midlands League, with yet another incarnation, Dunstable United, taking over their fixtures. The club eventually changed the 'United' back to 'Town' and have survived relatively unscathed, although Creasey Park is in quite a bad way. The unlucky covered terrace has collapsed back onto the perimeter fence and the ugly barn-like grandstand is in considerable disrepair, with every pane of glass in the glazed stand ends being broken and the roof

Champion Hill Stadium, Dulwich Hamlet

having numerous gaping holes. Creasey Park is one of the few grounds that would definitely benefit from knocking down the existing stand and replacing it with a shiny new modern structure.

DULWICH HAMLET
GROUND: Champion Hill Stadium, Edgar Kail Way, East Dulwich, London SE22
CURRENT CAPACITY: 3,000
RECORD ATTENDANCE: 1,835 v. Southport (FA Cup) 14/11/98
YEAR BUILT/OPENED: 1991
CURRENT LEAGUE: Ryman (Isthmian) League Division One (South)
CLUB FOUNDED: 1893
PREVIOUS GROUNDS: Woodwark Road; Dulwich Park; College Farm; Freeman's Ground; Champion Hill Ground (1912–91)

Don McLean sang of the 'day that music died', but in many ways 1991 was the year that non-League football died in London. In that year the largest non-League stadium in the capital, Dulwich Hamlet's Champion Hill, was demolished. It had been built in 1912 and had a massive and beautifully constructed pitch-length wooden main stand, as well as huge banks of terracing. The ground heaved to the tune of 20,500 people who witnessed the 1933 FA Amateur Cup final between Kingstonian and Stockton. However, by the 1980s the wooden stand had been condemned and partially closed. Additionally much of the terracing had become unsafe. In 1991 Sainsbury's made the club an offer they couldn't refuse for the site and the old stadium was razed to the ground. A supermarket went up in its place and the club was provided with a much smaller ground that partially covered the old site. There is shallow terracing around the ground and an attractive main stand, which is set off by a gable clock and fascia board, which

E

are attached to the large building behind the stand. This building houses all the social facilities, offices and changing rooms, as well as a health club. Ironically with the ground slightly more than 10 years old, it is rumoured that Dulwich Hamlet may be looking for a new venue in the not-too-distant future.

E

EASTBOURNE BOROUGH
GROUND: Priory Lane, Langney, Eastbourne, East Sussex
CURRENT CAPACITY: 2,500
RECORD ATTENDANCE: 1,400 v. Crystal Palace (Floodlight Opener) 1990
YEAR BUILT/OPENED: 1988
CURRENT LEAGUE: Dr Marten's (Southern) League Eastern Division
CLUB FOUNDED: 1966 as Langney FC
PREVIOUS GROUNDS: Princes Park; Adjacent pitch at Priory Lane

Once considered as young upstarts, Borough are now the highest ranked of Eastbourne's three senior clubs. Originally the club played on the old pitch, which was enclosed by hessian barriers on match days to allow the club to charge admission. The small stand is still standing on what is now the reserve pitch. Work began on the new site when the pitch was laid out in 1988 and has been steadily repaired ever since. The small wooden stand was complemented in the late 1990s by the construction of a huge clubhouse and dressing rooms behind the goal, which had a cover incorporated into its design. More recent developments include a 300-seater main stand and extensive covered terracing.

EASTBOURNE TOWN
GROUND: The Saffrons, Compton Place Road, Eastbourne, East Sussex
CURRENT CAPACITY: 3,000
RECORD ATTENDANCE: 7,378 v. Hastings United 1953
YEAR BUILT/OPENED: 1890
CURRENT LEAGUE: Rich City Sussex County League Division Two
CLUB FOUNDED: 1890
PREVIOUS GROUNDS: None

An ancient sporting venue that also hosts hockey and cricket, often hosting Sussex Cricket Club, as well as being home to Eastbourne Town for more than 100 years. The football side of the ground is beginning to show its considerable age and has suffered from a great deal of misfortune. The original grandstand was gutted by fire in 1967 and was replaced by the present covered terrace. In the mid-1990s one of the stands had its roof severely damaged by one of the many storms that batter this coastal location. However, watching a match at The Saffrons still transports you back to a bygone era.

EASTBOURNE UNITED
GROUND: The Oval, Channel View Road, Eastbourne, East Sussex
CURRENT CAPACITY: 3,000
RECORD ATTENDANCE: Not Known (11,000 at Lynchmere)
YEAR BUILT/OPENED: 1940
CURRENT LEAGUE: Rich City Sussex County League Division Two
CLUB FOUNDED: 1894 as 1st Sussex Royal Engineers
PREVIOUS GROUNDS: Clifton House; South Lynn; Lynchmere

The Oval, Eastbourne United

Even though the Princes Park Oval is a post-war venue, it gives the appearance of being somewhat older, being in a run-down state. When United's former ground at Lynchmere was seized for housing the council provided the club with a new site, which also had an athletic and cycling track. The club and supporters financed the construction of a clubhouse and later the current main stand. Later still a press box was fitted into one corner of the stand and the uncomfortable wooden-bench seating made way for the modern plastic variety. The ground also has a covered terrace opposite the main stand and stretches of shallow uncovered terracing.

EAST COWES VICTORIA ATHLETIC

GROUND: Beatrice Avenue Ground, Whippingham, Isle of Wight
CURRENT CAPACITY: 2,000
RECORD ATTENDANCE: 2,000 v. Poole Town (FA Cup) 16/10/48
YEAR BUILT/OPENED: 1912
CURRENT LEAGUE: Hampshire League Premier Division
CLUB FOUNDED: 1888
PREVIOUS GROUNDS: York Avenue; Norris Castle

The Beatrice Avenue Ground was first used in 1912 and had a wonderful wooden grandstand that was erected by local unemployed labourers. It stood in all its glory until 1994 when it was closed by the Wessex League ground-grading committee. It was replaced by the current structure, which, while perfectly acceptable and functional, is a poor replacement for its revered predecessor. The clubhouse was built in 1976 and floodlights erected a decade later. Fortunately the ground is protected by a covenant restricting its use to playing fields and therefore cannot be sold for

Beatrice Avenue Ground, East Cowes Victoria Athletic

commercial redevelopment. It is a real shame the old stand had to go as it was one of the oldest in Southern England.

EAST THURROCK UNITED

GROUND: Rookery Hill, Corringham, Essex
CURRENT CAPACITY: 3,000
RECORD ATTENDANCE: 947 v. Trevor Brooking's XI (Charity Match) 1987
YEAR BUILT/OPENED: 1985
CURRENT LEAGUE: Ryman (Isthmian) League One (North)
CLUB FOUNDED: 1969
PREVIOUS GROUNDS: Corringham Rec(1969–70); The Billet(1970–73, 1974–76); Grays Athletic FC (1973–74); Tilbury FC (1977–82); Thames Board Mills Ground (1982–84)

A relatively modern club that has settled nicely into their Rookery Hill ground after the nomadic years of their early existence. The club had despaired of ever owning their own ground when suddenly a piece of land became available adjacent to Corringham Marshes. Finance was hastily secured and the pitch laid and enclosed. The basic but functional stands were erected as the club progressed through the Essex Senior League, gaining promotion to the Isthmian League for the 1992/93 season.

EASTWOOD TOWN

GROUND: Coronation Park, Chewton Street, Eastwood, Nottinghamshire
CURRENT CAPACITY: 5,500
RECORD ATTENDANCE: 2,723 v. Enfield (FA Amateur Cup) 1965
YEAR BUILT/OPENED: 1965
CURRENT LEAGUE: Unibond (Northern Premier) League Division One
CLUB FOUNDED: 1953
PREVIOUS GROUNDS: Another ground also called Coronation Park(1953–65)

The club were formed in the year of Queen Elizabeth's Coronation, so it is therefore extremely appropriate that their ground was named after that royal event. Originally the ground was adjacent to the current venue and, since the club moved pitches in 1965, the original field has been converted into a bowling green. The old pitch was fairly unusual as it used a farmhouse for changing rooms and the covered area was dismantled and reassembled at the new site. Once settled into the new ground, the club erected a wooden stand in 1971, although much of it was destroyed in a gale. However, the club cleverly turned the undamaged section into a usable smaller cover. In recent years as the club has climbed the Northern League Pyramid, the ground has been extensively terraced. 1993 saw the erection of a smart new stand, loosely based on the design of the old stand from the original ground. Coronation Park is a fine venue, and one that just begs for a large crowd to gather.

EDGWARE TOWN
GROUND: White Lion Ground, High Street, Edgware, Middlesex
CURRENT CAPACITY: 5,000
RECORD ATTENDANCE: 8,500 v. Wealdstone (FA Cup) 18/10/47 or 29/10/49
YEAR BUILT/OPENED: 1939
CURRENT LEAGUE: Ryman (Isthmian) League Division Two
CLUB FOUNDED: 1939
PREVIOUS GROUNDS: None

The newly formed Edgware FC acquired the use of the field behind the White Lion Public House in 1939 and after the war the grandstand was opened and steep banking created around the ground. The covered terrace was erected a few years later. By the late 1970s the White Lion Ground had long since seen its better days and was crumbling badly. The lack of care eventually resulted in the old grandstand being totally destroyed by a fire in 1982. The club benefited from the insurance payout, which provided a new stand of almost identical size. The ground-share with long-time rivals Wealdstone, which started in 1995, has seen the ground gentrified further, but is still some way from its glory days of the 1940s and '50s.

White Lion Ground, Edgware Town

EGHAM TOWN

GROUND: Runnymeade Stadium, Tempest Road, Egham, Surrey
CURRENT CAPACITY: 5,500
RECORD ATTENDANCE: 1,400 v. Wycombe Wanderers (FA Cup) 07/10/72
YEAR BUILT/OPENED: 1963
CURRENT LEAGUE: Ryman (Isthmian) League Division One (South)
CLUB FOUNDED: 1963 re-formation of a club first founded in 1896
PREVIOUS GROUNDS: Angler's Rest; Manorcroft Road

This ground was only opened as recently as 1963 when the Town club was reformed after a gap of 24 years and leased a ground from the local council. The main stand went up in the early 1970s and since then the ground has acquired several areas of covered terracing. Since the Tempest Road ground was completely enclosed and the clubhouse opened, the ground has become a perfectly adequate Isthmian League set up.

ELY CITY

GROUND: Unwin Sports Ground, Downham Road, Ely, Cambridgeshire
CURRENT CAPACITY: 1,500
RECORD ATTENDANCE: 260 v. Soham Town Rangers (League) 12/04/93
YEAR BUILT/OPENED: 1986
CURRENT LEAGUE: Jewson Eastern Counties League Premier Division
CLUB FOUNDED: 1885
PREVIOUS GROUNDS: Paradise Ground (1890–1986)

The Robins are the oldest club in Cambridgeshire and played on the historic Paradise Ground until being forcibly relocated in 1986. The buildings at the old ground were condemned and were soon demolished. However the club were relocated to a large out-of-town venue, which came with planning permission for floodlights, a constant cause for the club's lack of progress at their former home. The Unwin Ground, named after the club's president, is a perfect venue for their current level in the

Unwin Sports Ground, Ely City

Pyramid. The ground is set off nicely by the unusually highly elevated grand-stand, erected in 1993, and is now fully enclosed from the adjacent reserve-team pitch.

ENFIELD
GROUND: Boreham Wood FC
CURRENT CAPACITY: 4,500
RECORD ATTENDANCE: 10,000 v. Tottenham Hotspur (at Southbury Road) 10/10/62
YEAR BUILT/OPENED: Ground-shared since 1999
CURRENT LEAGUE: Ryman (Isthmian) League Premier Division
CLUB FOUNDED: 1903 as Enfield Spartans
PREVIOUS GROUNDS: Bailey's Field(1983–96); Tuckers Field (1896–1900); Cherry Orchard Lane (1900–36); Southbury Road (1936–99)

Much has been written about the demise of Enfield's much loved Southbury Road ground. The problems really started when Saracens RUFC moved from Southgate to share at Enfield's ground. The large covered terrace opposite the main stand was demolished and had temporary open seating erected. However, when Saracens swiftly departed for Watford, the side was tarmacked over with no terrace or cover. The asset stripping of the club continued unabated in the late 1990s and the ground was lost to developers in 1999 and bulldozed with indecent haste. Various relocation plans were mooted at the Tesco Country Club in Cheshunt or Brimsdown Rovers ground at Goldsdown Road. Empty promises now see this once well-supported club playing to crowds of less than 100, miles away at Boreham Wood's

Meadow Park ground. Disgruntled and heartbroken officials and supporters have now formed their own club, Enfield Town, ironically ground-sharing at Brimsdown Rovers.

EPSOM & EWELL
GROUND: Banstead Athletic FC
CURRENT CAPACITY: 3,500
RECORD ATTENDANCE: 5,000 v. Kingstonian (FA Cup) 15/10/49 at West Street
YEAR BUILT/OPENED: Ground-shared since 1993
CURRENT LEAGUE: Ryman (Isthmian) League Division One (South)
CLUB FOUNDED: 1917 as Epsom FC
PREVIOUS GROUNDS: Horton Lane; West Street (1926–93)

In the modern era where ground-sharing is becoming an essential tool for survival, one of non-League football's most enduring arrangements sees Epsom & Ewell completing their ninth campaign sharing harmoniously at Banstead Athletic's Merland Rise ground. The club lost its own West Street ground in 1993 when a property developer secured the site for a housing complex. However, the longer the ground-share with Banstead endures, the less likely Epsom & Ewell are to find a suitable site for a ground of their own in what is a densely populated area.

ERITH & BELVEDERE
GROUND: Welling United FC
CURRENT CAPACITY: 5,500
RECORD ATTENDANCE: 5,573 v. Crook (FA Amateur Cup) 1949 at Park View
YEAR BUILT/OPENED: Ground-shared since 1999
CURRENT LEAGUE: Dr Marten's (Southern) League Eastern Division

CLUB FOUNDED: 1922 as a restructuring of Belvedere & District FC(1919)
PREVIOUS GROUNDS: Park View (1922–99)

In September 1997 Erith and Belvedere FC suffered a mortal blow when their 70-year-old main stand was gutted by a fire started by local vandals. The stand itself, which housed the original changing rooms, was built in 1924 from revenue gained from an exciting run to the final of the FA Amateur Cup. The ground was packed with an all-time record gate of 8,000 for a FA Cup tie with Coventry in 1932. By the late 1990s Park View was somewhat down at heel, with the covered terrace leaning precariously against the perimeter wall. The ground's aspect was spoilt by the construction of a bypass, although this made for an excellent panorama of the ground. Following the fire, the club removed the charred remains and soldiered on for a short while before cutting their losses and moving to ground-share at Welling United. In an interesting arrangement, Erith & Belvedere have their own stand and headquarters on one side of the ground while Welling's are on the opposite side.

ESH WINNING
GROUND: West Terrace, Waterhouses, County Durham
CURRENT CAPACITY: 3,500
RECORD ATTENDANCE: 900 v. Fantail (FA Sunday Cup) 1982
YEAR BUILT/OPENED: 1967
CURRENT LEAGUE: Albany Northern League Division One
CLUB FOUNDED: 1967 as Esh Winning Pineapple
PREVIOUS GROUNDS: None

Several incarnations of Esh Winning have been in existence since the village's first club, Esh Winning Rangers, were formed in 1889. Many of the clubs played at the

The main stand at Erith & Belvedere's Park View was gutted by fire in 1997

Stag Hill Recreation Ground but all subsequently disbanded until a Sunday side was formed in 1967 under the curious title of Esh Winning Pineapple. The club secured the use of the Welfare Ground of the disbanded Waterhouses Colliery, eventually purchasing the venue. They only converted to Saturday football, losing their interesting suffix in the process, as recently as 1980 by which time the ground had been developed to the first-class venue it is now. The twin stands with the unusual lofted roof spans set the ground off a treat. The ground's location in the beautiful Deerness Valley makes this a truly evocative venue.

EVESHAM UNITED
GROUND: Common Road, Evesham, Worcestershire
CURRENT CAPACITY: 2,000
RECORD ATTENDANCE: 2,338 v. West Bromwich Albion (Floodlight Opener) 18/07/92

YEAR BUILT/OPENED: 1968
CURRENT LEAGUE: Dr Marten's (Southern) League Western Division
CLUB FOUNDED: 1945 as Evesham Town
PREVIOUS GROUNDS: Crown Meadow (1945–68)

Considering the Common Road ground is less than 40 years old, it appears to be far older. The main stand followed the club from the Crown Meadow ground, having stood there since 1953. The clubhouse was opened in 1975 and floodlights came as recently as 1992 when Common Road was packed for the floodlight opening match against West Bromwich Albion. By far the most eye-catching feature of Common Road is the vast grass banking which comes down at a rakish angle from the railway line that sits on top of it. The banking provides not only a fine view of the ground, but also of this attractive market town. However,

West Terrace, Esh Winning

King George V Ground, Exmouth Town

despite the ground's relative modernity, the club plan to relocate to a new out of town venue in the near future.

EXMOUTH TOWN
GROUND: King George V Ground, Southern Road, Exmouth, Devon
CURRENT CAPACITY: 2,500
RECORD ATTENDANCE: 2,395 v. Liverpool (Friendly) 1987
YEAR BUILT/OPENED: 1964
CURRENT LEAGUE: Screwfix Direct Western League Division One
CLUB FOUNDED: 1933
PREVIOUS GROUNDS: Exmouth Cricket Club; Raleigh Park

Despite it's relatively recent vintage, the Southern Road ground is showing distinct signs of fraying round the edges. It has a nice aspect, being situated on the banks of the River Exe, but once inside, the ground is only basic. It has a clubhouse adjacent to the turnstiles and a small area of cover in the corner.

Opposite is a small main stand, block-built and uninteresting. The rest of the ground is hard standing without the merest whiff of terracing. The club's long-time former home at Maer is still in use by Exmouth Cricket Club.

FALMOUTH TOWN
GROUND: Bickland Park, Bickland Vale, Falmouth, Cornwall
CURRENT CAPACITY: 6,000
RECORD ATTENDANCE: 6,300 v. Oxford United (FA Cup) 03/11/62
YEAR BUILT/OPENED: 1957
CURRENT LEAGUE: Carlsberg South-Western League
CLUB FOUNDED: 1949
PREVIOUS GROUNDS: Union Corner Recreation Ground; Ashfield; Falmouth RUFC

The biggest and best ground in the Duchy, Bickland Park is a classic, albeit a relatively modern one. Town were offered a considerable sum to move from their riverside venue at Ashfield, and Shell even offered to build the club a new ground. The main stand is set into a huge grass bank and has the dressing rooms and a boardroom in its bowels. The two ends and opposite side all have cover that has been re-roofed numerous times due to frequent storm damage. The car-park end boasts a fine sweep of banked terracing and the ground is completed by something all 'new' grounds should have: part of their previous venue! The pay box at Bickland Park saw service at the old Ashfield ground. Of several fine Cornish grounds, Bickland Park is a real gem!

FARNBOROUGH TOWN
GROUND: Cherrywood Road, Farnborough, Hampshire

CURRENT CAPACITY: 4,163
RECORD ATTENDANCE: 3,581 v. Brentford (FA Cup) 22/11/95
YEAR BUILT/OPENED: 1976
CURRENT LEAGUE: Nationwide Football Conference
CLUB FOUNDED: 1967
PREVIOUS GROUNDS: Queens Road (1967-76)

Farnborough's ground is modern and somewhat dull. The original main stand was built onto the clubhouse wall and a 1990s extension sits uncomfortably alongside it. The rest of the ground is a mixture of covered and uncovered terrace. Cherrywood Road may well meet all the right ground-grading criteria but is terribly uninteresting. That said, it does serve the club well for its current needs. However, in recent months the club have actively looked for a ground-share (Aldershot and Kingstonian have been approached) while Farnborough either

Cherrywood Road, Farnborough Town

Throstle Nest, Farsley Celtic

totally redevelop Cherrywood Road or search for a site for a new stadium.

FARSLEY CELTIC
GROUND: Throstle Nest, Newlands, Farsley, Pudsey, West Yorkshire
CURRENT CAPACITY: 4,000
RECORD ATTENDANCE: Not Known (11,000 v. Tranmere at Elland Road)
YEAR BUILT/OPENED: 1948
CURRENT LEAGUE: Unibond (Northern Premier) League Division One
CLUB FOUNDED: 1908
PREVIOUS GROUNDS: Red Lane; Calverley Lane

The pitch-length covered terrace was built, and later extended, in 1974 from funds received from an FA Cup run that saw the side reach the first round, before losing to Tranmere Rovers in front of 11,000 at Elland Road. The main stand, belatedly replacing an earlier wooden structure, was erected in 1989. It features a smart cantilevered roof that gives an unobstructed view of the match. The long cover also has a centre section of seating with terracing to either side. The Throstle Nest ground is currently undergoing redevelopment that will see the ground turned into thoroughly modern venue.

FELIXSTOWE & WALTON UNITED
GROUND: Dellwood Avenue, Felixstowe, Suffolk
CURRENT CAPACITY: 2,000
RECORD ATTENDANCE: 1,500 v. Ipswich Town (Floodlight Opener) 25/01/91
YEAR BUILT/OPENED: 1902
CURRENT LEAGUE: Jewson Eastern Counties League Division One
CLUB FOUNDED: 2000 merger of Felixstowe Port & Town (1890) and Walton United
PREVIOUS GROUNDS: Felixstowe Tennis Club; Ferry Road; Adjacent pitch at current ground

Dellwood Avenue, Felixstowe & Walton United

Ironically, when Felixstowe Town merged with Essex & Suffolk Border League outfit Walton United in 2000, it was the second time in the club's history that they had done so. After World War Two Felixstowe FC merged with the original Walton United club to form Felixstowe United who later became Felixstowe Town. Something that has been more stable is the club's occupancy of Dellwood Avenue, now rapidly approaching its centenary. Originally the club played on the pitch adjacent to the present site, which was shared with the cricket club, but when they relocated a remarkable piece of ingenuity saw the existing wooden stand moved to face the new, enclosed, pitch. The fascia board and stand back were simply switched to the opposite side and the benched seating was rearranged. The club had a terrible time in securing planning permission for floodlights. Protesting neighbours saw to it that several applications turned down

and the club were forced to find the extra funds to pay for hydraulically operated pylons that would be raised and lowered after every game.

FISHER ATHLETIC (LONDON)
GROUND: Surrey Docks Stadium, Salter Road, London SE16
CURRENT CAPACITY: 5,300
RECORD ATTENDANCE: 4,283 v. Barnet (Conference) 04/05/91
YEAR BUILT/OPENED: 1982
CURRENT LEAGUE: Dr Marten's (Southern) League Eastern Division
CLUB FOUNDED: 1908 as Fisher Athletic
PREVIOUS GROUNDS: Bermondsey Park; London Road, Mitcham

Fisher Athletic have led a strangely nomadic existence since their original formation in 1908. They played initially on several sites in Bermondsey, first playing youth-team football. Eventually

Surrey Docks Stadium, Fisher Athletic

the club disbanded but reformed and relocated many miles to the south-west in Mitcham. They eventually worked their way up to the Spartan League, winning the Senior Division in 1981 and 1982. They successfully applied to join the Southern League, having acquired the lease on a brand new ground at Surrey Docks. The move coincided with huge on-field success. The club enjoyed a four-season spell in the Conference between 1987 and 1991. However, recent seasons have seen financial hardship at the club and a consequent slide down the leagues. The stadium is perfect for their current status, with an unusual main stand, complete with exposed steelwork and the always-impressive backdrop of the towering Canary Wharf.

FLACKWELL HEATH
GROUND: Wilks Park, Heath End Road, Flackwell Heath, Buckinghamshire
CURRENT CAPACITY: 2,000

RECORD ATTENDANCE: 4,500 v. Oxford United (Charity Match) 1986
YEAR BUILT/OPENED: 1946
CURRENT LEAGUE: Ryman (Isthmian) League Division Two
CLUB FOUNDED: 1907
PREVIOUS GROUNDS: Recreation Ground (1907–39)

A small village ground that only ever had the changing room as a permanent structure. The overhang from this had provided the ground's only cover until the club decided to apply for Isthmian League membership in 1984. While the ground was suitable for their Athenian League membership, a league that would fold at the end of the season, the step up in status required floodlights and the construction of a new stand. These were completed in time to play in the Isthmian League for the 1984/85 campaign. However, since then, unlike many Ryman League grounds, the ground has seen little development.

Calthorpe Park, Fleet Town

FLEET TOWN
GROUND: Calthorpe Park, Crookham Road, Fleet, Hampshire
CURRENT CAPACITY: 2,000
RECORD ATTENDANCE: 1,050 v. Coventry City (Friendly) 1991
YEAR BUILT/OPENED: 1923
CURRENT LEAGUE: Dr Marten's (Southern) League Western Division
CLUB FOUNDED: 1947 re-formation of a club originally formed in 1890
PREVIOUS GROUNDS: Watson's Meadow

The Calthorpe Park site was left to the town by Lord Calthorpe in 1923 under the condition that it would be used in perpetuity for the staging of football. The ground remained virtually untouched until 1991 when a major fire gutted the wooden stand. The whole of that side of the ground was rebuilt and now has a smart modern stand and gatehouse. The clubhouse was also modernized. The mid-1990s saw the club playing at its highest level, in the Southern League, but high travelling expenses and poor form saw the club step down to the Wessex League in 2000. After a couple of seasons of consolidation and restructuring, Fleet were able to regain their place in the Dr Marten's League when they finished runners-up to Andover in the Wessex League at the end of the 2001/02 season.

FLEETWOOD TOWN
GROUND: Highbury Stadium, Park Avenue, Fleetwood, Lancashire
CURRENT CAPACITY: 4,000
RECORD ATTENDANCE:6,150 Fleetwood Town v. Rochdale (FA Cup) 13/11/65
YEAR BUILT/OPENED: 1939
CURRENT LEAGUE: North West Counties League Division One
CLUB FOUNDED: 1997 as Fleetwood Wanderers
PREVIOUS GROUNDS: None

Highbury Stadium, Fleetwood Town

The Highbury Stadium ground was opened in August 1939 and was built next to one of the original club's many former grounds, The Memorial Park. In the same month war broke out and the ground wasn't used again until 1946, when the main stand had been augmented by a large covered terrace. However, this new structure lasted just two years when the council allowed its demolition to cater for the installation of a cinder speedway track. The speedway club folded after just three years in 1952. When the speedway track was removed, the small cover erected opposite the main stand was left stranded some distance from the pitch and never relocated. The town has seen several senior football clubs come and go, with Fleetwood Freeport being the latest incumbents of this unusual ground. Recently the club purchased some plastic seats from the demolished stand at Blackpool's Bloomfield Road ground and hope to install them in the main stand in place of the numbing wooden benching that provides seating accom-

modation. During the summer of 2002 the club changed its suffix from Freeport to Town.

FOLKESTONE INVICTA
GROUND: New Pavilion, Cheriton Road, Folkestone, Kent
CURRENT CAPACITY: 6,500
RECORD ATTENDANCE: 2,332 v. West Ham United (Friendly) 1996
YEAR BUILT/OPENED: 1914
CURRENT LEAGUE: Dr Marten's (Southern) League Premier Division
CLUB FOUNDED: 1936
PREVIOUS GROUNDS: South Road

An old amateur club, Invicta came to prominence in 1991 when the town's senior club, Folkestone Town, succumbed to years of financial troubles and folded. Invicta were playing at County League level and not even in the town, but along the coast at Hythe when the Cheriton Road ground suddenly became vacant. The club seized the opportunity, took over the ground, slowly climbed the divisions and have returned Southern League foot-

Cheriton Road, Folkestone Invicta

ball to the Kent town. Cheriton Road, awash with all manner of sporting facilities, saw its football ground opened in 1914 and on joining the Southern League in 1923, Town erected a huge wooden grandstand. In 1958, 7,881 crammed into the ground to witness a Kent Senior Cup tie with Margate and with the revenue from that match the club erected a long covered terrace on the Cheriton Road side of the ground. In 1974 the grandstand, just past its 50th year, was burned down and replaced with the modern 900-seater stand. Although the stand is perfectly serviceable, the view of the game is somewhat spoilt by the roof supports. That said, it's great to see Cheriton Road back in the upper echelons of football for it could have been so different if Invicta had shown less ambition.

FORD UNITED
GROUND: Oakside Stadium, Station Road, Barkingside, Essex
CURRENT CAPACITY: 3,000
RECORD ATTENDANCE: Not Known
YEAR BUILT/OPENED: 1957

CURRENT LEAGUE: Ryman (Isthmian) League Premier Division
CLUB FOUNDED: 1958 merger of Briggs Sports (1934) and Ford Sports (1934)
PREVIOUS GROUNDS: Rush Green Road (1958–2001)

Formed from a merger of two of Dagenham's six senior clubs in the 1950s, the club decided to relocate to Rush Green Road where they would develop excellent sporting and social club facilities. Originally Ford Sports played at Kent Avenue close to the massive Ford car works. Brigg Sports, the works team from the Briggs Motor Bodies Company, played at Victoria Road, the current Dagenham and Redbridge Ground. The Rush Green Road ground boasted an unusual concrete main stand and facilities well up to Ryman League standard. However, in the summer of 2001 the club found themselves in breach of Ryman League rules when the parent company offered them only an annually renewable lease on the venue. The League required a more permanent arrangement and the club were forced to relocate to Oakside, home of the financially struggling Essex Senior League outfit Barkingside. Ford bought out the lease and Barkingside now find themselves tenants at their own ground. Ironically, Oakside had seen some considerable development in the late 1990s in an attempt to get Barkingside into the Ryman League, but the project ended in the club's financial ruin. In another twist of fate, Oakside was built in 1957, a year before Rush Green Road.

FOREST GREEN ROVERS

GROUND: The Lawn, Nympsfield Road, Forest Green, Nailsworth, Gloucestershire
CURRENT CAPACITY: 5,000
RECORD ATTENDANCE: 3,002 v. St Albans City (FA Trophy) 18/04/99
YEAR BUILT/OPENED: c. 1918
CURRENT LEAGUE: Nationwide Football Conference
CLUB FOUNDED: 1890
PREVIOUS GROUNDS: Numerous pitches

The Lawn has been in use by Forest Green Rovers since World War One, but has only seen major development since 1945. Rovers have continued expansion in modern times to keep pace with their notable rise to the top level of the non-League game. The old dressing room block dated from 1950 and, 10 years later, the ground was closed for a season to allow the pitch to be levelled. The new main stand, built in 1996, incorporates club offices and underground changing rooms. Rovers were strangely reticent in acquiring floodlights, purchasing a set as recently as 1981. In the best tradition of non-League grounds, The Lawn boasts a piece of another old stadium, the turnstiles having been salvaged from Bedford Town's former ground, The Eyrie.

FRICKLEY ATHLETIC

GROUND: Westfield Lane, South Elmsall, Pontefract, West Yorkshire
CURRENT CAPACITY: 6,000
RECORD ATTENDANCE: 6,500 v. Rotherham United (FA Cup) 20/11/71

The Lawn, Forest Green Rovers, heaving with a record gate of 3,002

YEAR BUILT/OPENED: 1925
CURRENT LEAGUE: Unibond (Northern Premier) League Premier Division
CLUB FOUNDED: 1910
PREVIOUS GROUNDS: Numerous pitches

The ground was first used in 1925, with the vast main stand built a year later, by striking miners participating in the General Strike. The superb covered terrace is of more recent vintage, having been erected in the immediate post-war years. The local colliery was closed in the recession years of the 1970s and the club changed its suffix from Colliery to Athletic. By the mid-1980s Frickley had risen to the top level of the non-League ladder, then called the Alliance Premier League, but have suffered leaner times since. Not much has changed at Westfield Lane in recent years other than in 1991 when the ground suffered severe storm damage, most notably when a floodlight pylon collapsed through the main stand roof. After several months of insurance wrangles and fundraising, the now 75-year-old stand was fitted with a brand-new roof.

FROME TOWN
GROUND: Badgers Hill, Berkeley Road, Frome, Wiltshire
CURRENT CAPACITY: 5,000
RECORD ATTENDANCE: 8,000 v. Leyton Orient (FA Cup) 20/11/54
YEAR BUILT/OPENED: 1904
CURRENT LEAGUE: Screwfix Direct Western League Premier Division
CLUB FOUNDED: 1904
PREVIOUS GROUNDS: None

Badgers Hill is now fast approaching its centenary and is now beginning to look its age. The wooden stand on the Berkeley Road side is a 1930s structure that replaced the original main stand erected in 1907. The banking and shallow covered terraces, built at a strangely obtuse angle to the touchline, were parts of huge improvements that Frome undertook in order to stage their FA Cup tie in 1954 against Leyton Orient. The effort was rewarded with the ground's all-time record gate, which is unlikely to ever be surpassed. Even though it is fraying around the edges, Badgers Hill is more than adequate for Town's current ambitions.

G

GAINSBOROUGH TRINITY
GROUND: Northolme, North Street, Gainsborough, Lincolnshire
CURRENT CAPACITY: 4,000
RECORD ATTENDANCE: 9,760 v. Scunthorpe United (Midland League) 06/09/48
YEAR BUILT/OPENED: 1873
CURRENT LEAGUE: Unibond (Northern Premier) League Premier Division
CLUB FOUNDED: 1873
PREVIOUS GROUNDS: Pringle Hill; Moreton Terrace; The Beslings; Gamble's Field; Trentbridge; Middlefield; Ropery Road (all used when Northolme was in use for cricket)

A historic venue that was first used for cricket in 1853. Trinity were formed in 1873 and had to play second fiddle to cricket for many years, often starting and finishing seasons at a variety of different venues. In 1896 they were admitted into

Northolme, Gainsborough Trinity

the Football League and spent a 16-season stint in that competition before rejoining the Midland League. The current main stand is a modern structure opened in 2000 but built deliberately to give the same visual appearance of its wooden predecessor built in 1949. This stand had itself replaced an earlier structure burned to ashes by vandals during World War Two. The lengthy cover on the opposite side was built in the early 1950s. The ground was purchased by the Supporters' Club in recent years and their sympathetic redevelopment of this historic venue has won widespread and deserved praise.

GARFORTH TOWN
GROUND: Wheatley Park Stadium, Cedar Ridge, Garforth, West Yorkshire
CURRENT CAPACITY: 3,000
RECORD ATTENDANCE: 1,014 ex-Leeds v. ex-Aston Villa 1999
YEAR BUILT/OPENED: 1998
CURRENT LEAGUE: Northern Counties East League Premier Division
CLUB FOUNDED: 1964 as Miners Arms FC
PREVIOUS GROUNDS: Swillington Miners Welfare; Micklefield Miners Welfare; Brierlands Lane

Garforth Town have come a long way since they were formed as a Sunday League side in 1964. Their former home at Brierlands Lane was preventing the club progressing up the pyramid due to residents successfully appealing against planning permission for floodlights. The problem was solved by Wheatley Construction, who offered to build a new stadium for the club close to the existing ground but further away from the housing developments. In return Wheatley built on the existing ground and provided an excellent facility for Town at Cedar

Ridge. They now boast a superb clubhouse and a floodlit ground, with the centrepiece being a fantastic 300-seater stand with a raised cantilevered roof, which is unique in design in this country, although reminiscent of some new smaller European venues. A rare example of a football club working in harmony with a property developer for mutual benefit.

GATESHEAD
GROUND: International Stadium, Neilson Road, Gateshead, Tyne & Wear
CURRENT CAPACITY: 11,500
RECORD ATTENDANCE: 11,750 v. Newcastle United (Friendly) 07/08/95
YEAR BUILT/OPENED: 1968
CURRENT LEAGUE: Unibond (Northern Premier) League Premier Division
CLUB FOUNDED: 1977
PREVIOUS GROUNDS: None

A complex history in the area sees the latest Gateshead club originally being called South Shields (and later Gateshead Utd) and the most recent South Shields club starting out as Gateshead! The original and former Football League club, Gateshead FC folded in 1972 and not long afterwards the redundant Redheugh Park was demolished. The great old venue had begun crumbling and all but useless when in 1968 the local council opened the Municipal Stadium, later to be renamed the International Stadium. Initially Gateshead Town played there but disbanded, then Gateshead United folded before regrouping as the present-day club. Should the current club obtain a decent level of success, they certainly have a Football League standard venue at their disposal.

GILLINGHAM TOWN
GROUND: Hardings Lane, Gillingham, Dorset
CURRENT CAPACITY: 2,000
RECORD ATTENDANCE: Not Known
YEAR BUILT/OPENED: 1925

International Stadium, Gateshead

Hardings Lane, Gillingham Town

CURRENT LEAGUE: Dorset Premier League
CLUB FOUNDED: 1879
PREVIOUS GROUNDS: Chantry Fields (1879–1914); High Street Ground (1919–25)

The Hardings Lane ground has been used for football since 1925 but had previously seen use as the town's showground. Despite its close proximity to the town centre, the ground has beautiful rural views from virtually every aspect. It is the venue's exposed location that has seen the old wooden stand buffeted by strong winds over the years and, as a result, supporting wooden struts have been used at the rear and sides of the structure. The nearby Waterloo-Exeter railway flashes past the ground regularly and a superb view of Hardings Lane is obtained from Gillingham rail station.

GLOUCESTER CITY
GROUND: Meadow Park, Sudmeadow Road, Hempsted, Gloucester, Gloucestershire
CURRENT CAPACITY: 3,500
RECORD ATTENDANCE: 4,000 v. Dagenham & Redbridge (FA Trophy) 12/04/97
YEAR BUILT/OPENED: 1986
CURRENT LEAGUE: Dr Martens (Southern) League Western Division
CLUB FOUNDED: 1889
PREVIOUS GROUNDS: Longlevens (1935–1965); Horton Road (1965–1986)

Gloucester City have led a nomadic existence since their formation in 1889. The club went to and from various grounds, each with their own problems, until settling at Longlevens in 1935. The ground was out-of-town and when the club were offered a substantial amount of money by a housing developer in 1960 they began to search for a new ground. Horton Road took four years to acquire and develop but was never built to the originally intended grand scale. This was due to lack of support and finance. Dog racing, introduced in the 1970s, was a financial

Meadow Park, Gloucester City

disaster, and coupled with the pitch's poor drainage, the club sold the ground to builders in 1979. As part of the sale City were provided with a new stadium at Sudmeadow Road although it was not completed until 1986. The club now have an excellent modern stadium and a vibrant social club, and despite financial problems in recent years, have continued to develop this fine venue.

GODALMING & GUILDFORD

GROUND: Weycourt, Meadrow, Godalming, Surrey
CURRENT CAPACITY: 1,500
RECORD ATTENDANCE: 600 ex-Guildford City XI v. ex-League XI (Benefit Match) 1991
YEAR BUILT/OPENED: 1971
CURRENT LEAGUE: Combined Counties League
CLUB FOUNDED: 1950 as Godalming United
PREVIOUS GROUNDS: Recreation Ground (1950–71); Broadwater Park

An interesting story surrounds Weycourt with this now pleasant little venue being developed by means of begging and borrowing. Farncombe FC had collapsed in 1970 leaving the ground in Meadrow unused. Godalming United took over the debts and tenancy of the disbanded clubs and after realigning the pitch, renamed the ground Weycourt. Waverley Council helped the club out when drainage problems and subsidence befell the new pitch, providing finance for new topsoil and a temporary home at Broadwater Park. In 1985, another nearby club Addlestone and Weybridge collapsed and Godalming United purchased the stand (£225) and post and rail fence (£50) from the old Liberty Lane ground before it was demolished. The stand was re-erected at Weycourt and fitted with new plastic seating and a smart fascia board. In 1991, the Guildford Football Appeal (formed to try to return the name of Guildford to senior football following the demise of Guildford City and the loss of their cher-

Weycourt, Godalming & Guildford

ished St Josephs Ground in 1977) provided the finance to purchase floodlights
for Weycourt. The condition was that
'Guildford' would be incorporated into
the club's name. The ground as it stands
now was completed in 1994 when, in
another bout of recycling, the club purchased a turnstile from the demolished
Millwall ground at The Den.

GOOLE
GROUND: Victoria Pleasure Grounds,
Marcus Street, Goole, East Yorkshire
CURRENT CAPACITY: 3,000
RECORD ATTENDANCE: Not Known
YEAR BUILT/OPENED: 1888
CURRENT LEAGUE: Northern Counties
East League Premier Division
CLUB FOUNDED: 1997
PREVIOUS GROUNDS: None

Goole are a recently formed club rising
out of the ashes of the defunct Goole

Town club and taking over the latter's
occupancy of the ancient Victoria
Pleasure Grounds. The grounds were
opened in August 1888 and rugby was
first played on the site. However, the
ground has since been used to stage
rugby league, cricket, wrestling and even
heavy horse shows! The demise of the
Town club in 1996 was symptomatic of
the decline of the ground. The once
impressive Town End Spion Kop crum-
bled away due to neglect and the rest of
the ground fell into disrepair. The only
existing stand straddles a large section of
terrace and houses a small seated area.
There was another stand opposite but
this was unable to withstand the buffet-
ing of North Sea gales. It was blown
down in 1993 and never replaced. The
ground has an interesting industrial
backdrop, with one particularly oddly
shaped chimney. You will have to go to
see what I mean!

Victoria Pleasure Grounds, Goole

GRANTHAM TOWN

GROUND: South Kesteven Stadium, Trent Road, Grantham, Lincolnshire
CURRENT CAPACITY: 7,500
RECORD ATTENDANCE: 3,695 v. Southport (FA Trophy) 14/03/98
YEAR BUILT/OPENED: 1990
CURRENT LEAGUE: Dr Marten's (Southern) League Premier Division
CLUB FOUNDED: 1874 as Grantham FC
PREVIOUS GROUNDS: London Road (1874–1990)

The Gingerbreads vacated their ancient London Road ground in 1990, having been major players in the construction of a new council-owned stadium to the south of the Lincolnshire town. Ironically, the football club went from sharing a ground with the town's cricket club to sharing it's new ground with the town's athletes. Although the club now unquestionably enjoy better facilities than they ever could have imagined, there has always been an uneasy acceptance of football grounds with athletics tracks. That said, South Kesteven is without doubt one of the better conceived of the dual-purpose stadia. The vast main stand is complemented by a large covered terrace opposite, which gives the ground a more enclosed and intimate feel. The roofs of both cantilever stands with the exposed framework are particularly impressive at non-League level.

GRAVESEND & NORTHFLEET

GROUND: Stonebridge Road, Northfleet, Kent
CURRENT CAPACITY: 3,300
RECORD ATTENDANCE: 12,036 v. Sunderland (FA Cup) 12/02/63
YEAR BUILT/OPENED: 1905
CURRENT LEAGUE: Nationwide Football Conference
CLUB FOUNDED: 1946 Merger of

Stonebridge, Gravesend & Northfleet

Gravesend United (1893) and
Northfleet United (1890)
PREVIOUS GROUNDS: Gravesend:
Central Avenue Northfleet: Old Perry
Street; Collins' Meadow; Portland
Meadow

This classic ground has been home to
Northfleet United and the latterly
merged club since 1905, and is leased
from the cement manufacturers, Blue
Circle. The vast main stand was erected
in 1914 and complemented a smaller
stand on the Stonebridge Road side of
the ground erected some six years later.
The smaller stand was later demolished
and replaced by the present large covered terrace in 1959, which matched the
then seven-year-old cover behind the
East goal. In 1980 the Swanscombe End
was reterraced to modern safety standards. All the developments at the
ground over the years have been sympathetic and in keeping with the site's great
age, but have been done in such a manner that Stonebridge Road remains well
up to modern ground-grading criteria.
For that the club's management should
take a well-deserved bow and promotion
to the Football Conference after winning
the 2001/02 Ryman League Championship
is a suitable reward for their endeavours.

GRAYS ATHLETIC
GROUND: Recreation Ground, Bridge
Road, Grays, Essex
CURRENT CAPACITY: 4,500
RECORD ATTENDANCE: 9,500 v.
Chelmsford City (FA Cup) 31/10/59
YEAR BUILT/OPENED: 1890
CURRENT LEAGUE: Ryman (Isthmian)
League Premier Division
CLUB FOUNDED: 1890
PREVIOUS GROUNDS: The Hoppit

A once-vast ground, the Recreation
Ground dates from 1890 when it was
used by Grays Town. Athletic used a
ground called The Hoppit in Little
Thurrock. Town eventually faded from

the scene and Athletic took residency at the ground. The ground originally provided the space for greyhound racing and athletics but on all sides the spread of housing has encroached to reduce the size and capacity of the ground. The current main stand, called the Smallcombe Stand after a club stalwart, dates from 1952. This replaced a stand that was to find a new home at Aveley's Mill Field ground. The excellent grandstand on the east side of the ground was burned down in 1983 and the land it occupied was sold for a flat development that houses the dressing rooms underneath. Although considerably reduced in stature, the Recreation Ground is still an impressive venue with a clubhouse overlooking an indoor five-a-side pitch, which generates welcome revenue for the club.

GREAT WAKERING ROVERS
GROUND: Burroughs Park, Little Wakering Hall Lane, Great Wakering, Essex
CURRENT CAPACITY: 2,100
RECORD ATTENDANCE: 659 v. Potters Bar Town (FA Vase) 07/02/98
YEAR BUILT/OPENED: 1987

CURRENT LEAGUE: Ryman (Isthmian) League Division One (North)
CLUB FOUNDED: 1919
PREVIOUS GROUNDS: Wakering Recreation Ground

This village club have come a long way in a short time having moved into senior football from the Essex Intermediate League in 1992. Five years previously the Rovers had successfully acquired land adjacent to their Recreation Ground home occupied by disused allotments and commenced work on their own ground, which would be named after the club's president, Roger Burroughs. Since senior status was attained the ground's development has been rapid. Between 1992 and 1994, the ground was fully enclosed, the clubhouse built and floodlights erected. A stand was built on the north side of the ground but for several years had no back to it, therefore offering shelter from the rain but not the wind. On gaining promotion to the Ryman League, Rovers completed this stand and installed seats. A further covered area was added on the opposite side, replacing an older tin shelter. Burroughs Park is now

Burroughs Park, Great Wakering Rovers

117

Wellesey Recreation Ground, Great Yarmouth Town

an excellent little venue but the dreaded ground-grading rules have robbed the venue of a nice little local touch. The path around the pitch was originally made of crushed cockleshells but this has now been replaced by the more politically-correct paving slabs.

GREAT YARMOUTH TOWN
GROUND: Wellesey Recreation Ground, Wellesey Road, Great Yarmouth, Norfolk
CURRENT CAPACITY: 3,600
RECORD ATTENDANCE: 8,944 v. Crystal Palace (FA Cup) 21/11/53
YEAR BUILT/OPENED: 1897
CURRENT LEAGUE: Jewson Eastern Counties League Premier Division
CLUB FOUNDED: 1897
PREVIOUS GROUNDS: Old Recreation Ground (1897)

Without doubt, the grandstand at the Wellesey is the single most photographed ground in non-League history. It is understandable as everything about its construction is aesthetically pleasing. From the dog-tooth fascia board, turned roof supports, roof gable and pierced roof ends down to ornate dressing room window frames it is just a joy. The opposite side of the ground has an unattractive run of covered benching. However it is the 1,000-seater stand, built in the summer of 1906, that is the ground's pride and joy. It even manages to avert the eye from the ghastly all-weather athletics track that replaced a cinder track in the early 1990s. It was also during that time that the stand was closed for patronage under the Safety of Sports Ground Act due to the presence of large amounts of inflammable timber. However, the preservation order on the stand assures its survival for many future generations to enjoy.

GRESLEY ROVERS

GROUND: Moat Ground, Moat Street, Church Gresley, Swadlincote, Derbyshire
CURRENT CAPACITY: 2,000
RECORD ATTENDANCE: 3,950 v. Burton Albion (Birmingham League) 1957
YEAR BUILT/OPENED: 1909
CURRENT LEAGUE: Dr Martens (Southern) League Western Division
CLUB FOUNDED: 1882
PREVIOUS GROUNDS: Mushroom Lane 1882–1895; Church Street 1895–1909

The club have been trying to move to a more spacious and modern ground since the mid-1990s but still remain at Moat Street, which has been home for more than 90 years. The most striking feature of the ground is not the main stand, a relatively modern structure erected in 1990, but the two ends and the Queen St side, which are so tightly hemmed in by housing that they must have the narrowest stands in the country! How they crammed in nearly four thousand for a local derby with Burton Albion in the late 1950s just beggars belief. Personally, I hope the Moat Ground can survive the increasingly stringent Dr Martens League ground grading-criteria as, even with its current safety level for capacity, to witness a match in a packed Moat Street is a tremendous experience.

GUISELEY

GROUND: Nethermoor, Otley Road, Guiseley, West Yorkshire
CURRENT CAPACITY: 3,000
RECORD ATTENDANCE: 2,486 v. Bridlington Town (FA Vase) 24/03/90
YEAR BUILT/OPENED: 1909
CURRENT LEAGUE: Unibond (Northern Premier) League Division One
CLUB FOUNDED: 1909
PREVIOUS GROUNDS: None

Guiseley have always played at Nethermoor, which was nothing more than a field in the early days. Until 1935 the only building was the wooden scout hut that served as changing rooms. In that year the club acquired a grandstand

Moat Ground, Gresley Rovers

Nethermoor, Guiseley

from the Harry Ramsden's fish and chip shop further down Otley Road. It was used on the chip shop grounds for brass band recitals but was sold to the football club for only £50. A roof was added and, apart from a few licks of paint, has remained unchanged ever since. The clubhouse was opened in the mid-1970s and new changing rooms came in 1983. Previously the club shared facilities with the adjacent cricket club. The club's penchant for obtaining bargain buys continued and in 1987 they purchased a second-hand set of floodlights that had seen service at a British Rail goods yard in nearby Bradford. In another example of making do, the club converted existing tennis courts into an all-weather training surface. The club's promotion to the Northern Premier League in 1991 was subject to the construction of an additional cover on the cricket-ground side of Nethermoor. It is a superb venue and an excellent example of all that is charming in non-League football ethics. In recent years the ground has been used as the backdrop for the popular television series, *Playing The Field*. However, a problem on the horizon was the club's inability to secure a lease beyond 2003 or, indeed, planning permission for ground improvements. As a result, the club was contemplating taking the dramatic decision during 2002 of relocating to Cougar Park, home of Keighley Cougars RLFC. However, a ballot of supporters vetoed the plans and a working party was set up to spruce up the Nethermoor ground. The abandonment of Nethermoor would have been very sad as a visit for a match followed by fish and chips at the original Harry Ramsden's just cannot be beaten!

H

HALESOWEN HARRIERS

GROUND: Hayes Park , Park Road,
Colley Gate, Halesowen, West Midlands
CURRENT CAPACITY: 4,000
RECORD ATTENDANCE: 750 v.
Wolverhampton Wanderers (Friendly)
1985
YEAR BUILT/OPENED: 1984
CURRENT LEAGUE: Midland Alliance
CLUB FOUNDED: 1961
PREVIOUS GROUNDS: Senellys Park;
Cooksey Lane; Halesowen Town FC

Halesowen Harriers were originally a
Sunday club and only converted to senior
Saturday football in 1984 when they
acquired their current ground in Park
Road. The new venue was just down the
road from Halesowen Town's
ground – Harriers' home for the previous 14 years. The creation of Hayes Park
was the vision of one man, Derek Beasley.

The site was a heavily sloping hill and the
excavation and levelling of the pitch was
an impressive engineering achievement.
Some of the excess soil was used to create the impressive banking all around the
ground. An expert on turf technology
who listed Wembley among his projects,
was enlisted to ensure the new pitch
would drain well in a marshy area.
Covered accommodation at the ground
is provided by a small brick-built stand
behind the east goal and a low cover on
the south side of the ground. The ground
is approached from Park Road up a steep
and windy path and, carrying on past the
turnstile block, you will find the club's
impressive all-weather training surface.

HALESOWEN TOWN

GROUND: The Grove, Old Hawne
Lane, Halesowen, West Midlands
CURRENT CAPACITY: 5,000
RECORD ATTENDANCE: 5,000 v.
Hendon (FA Cup) 19/11/55
YEAR BUILT/OPENED: 1884
CURRENT LEAGUE: Dr Marten's
(Southern) League Western Division

Hayes Park, Halesowen Harriers

The Grove, Halesowen Town

CLUB FOUNDED: 1873
PREVIOUS GROUNDS: Two grounds in Hasbury

A classic ground, and just about the oldest stadium in the West Midlands. On one side, The Grove has a large and impressive sweep of terracing. Opposite is the modern main stand known as The Harry Rudge Stand, which was opened in 1987 and replaced a low and oddly angular wooden stand dating from the pre-World War Two era. The old surviving part of The Grove is the Hawne Lane end covered terrace, opened in 1952. The former ash banking underneath has been replaced in more recent times by modern terracing. Until the mid-1970s the ground was three sided, sharing boundaries with the cricket club. The cricketers departed and the ground was at last fully enclosed with the large uncovered terrace. Only in the mid-1980s did the ground have its own dressing rooms with players previously changing on the other side of the recreation ground before trotting over the cricket area and entering the football pitch. The Grove also boasts a fine clubhouse, which has seen extensive refurbishment since a terrible fire in 1996.

HALIFAX TOWN
GROUND: The Shay, Shaw Hill, Halifax, West Yorkshire
CURRENT CAPACITY: 9,900
RECORD ATTENDANCE: 36,885 v. Tottenham Hotspur (FA Cup) 14/02/53
YEAR BUILT/OPENED: 1921
CURRENT LEAGUE: Nationwide Football Conference
CLUB FOUNDED: 1911
PREVIOUS GROUNDS: Sandhall Lane (1911–15), Exley (1919–21)

Halifax Town have the dubious honour of being the first club to be relegated from the Football League on two occasions. The Shay has seen some history including the club's initial acceptance into Division Three North in 1921. The first stand at The Shay was purchased from Manchester City and transported from City's old ground at Hyde Road. In recent years, The Shay has survived the loss of the speedway club that shared the ground from 1948 and also the threat of closure by its owners, Calderdale council. The council originally planned to rehouse The Shaymen at the town's rugby league stadium at Thrum Hall. However, the council changed its mind and the Halifax Blue Sox eventually moved into The Shay. The ground has been upgraded with both ends now boasting steep covered terraces. The main stand was originally a covered terrace that had seating installed to the left-hand side. This has now been fully turned over to seating. The former main stand was demolished in 2000 as was the last remaining section of speedway track. The new structure has been built at an

amazingly slow rate, apparently hampered by funding problems. Although the present venue has an impressive capacity, it seems hard to imagine nearly 37,000 packing into the ground for a FA Cup tie in 1953.

HALLAM
GROUND: Sandygate, Sandygate Road, Crosspool, Sheffield, South Yorkshire
CURRENT CAPACITY: 1,000
RECORD ATTENDANCE: 2,000 v. Hendon (FA Amateur Cup) 1959
YEAR BUILT/OPENED: 1860
CURRENT LEAGUE: Northern Counties East League Premier Division
CLUB FOUNDED: 1860
PREVIOUS GROUNDS: None

A truly historic club and ground, which saw its first match on Boxing Day 1860 against the world's oldest football club, Sheffield. The ground was originally owned by the landlord of The Plough public house over the road. At first the team played on the lower field until the

The Shay, Halifax Town

Sandygate, Hallam

ground was redesigned in 1865 to accommodate cricket. The club were unceremoniously booted out of Sandygate in 1933 when the landlord rented it out to other clubs including Crookes Working Mens Club, St Phillips Church Institute and Fullwood. Fortunately for Hallam, The Plough had a new landlord by 1946 and they resumed tenancy of the ground. The first structure built at Sandygate was a coin-operated toilet block in 1948. Six years later, the club opened a grandstand after securing a proper lease on the venue. A pavilion was opened in 1964, with the grounds first changing rooms. Previously changing facilities were only available at the hostelry over the road. The Sandygate ground was nearly sold for housing in 1972 by then-owners, Whitbreads, but the deal mercifully fell through when planning permission was withheld. In a complete change of heart Whitbreads contributed to repairs following storm damage at the ground and gave the club

a 99-year lease on the ground for £50,000. With their future now secure, floodlights were erected in 1992 and seven years later a brand-new main stand was opened. Despite its recent modernization, Sandygate remains a breathtakingly historic and atmospheric ground.

HALSTEAD TOWN
GROUND: Rosemary Lane, Broton Industrial Estate, Halstead, Essex
CURRENT CAPACITY: 2,000
RECORD ATTENDANCE: 4,000 v. Walthamstow Avenue (Essex Senior Cup) 1949
YEAR BUILT/OPENED: 1948
CURRENT LEAGUE: Jewson Eastern Counties League Division One
CLUB FOUNDED: 1879
PREVIOUS GROUNDS: Coggeshall Pieces; Three Gates; Cortaulds Club

An interesting ground located in a less-than-prepossessing industrial estate, although once in the ground, the outlook

Rosemary Lane, Halstead Town

is surprisingly rural with open fields tailing off to the distance. When Halstead re-emerged after World War Two they, like many clubs, found that their old ground was no longer usable for football, having been turned over to agriculture to aid the war effort. The club eventually secured a piece of land, a former sandpit, next to the town's bowling green. Volunteers ensured the ground was enclosed and a car park was laid. The club secured a building from the Ministry of Supply for use as a clubhouse only to lose the pre-fabricated unit when it was stolen in transit! Instead the club funded their own clubhouse building at a cost of £900. The current main stand, an impressive pitched roof structure, was erected in the summer of 1950. The pitch was railed off with a bargain buy from the former sea defences at Walton-on-the-Naze. In recent times the ground has remained relatively untouched apart from new perimeter fencing and, in 1997, plastic seating was installed in the main stand,

replacing the old wooden benches.

HAMPTON & RICHMOND
GROUND: Beveree Stadium, Beaver Close, Hampton, London TW12
CURRENT CAPACITY: 3,000
RECORD ATTENDANCE: 1,027 v. Aldershot (League) 15/03/97
YEAR BUILT/OPENED: 1921
CURRENT LEAGUE: Ryman (Isthmian) League Premier Division
CLUB FOUNDED: 1921 as Hampton FC
PREVIOUS GROUNDS: Hatherop Recreation Ground (1921–59)

The Beveree has always been home to Hampton except for seven years when they were forced off the ground following skulduggery by local rivals, Twickenham Town. Town's chairman, who was also the local mayor, contrived to get Twickenham the lease on the as-yet-undeveloped ground. By the time Twickenham vacated the Beveree and eventually folded, the ground boasted a

Beveree Stadium, Hampton & Richmond

railed-off pitch and a small stand that would be replaced by the present main stand in 1964. Three years later floodlights and the spacious clubhouse were opened. The covered terrace on the far side of the ground was erected in 1970. Interestingly the present main stand has seats acquired from two old grounds, Leytonstone's Granleigh Road and Wimbledon's Plough Lane. Another item with a sporting past are the turnstiles, which were rescued from the old racecourse at nearby Hurst Park. In more recent years the Beveree has been completely terraced all around the ground and, in 1999, the club opened a magnificent new stand behind the south goal. The Beveree has been developed with loving care into one of the Ryman League's most attractive venues.

HAREFIELD UNITED
GROUND: Preston Park, Breakespeare Road, North Harefield, Middlesex
CURRENT CAPACITY: 2,000

RECORD ATTENDANCE: 430 v. Bashley (FA Vase) 1990
YEAR BUILT/OPENED: 1963
CURRENT LEAGUE: Minerva Spartan South Midlands League Premier Division
CLUB FOUNDED: 1868
PREVIOUS GROUNDS: Taylors Meadow

Considering its location, just within the M25, Harefield United's Preston Park is an amazingly rural little ground. An ancient club who were formed as early as 1868, Harefield spent many years playing local football in the Uxbridge and District League. The club really came to the fore in 1963 when they stepped up to the old Parthenon League. At the same time they moved into Preston Park, gradually building up the facilities. The pitch was railed off and a small seated stand erected on the far side. Isthmian League football came in 1984 and with it, floodlights and another area of cover. However, The Hares found the Isthmian League a real struggle and, coupled with ground-grading issues, the club were demoted to the Spartan League in 1996. The club's former undeveloped ground at Taylors Meadow is still in use for local football.

HARLOW TOWN

GROUND: Harlow Sports Centre, Hammarskjold Road, Harlow, Essex
CURRENT CAPACITY: 10,000
RECORD ATTENDANCE: 9,723 v. Leicester City (FA Cup) 08/01/80
YEAR BUILT/OPENED: 1960
CURRENT LEAGUE: Ryman (Isthmian) League Division One (North)
CLUB FOUNDED: 1879
PREVIOUS GROUNDS: Harlow College (1879–85); Green Man Field (1885–95, 1922–60); Marigolds Field (1895–1922)

Although Harlow is designated a 'new town', the town is actually much older as is its football club, which was founded in 1879, playing on a pitch at Harlow College. They then played on the field at the rear of The Green Man public house before a spell at a site called Marigolds. From 1922 Harlow returned to The Green Man field and developed the venue to a high standard, although space was limited. So when a new sports centre was opened in the town in 1960, the club opted to relocate to the larger venue. The original stand at the Sports Centre ground was a long, low-roofed affair although this was replaced by the current grandstand in 1972 at a cost of £15,000. Floodlights came in January 1970 after the committee purchased the pylons from The Hive, the home of the defunct Brentwood Town. The ground is steeply banked and in 1998 the club erected a token covered stand opposite the main stand to comply with Isthmian League ground-grading rules. After the club's epic 1979 FA Cup run, which bought the record gate to the Sports Centre, most of the 1980s were spent looking for an out-of-town site for a new ground. In 1985 plans were unveiled for the construction of a new stadium on the Roydon Road although numerous delays

Harlow Sports Centre, Harlow Town

Wetherby Road, Harrogate Town

meant work did not commence until 1991. A clubhouse and the framework for a stand were built when the project abruptly ran out of money. Unfortunately the club had registered the new ground as their headquarters and therefore were left without a suitable ground. They were unable to field a side for the 1992/93 campaign. The following season saw Harlow return to the Sports Centre where they continue to reside while the Roydon Road ground remains half built.

HARROGATE TOWN
GROUND: Wetherby Road, Harrogate, North Yorkshire
CURRENT CAPACITY: 3,800
RECORD ATTENDANCE: 4,280 v. Harrogate RA (Whitworth Cup Final) 1950
YEAR BUILT/OPENED: 1920
CURRENT LEAGUE: Unibond (Northern Premier) League Premier Division
CLUB FOUNDED: 1919 as Harrogate FC
PREVIOUS GROUNDS: Starbeck Lane (1919–20)

A pleasant venue in a historic market town, the Wetherby Road ground has been home to Harrogate Town since their second season of existence. Their first, 1919/20, was spent at a sloping field in Starbeck Lane. The present ground has a smart, modern main stand on the far side, opened in August 1990. The near side has a long section of covered terrace with the centre section equipped with seating. The Town End is relatively undeveloped while the opposite end has all the social and official facilities and a small area of seating. In recent years the club have upgraded their floodlights and improved the turnstile block. The club have built an impressive home in an area renowned for difficulties in gaining planning permission.

HARROW BOROUGH
GROUND: Earlsmead, Carlyon Avenue, South Harrow, Middlesex
CURRENT CAPACITY: 3,000
RECORD ATTENDANCE: 3,000 v. Wealdstone (FA Cup) 05/10/46

YEAR BUILT/OPENED: 1934
CURRENT LEAGUE: Ryman (Isthmian)
League Premier Division
CLUB FOUNDED: 1933 as Roxonian FC
PREVIOUS GROUNDS: Northolt Road
(1933–34)

The club's first ground at Northolt Road had been open barely four months when Roxonians were informed that they would be ejected from the venue at the end of their inaugural campaign. The club took the setback well and parted with £1,625, with which to purchase the current site in Carlyon Avenue. Amazingly, the ground was ready for use in August 1934 after a summer of hard work to shape the new site into a football ground. Within four years, fundraising had resulted in the new ground boasting a superb pavilion and a wooden main stand donated to the club by the Champniss family. This stand stood until replaced in 1997 with the present structure, itself part funded by a considerable donation from the Football Trust. It was the first major work at the ground since the mid-1970s when the second pitch was sold to a developer. The funds generated saw floodlights, a new clubhouse and terracing laid all around the ground. So much work was carried out during the early 1970s that the club were forced to play all their home games in the 1973/74 campaign at opponents' venues. Recent developments have seen Earlsmead given a fresh air of respectability.

HARWICH & PARKESTON
GROUND: Royal Oak, Main Road, Dovercourt, Essex
CURRENT CAPACITY: 5,000
RECORD ATTENDANCE: 5,649 v. Romford (FA Amateur Cup) 1938
YEAR BUILT/OPENED: 1898
CURRENT LEAGUE: Jewson Eastern Counties League Premier Division
CLUB FOUNDED: 1875
PREVIOUS GROUNDS: Phoenix Field; Barrack Field; Hamilton Park

Earlsmead, Harrow Borough

Royal Oak, Harwich & Parkeston

One of the most historic of Essex grounds, The Royal Oak ground opened for business in 1898. It was a good financial move for The Shrimpers as their ground at the Phoenix Field was so close to the North Sea that the club went through a considerable amount of footballs during the course of a season! The ground has suffered the loss of a superb covered terrace, opposite the main stand, in 1979 and 16 years later the open terrace at the south end was deemed unsafe and was demolished. The removal of the terrace has left the dressing rooms stranded some way distant from the rest of the ground. However, the ground retains its famous main stand, erected in November 1948. Its fame, or perhaps infamy, stems from the unusually sharp sightlines caused by the angle of construction of the stand. Visitors of a vertiginous disposition may need to view the game from ground level. The current ground is completed by the covered ter-race at the Main Road end, which features quite possibly the deepest steps of terracing in the country. In short the Royal Oak is an essential and quirky visit. The most recent threat to this dear old ground came in 2001 when the club turned down a sizeable offer from the supermarket chain, Lidl.

HASTINGS UNITED
GROUND: The Pilot Field, Elphinstone Road, Hastings, East Sussex
CURRENT CAPACITY: 4,050
RECORD ATTENDANCE: 4,888 v. Nottingham Forest (Friendly) 23/06/96
YEAR BUILT/OPENED: 1921
CURRENT LEAGUE: Dr Marten's (Southern) League Premier Division
CLUB FOUNDED: 1894 as Hastings & St Leonards Amateurs
PREVIOUS GROUNDS: The Firs (1921–23, 1948–73, 1976–85); Pilot Field (1923–48); Bulverhythe Recreation Ground (1973–76)

The Pilot Field and 'the upper ground' known as The Firs, current home of St Leonards, have had a quite remarkable and at times torrid history. Town were formed in 1894 and had three separate spells playing at the top pitch. However, the club played at The Pilot Field between 1923 and 1948. The council had opened both grounds in 1921 at a cost of £32,000. In 1923, the current vast main stand at the Pilot Field was opened at an additional cost of £8,000. In 1948 a professional club, Hastings United, were formed and Town returned to the smaller ground at The Firs. Speedway had come to the Pilot Field in 1948 and some of the old track still remains today. However, after one season racing was banned by the council after complaints of noise from neighbours. The 1950s saw some huge crowds at the Pilot Field, the largest being 12,727 for the visit of Norwich City in a FA Cup tie in January 1954. By 1985, Hastings United had folded following bankruptcy. Town seized the opportunity to return to the Pilot Field and took United's place in the Southern League. The club remain in this vast venue despite modest support but strangely even after some 15 years the ground still displays a couple of signs with the name of the long-defunct Hastings United. In the light of this, and to complicate the story still further, Hastings Town opted to change its name during the summer of 2002 to... Hastings United!

HAVANT & WATERLOOVILLE

GROUND: Westleigh Park, Martin Road, Havant, Hampshire
CURRENT CAPACITY: 4,500
RECORD ATTENDANCE: 3,500 v. Wisbech Town (FA Vase) 1986
YEAR BUILT/OPENED: 1983
CURRENT LEAGUE: Dr Marten's (Southern) League Premier Division
CLUB FOUNDED: 1998 merger of

The Pilot Field, Hastings United

H

Havant Town (1958) and Waterlooville
(1902)
PREVIOUS GROUNDS: Havant: Front
Lane Waterlooville: Hart Plain Park;
Convent Ground; Rowlands Avenue;
Jubilee Park

Waterlooville played at Jubilee Park – a
modern ground opened in September
1957 – until severe financial difficulties
forced them to sell up in 1998. Rather
than fold up and die, the club merged
with Havant Town and relocated to
Town's Westleigh Park some four miles
away. This ground is quite remarkable in
its own right, having been built as
recently as 1983. However it does look
considerably older than that. The main
stand is a largely timber affair with numerous roof supports giving the appearance
of a not-so-modern design. There is also
ample covered terracing and a large,
grassed bank. The front of the ground
houses the turnstile block, one turnstile
having been acquired from nearby
Portsmouth when new turnstiles were

installed at Fratton Park. With a long-term
lease acquired on Westleigh Park, football
in this corner of East Hampshire has a
secure future.

HAVERHILL ROVERS
GROUND: Hamlet Croft, Haverhill,
Suffolk
CURRENT CAPACITY: 3,000
RECORD ATTENDANCE: 1,537 v.
Warrington (FA Vase) 1987
YEAR BUILT/OPENED: 1926
CURRENT LEAGUE: Jewson Eastern
Counties League Division One
CLUB FOUNDED: 1886
PREVIOUS GROUNDS: Seven Acres
(1886–1926); Recreation Ground (1962)

Hamlet Croft is a pleasant venue with all
facilities sitting on the top of a steep grass
bank which gives an indication of the
severe latitudinal slope that hampered
players until its levelling in 1962. The club
moved to the ground in 1926 having
played at Seven Acres for many years. The
ground's only stand was opened in 1935

Hamlet Croft, Haverhill Rovers

at a cost of £250. Due to the rotting of the wooden back and side panels and general wear and tear, the stand was renovated in recent years with metal cladding. The clubhouse, changing rooms and tea bar are also on this side of the ground. This elevated view also allows drivers to park up and watch the action as if they were at the drive-in movies. Behind the Town End goal the club has a training area. Although Hamlet Croft remains perfectly adequate for Haverhill's current ambitions, the club have been considering sites for a new home for several years.

HAYES
GROUND: Townfield, Church Road, Hayes, Middlesex
CURRENT CAPACITY: 6,500
RECORD ATTENDANCE: 15,370 v. Bromley (FA Amateur Cup) 10/02/51
YEAR BUILT/OPENED: 1920
CURRENT LEAGUE: Ryman League Premier Division
CLUB FOUNDED: 1908 as Botwell Mission

PREVIOUS GROUNDS: Botwell Common (1908–20)

Botwell Mission acquired Townfield, or Cox's Meadow as it was known, in 1920 and it was regarded to be a far superior venue than their previous home at Botwell Common, off Coldharbour Lane. Within four years of the move, The Missioners had changed their name to Hayes. In 1925, the club cobbled together enough money to build a wooden grandstand, which stood until the 1960s when it was replaced by the present brick-built structure. The old main stand, the covered terrace opposite and the vast banks around the ground allowed more than 15,000 to cram into Townfield for an Amateur Cup tie in 1951. The post War years saw the replacing of the old clubhouse, a victim of a direct hit from the Luftwaffe, which also saw the club lose all its records. The Townfield ground is a relatively large venue by today's standards and boasts ample terracing. The ground has had

Townfield, Hayes

cosmetic improvements in recent years courtesy of the £600,000 the club received in 1995 when one of their 'old boys', Les Ferdinand, was sold by Queens Park Rangers to Newcastle United. The windfall also ended a protracted period of financial worries at Church Road.

HAYWARDS HEATH TOWN
GROUND: Hanbury Park Stadium, Allen Road, Haywards Heath, West Sussex
CURRENT CAPACITY: 3,000
RECORD ATTENDANCE: 4,000 v. Horsham (Metropolitan League) 23/08/52
YEAR BUILT/OPENED: 1952
CURRENT LEAGUE: Rich City Sussex County League Division Three
CLUB FOUNDED: 1888 as Haywards Heath Excelsior
PREVIOUS GROUNDS: Muster Green; Recreation Ground; Victoria Park

While Haywards Heath Town have struggled in the lower reaches of the Sussex County League in recent years, their superb Hanbury Park Stadium remains among the finest in Sussex. The club were formed in 1888 as Hayward Heath Excelsior, merging with Haywards Heath Juniors seven years later. The club moved into the current ground in 1952 and that was a springboard to their heyday in that decade when they had a 10-season spell in the Metropolitan League. That competition provided the ground's record gate when 4,000 people saw the local derby with Horsham in 1952. The club's elevation to the Metropolitan League came after being crowned Sussex County League champions two seasons running in 1949/50 and 1950/51. The club's unprecedented success culminated in winning the Sussex Senior Cup in 1958. The club rejoined the County League in 1961, winning the title again in 1969/70

Hanbury Park Stadium, Haywards Heath Town

although they then went into a spiral of decline throughout the late 1970s and '80s. The ground remains impressive, the superb pitched roof main stand accommodates 500 seated spectators and houses the changing rooms. However, much of the wooden-bench seating is in a decayed state and some sections are periodically cordoned off to spectators. The banking around the ground could accommodate 3,000 in the unlikely event that Town enjoy a renaissance. It is a crying shame that the team's woeful recent record means that that renaissance looks further away than ever.

HEDNESFORD TOWN

GROUND: Keys Park, Hill Street, Hednesford, Staffordshire
CURRENT CAPACITY: 6,000
RECORD ATTENDANCE: 3,169 v. York City (FA Cup) 13/01/97
YEAR BUILT/OPENED: 1995
CURRENT LEAGUE: Dr Marten's (Southern) League Premier Division
CLUB FOUNDED: 1880
PREVIOUS GROUNDS: The Tins (1880–1904); Cross Keys (1904–95)

Hednesford Town's old ground at Cross Keys was bulldozed and levelled inside a week during 1995 having stood for more than 90 years. It was a real shame as it was a unique ground in many ways and once held 10,000 for a FA Cup tie with Walsall in 1919. Although it remained a sizeable venue, the cost of bringing Cross Keys up to Conference standard meant it effectively had come to the end of its serviceable life. The new ground was built a few hundred yards up the road and was officially opened in August 1995 with a visit from Walsall. The main stand is a superb structure with a tall roofline and roof supports that do not impair the view of spectators. To the rear of the main stand is an impressive two-story building. The lower level houses the dressing

Keys Park, Hednesford Town

rooms and club offices while the upper has the boardroom and a plush function suite. Both ends of Keys Park have ample covered terracing, while, until recently, the side opposite the main stand had a full-length uncovered terrace. However, despite relegation from the Conference at the end of the 2000/01 season, Hednesford persevered and erected a cover over the open side during the summer of 2001. Keys Park now has everything in place for a push towards Football League status, the players just need to keep their end of the bargain!

HEMEL HEMPSTEAD TOWN
GROUND: Vauxhall Ground, Adeyfield Road, Hemel Hempstead, Hertfordshire
CURRENT CAPACITY: 3,000
RECORD ATTENDANCE: 2,020 v. Watford (Friendly) 1985
YEAR BUILT/OPENED: 1972
CURRENT LEAGUE: Ryman (Isthmian) League Division One (North)
CLUB FOUNDED: 1885 as Apsley FC

PREVIOUS GROUNDS: Salmon Meadow; Crabtree Lane

This Hertfordshire town expanded massively during the 1960s and '70s with housing and industry taking all before them, including Hemel Hempstead's long-standing home in Crabtree Lane. This was an impressive town centre ground with a sizeable grandstand. They relocated to a new venue to the east of the town in the Adeyfield area. They also, at this time, merged with local rivals Hemel Hempstead United. The Vauxhall ground is just over 30 years old, but is decidedly worse for wear. It has suffered greatly from the unwanted attention of vandals, including a serious blaze that gutted the clubhouse in 1992. The trouble with the Vauxhall Road ground is that it has no immediate focal point. The far side is a fairly unremarkable covered terrace and the main stand is also a dull affair. It has a low roof and a bare minimum of seats. Despite its rel-

Vauxhall Ground, Hemel Hempstead

Claremont Road, Hendon

ative youth, the club has struggled in recent years to keep it up to Ryman League standard.

HENDON
GROUND: Claremont Road, Cricklewood, London WW2
CURRENT CAPACITY: 3,000
RECORD ATTENDANCE: 9,000 v. Northampton Town (FA Cup) 22/11/52
YEAR BUILT/OPENED: 1926
CURRENT LEAGUE: Ryman (Isthmian) League Premier Division
CLUB FOUNDED: 1908 as Hampstead Town
PREVIOUS GROUNDS: Kensal Rise (1908–12); Avenue Ground (1912–26)

Interestingly, Hendon's two previous grounds were both subsequently used by other clubs. The National Athletics Stadium in Kensal Rise was used by QPR and the Avenue Ground was used for Isthmian League football by the Civil Service club. In May 1926, the local council offered the club a new site at Claremont Road. Within weeks the ground was levelled and the present main stand erected. The stand has only ever been cosmetically enhanced, most notably in 1993 when plastic seats acquired from Watford were installed, replacing the wooden benching. Opposite the main stand is the cavernous Gordon Raymond covered terrace on which, apparently, you can see the club's previous name of Golders Green faintly outlined on the roof. The name was painted out during World War Two to confuse enemy bombers. The remainder of the ground has copious concrete terracing, which replaced railway sleepers that previously did the job. Floodlights came to Claremont Road in 1962 and were improved nine years later. The smart clubhouse, a modern structure that replaced the old wooden pavilion, stands just outside the entrance. Despite modern safety constraints, Claremont Road remains a large venue and it was no surprise that the ground was considered by Barnet when the then-Football League club were looking for alternatives to their decrepit Underhill ground.

H

HEREFORD UNITED
GROUND: Edgar Street, Hereford, Hereford & Worcestershire
CURRENT CAPACITY: 8,843
RECORD ATTENDANCE: 18,114 v. Sheffield Wednesday (FA Cup) 04/01/58
YEAR BUILT/OPENED: c1910
CURRENT LEAGUE: Nationwide Football Conference
CLUB FOUNDED: 1924 merger of St Martins and RAOC
PREVIOUS GROUNDS: None

Edgar Street was originally a sports ground owned by the cider makers Bulmers and was used for various sports and by various football clubs including the most senior side in the area, Hereford City. City would eventually fold in 1939, and were eclipsed by Hereford United – a merger of two minor clubs who had shared Edgar Street since August 1924. Edgar Street nowadays has a dramatically reduced capacity and the club have always suffered from planning restrictions limiting the height of buildings in the town to only 45 ft. The ground has two early examples of cantilever-roofed stands. The older was erected in 1968 and extended in 1989 and is called the Merton Stand. The second was erected during their early years of Football League membership in 1974 when a five-row tier of seating was added over an existing terrace. This extremely narrow stand – the Len Weston Stand – is a remarkable feat of ingenuity considering the lack of space. The two ends, the Meadow End and Blackfriars Street End, have interesting curved covered terraces. The latter suffered storm damage to its roof in January 2002. While Hereford's relegation from the Football League in 1997 was a bitter blow for the town, it also ensured that their delightful archaic ground will remain untouched for a while longer.

HERTFORD TOWN
GROUND: Hertingfordbury Park, West Street, Hertford, Hertfordshire
CURRENT CAPACITY: 6,500
RECORD ATTENDANCE: 5,000 v. Kingstonian (FA Amateur Cup) 1956
YEAR BUILT/OPENED: 1908
CURRENT LEAGUE: Ryman (Isthmian) League Division One (North)
CLUB FOUNDED: 1908 merger of Port Vale Rovers and Hertford Blue Cross
PREVIOUS GROUNDS: Port Vale Rovers: Hartham Park

Hertingfordbury Park remains a fine venue as it rapidly approaches its centenary. The club formed in 1908 when Port Vale Rovers and Hertford Blue Cross merged and decided to play at the latter's home ground. The ground is accessed down a narrow lane that crosses over the River Lea. It has an impressive brick-built stand, erected in 1959, which houses changing rooms and a modest boardroom. Earlier in 1950, the covered terracing on the river side, which was later extended, and car-park end were built. The current floodlights were opened in 1965 and replaced an inferior set that had stood for nine years. The clubhouse on the ground has led an interesting life. The original wooden building was replaced with a larger building in 1974 but this was burned to the ground in 1991. This was replaced by the large portakabin that currently serves adequately as a social club.

HEYBRIDGE SWIFTS
GROUND: Scraley Road, Heybridge, Essex

Hertingfordbury Park, Hertford Town

CURRENT CAPACITY: 3,000
RECORD ATTENDANCE: 2,477 v.
Woking (FA Trophy) 22/03/97
YEAR BUILT/OPENED: 1966
CURRENT LEAGUE: Ryman (Isthmian)
League Premier Division
CLUB FOUNDED: 1880
PREVIOUS GROUNDS: The Plains;
Bentalls Sports Ground; Sadd's Athletic
FC

As with Wivenhoe's Broad Lane ground, Heybridge's Scraley Road ground was once a carrot field before the club acquired the site in 1966. The club had spent a couple of unhappy seasons ground-sharing at Sadd's Athletic after the demise of their former home at Bentalls. The sports and recreation ground at Bentalls – Swifts' home since 1890 – had been bought by a company called Acrow and both the Swifts and Heybridge Cricket Club were turned out without warning. The club also found that a lot of their equipment had either been thrown out or destroyed. The club were on the verge of folding when the carrot field was made available at the 11th hour. The Scraley Road ground was quickly railed off and the current wooden stand at the Town End was soon erected. The large stand on the east side of the ground dates from 1996. The cover at the south end of the ground was started in late 1995, but gales blowing off the River Blackwater saw the preliminary shell of the stand destroyed. Scraley Road was briefly closed by the council due to safety concerns. However, the stand was eventually rebuilt. The now well-developed ground has an excellent clubhouse with a grassed area inside the ground, equipped with picnic tables. Perfect for watching a match on a warm, sunny afternoon.

HINCKLEY UNITED
GROUND: Middlefield Lane, Hinckley, Leicestershire

139

H

Scraley Road, Heybridge Swifts

CURRENT CAPACITY: 5,000
RECORD ATTENDANCE: 5,410 v.
Nuneaton (Birmingham Combination)
26/12/49
YEAR BUILT/OPENED: 1940
CURRENT LEAGUE: Dr Marten's
(Southern) League Premier Division
CLUB FOUNDED: 1997 merger of
Hinckley Athletic (1889) and Hinckley
Town (1958)
PREVIOUS GROUNDS: Athletic:
Hollywell Lane; Westfield; Coventry
Road; Leicester Road

Hinckley United were formed in 1977
when the town's two senior sides, Athletic
and Town, joined forces and opted to play
at Hinckley Athletic's Middlefield Lane
ground. The Athletic club, ironically then
known as Hinckley United, had moved to
Middlefield Lane in 1946, although the
ground had already been in use for greyhound racing since 1940. The pitch was
dug up and relaid in the summer of 1947,
with surplus earth being banked up on
one side of the ground. The stand on this
side was not built until 1950 after a
lengthy fundraising appeal. By then the
ground had already seen its biggest-ever
crowd when the visit of neighbours,
Nuneaton Borough, filled the ground
with more than 5,000 spectators. The
1950 stand had changed little since it was
built except for the addition, in 1993, of
plastic seating cast aside by Leicester City.
The 1950s saw continued development at
Middlefield Lane with a new clubhouse
(replaced in 1977), terracing and a large
cover opposite the main stand. This cover
was blown down in 1985 and eventually
replaced in 1999 with an impressive pitch-
length structure bearing the newly
merged club's name on its fascia board.
Floodlights came in 1979 although these
would be replaced by a more modern set
in 1991. The joining of forces has resulted
in a bright new future for Hinckley football and the club are now looking at a new
Conference standard ground to be built,
subject to planning permission, close to

Middlefield Lane, Hinckley United

Hinckley Town's old Leicester Road ground.

HISTON
GROUND: Recreation Ground, Bridge Road, Impington, Cambridgeshire
CURRENT CAPACITY: 3,250
RECORD ATTENDANCE: 2,400 v. Kings Lynn (FA Cup) 15/10/49
YEAR BUILT/OPENED: 1904
CURRENT LEAGUE: Dr Marten's (Southern) League Eastern Division
CLUB FOUNDED: 1904 as Histon Institute
PREVIOUS GROUNDS: None

The club have played on the Recreation Ground since their formation as Histon Institute in 1904. The ground was re-aligned in 1962 when the existing stand was demolished and the pitch bulldozed to make way for the new B1049 trunk road. The new ground was ready for use in 1964, with an interesting combined clubhouse and elevated stand. The roof of the clubhouse extends backwards to provide the roof for the stand, which is supported on half a dozen trusses. The seats are accessed by a metal staircase to the side. There was, by design, an area of cover underneath the stand. However, when Histon gained promotion to the Dr Marten's League in 2000, the standing area was lost as the stand had an extension added down to ground level providing several extra tiers of seats. The only problem is that the roof does not cover the new section of seats. As the club progresses, it will look to develop the ground further and hopefully this will result in the removal of the ugly, disused all-weather surface at one end of the ground. It was built in the mid 1980s but was most recently in use as additional car parking space.

HITCHIN TOWN
GROUND: Top Field, Fishponds Road, Hitchin, Hertfordshire
CURRENT CAPACITY: 4,000

RECORD ATTENDANCE: 7,878 v.
Wycombe Wanderers (FA Amateur Cup)
18/02/56
YEAR BUILT/OPENED: 1871
CURRENT LEAGUE: Ryman (Isthmian)
League Premier Division
CLUB FOUNDED: 1928
PREVIOUS GROUNDS: None

Top Field is one of the country's oldest football grounds, having staged one of the first-ever FA Cup ties against Crystal Palace. In fact, the original Hitchin Football Club donated £25 to the cost of the original FA Cup trophy. There is a bizarre, but enduring, covenant on the Top Field that allows the society of local farmers, The Cow Commoners, to run their herds across the field once a year! Although the covenant has not been taken up for a vast number of years, the club are not allowed to build permanent buildings on the site. Therefore, the tremendous main stand and extensive wooden terracing could have to come down at any time. The original Hitchin club folded before World War Two when their grandstand was burned to the ground. The current club formed as late as 1928 when they also opened the current grandstand. The wooden terracing was finished in the 1950s and the only changes since then have been floodlighting in 1962 and a new wooden boundary fence in the mid-1990s. In the 1960s the club had the world's first Football Museum, with a plethora of early football memorabilia. After its closure the exhibits were stored out of public view in the bowels of Hitchin Museum, although many are now on display in the National Football Museum at Preston North End's Deepdale Stadium – an appropriately ancient venue.

HOLKER OLD BOYS

GROUND: Rakesmoor Lane, Hawcourt, Barrow-in-Furness, Cumbria
CURRENT CAPACITY: 2,500
RECORD ATTENDANCE: 1,240 v. Barrow (ATS Trophy) 16/01/96
YEAR BUILT/OPENED: 1968
CURRENT LEAGUE: North West Counties League Division Two
CLUB FOUNDED: 1936
PREVIOUS GROUNDS: Thorncliff Road (1936–68)

The club were formed in 1936 by former pupils of the Holker Street school and not, as is often incorrectly assumed, by dissident Barrow supporters! In 1968 the club, then in the Furness League, acquired a small plot of land on the outskirts of the town in Hawcoat. The first building on the new ground was the clubhouse, sympathetically extended in 1981. In recent years, the club's promotion to the North West Counties League in 1991 has seen Rakesmoor Lane completely revamped. As you enter through the modern turnstile block, a seated stand sits somewhat strangely along the South End by-line. The now fully enclosed ground sports a covered stand down one side to give the feel of a proper ground. Not surprisingly, Rakesmoor Lane's record gate came for a cup tie against their more senior neighbours.

HORDEN COLLIERY WELFARE

GROUND: Welfare Ground, Park Road, Horden, County Durham
CURRENT CAPACITY: 3,000
RECORD ATTENDANCE: 8,000 v. Blyth Spartans (FA Cup) 13/11/57
YEAR BUILT/OPENED: 1908
CURRENT LEAGUE: Albany Northern League Division Two

Rakesmoor Lane, Holker Old Boys

CLUB FOUNDED: 1908 as Horden Athletic
PREVIOUS GROUNDS: None

A gritty, working town, Horden is a somewhat desolate place, particularly since the colliery closure in 1986. However the old Welfare Ground, the centre of the town's sporting activities since 1908, remains in good shape. The area around Park Road gives an indication of its industrial heritage, with rows and rows of small, terraced, miners' houses. The grandstand at the ground is old, although the exact date of construction remains unknown. The early 1990s saw the old roof and side panels replaced with modern metal cladding, giving the old stand a new lease of life. The club's halcyon days of the 1960s saw the old railway sleepers replaced with proper concrete terracing, although this new terracing was condemned as unsafe during the

1980s. Even though the club has struggled in recent years, the terracing is gradually being repaired and the old ground looks better than it has done for many years.

HORNCHURCH
GROUND: Bridge Avenue, Upminster, Essex
CURRENT CAPACITY: 3,000
RECORD ATTENDANCE: 3,000 v. Chelmsford City (FA Cup) 15/10/66
YEAR BUILT/OPENED: 1952
CURRENT LEAGUE: Ryman (Isthmian) League Division One (North)
CLUB FOUNDED: 1923 as Upminster FC
PREVIOUS GROUNDS: Recreation Ground (1923–52)

Opened by the council in November 1952, the home to Hornchurch is a somewhat uninspiring ground. However dull, it was a vast improvement on their previ-

Welfare Ground, Horden Colliery Welfare

ous stadium – an unenclosed field that prevented the taking of admission money. The ground has changed little in the intervening 50 years, save for the addition of the clubhouse on top of the bank at the car-park end. The main stand is on the far side of the ground and is in keeping with the functional but unremarkable surroundings. On the near side there is a small collection of covered stands and a wooden director's stand. In 1961 the Upminster club merged with local rivals Upminster Wanderers and after being called Hornchurch & Upminster for several years, they took the current title. Hornchurch share the ground with Havering Athletics Club.

HORSHAM
GROUND: Queen Street, Horsham, West Sussex
CURRENT CAPACITY: 4,500
RECORD ATTENDANCE: 8,000 v. Swindon Town (FA Cup) 26/11/66
YEAR BUILT/OPENED: 1904
CURRENT LEAGUE: Ryman (Isthmian) League Division One (South)
CLUB FOUNDED: 1885
PREVIOUS GROUNDS: Horsham Park; Hurst Park; Springfield Park

A pleasant venue, the Queen Street ground is one of the more individual grounds in the Ryman League. Opened in 1904, the ground's most noticeable feature is the splendidly constructed main stand erected in 1928. To the side of the stand is the entrance to the changing rooms, set off with a smart nameboard. The stand itself has a flat roof with unusual screen ends and the detail of false doors at the front are a welcome focal point. The attention to detail extends to the turnstile block, which has its own roof complete with slates. The side opposite the stand and one end have substantial covered terraces. The Queen Street end is open terracing. This substantial ground has needed little to bring it in line with modern requirements, so retains its individuality as it approaches its centenary. The adjacent set of flood-

Queen Street, Horsham

lights belong to Gorings Mead, home to Sussex County League outfit Horsham YMCA since 1924.

HUCKNALL TOWN
GROUND: Watnall Road, Hucknall, Nottinghamshire
CURRENT CAPACITY: 5,000
RECORD ATTENDANCE: 1,436 v. Ilkeston Town (FA Cup) 28/10/00
YEAR BUILT/OPENED: 1954
CURRENT LEAGUE: Unibond (Northern Premier) League Premier Division
CLUB FOUNDED: 1945
PREVIOUS GROUNDS: Wigwam Park (1946–54)

The club is a relative newcomer to the upper echelons of the non-League pyramid, having been a Notts Alliance League club as recently as 1989. The change of fortune coincided with the club changing its name from Hucknall Colliery Welfare, following the pit closure in 1988. Since then the club has rocketed through the Central Midlands League and the Northern Counties (East) League, before gatecrashing the Northern Premier League in 1997. The ground is on pit land, as was their first ground off Wigwam Lane. Originally the players changed in the pit baths, until the present ground was re-aligned and enclosed. The present dressing rooms date from 1962. The turnstiles were acquired from Walsall's old Fellow's Park ground and in 1990 the old stand was replaced by a sizeable pitch-length covered stand with ample seating in 1990. Rumours of a merger with nearby neighbours Hucknall Rolls Royce Welfare persist, with Watnall Road becoming the first team's pitch and Hucknall Rolls Royce's becoming the reserves headquarters.

HUNGERFORD TOWN
GROUND: Town Ground, Bulpit Lane, Hungerford, Berkshire
CURRENT CAPACITY: 3,000
RECORD ATTENDANCE: 1,684 v. Sudbury Town (FA Vase) 1989
YEAR BUILT/OPENED: 1886

Tameside Stadium, Hyde United

CURRENT LEAGUE: Ryman (Isthmian) League Division Two
CLUB FOUNDED: 1886
PREVIOUS GROUNDS: None

The Bulpit Lane ground has been home to Hungerford since their formation in 1886 and is now well over 100 years old. There are now two seated stands at the ground, with the older grandstand dating from 1950, complete with old cinema seats. The more recent stand on the opposite side was erected in 1981, although the plastic seating is a more recent addition. The clubhouse was erected in 1972 after the club acquired a disused building from Hungerford British Legion. A function room was added to the end of the clubhouse a few years later. The current dressing rooms date from the same period. Although Hungerford have never been a well-supported club, not helped by the lack of local derbies due to their distance from other Ryman League clubs, Bulpit Lane

remains an interesting and ancient footballing arena.

HYDE UNITED
GROUND: Tameside Stadium, Walker Lane, Hyde, Greater Manchester
CURRENT CAPACITY: 4,000
RECORD ATTENDANCE: 9,500 v. Nelson (FA Cup) 11/11/50
YEAR BUILT/OPENED: 1887 as Ewen Fields
CURRENT LEAGUE: Unibond (Northern Premier) League Premier Division
CLUB FOUNDED: 1919
PREVIOUS GROUNDS: Townend Street (1919–20)

In 1986 the Hyde United Supporters Club sold the freehold of the Ewen Fields to Tameside Council. The reasons were manifold. The ground had been home to Hyde, except for one season, since 1887 and as such was beginning to creak at the seams. Furthermore, Tameside Council's plans for the stadium to be turned into a sport and leisure centre for the whole community were too good to resist. Indeed 1887 was an eventful year for Hyde as they set an unenviable record for losing a FA Cup tie by a still-record score of 26-0 to Preston North End at Deepdale. The Ewen Fields had had a chequered history, including being commandeered by the military during World War One, where it was turned into a vegetable patch to aid the war effort. When the club reformed after the war, they had to spend the 1919/20 campaign on a field off Townend Street while their old ground was returfed and patched up. It was built up to a substantial ground, capable of holding a near-10,000 gate for an FA Cup tie with Nelson in 1950. Following the council takeover, all the stands were systematically pulled down and replaced – the main stand being particularly notable for its unusual roof finial. However, the council replaced the turf with an artificial Baspograss pitch. The turf was restored when the Football Association banned plastic pitches in the late 1980s. The Tameside Stadium is an excellent modern venue that gives no indication to its lengthy history.

I

IBSTOCK WELFARE
GROUND: Welfare Ground, Leicester Road, Ibstock, Leicestershire
CURRENT CAPACITY: 2,000
RECORD ATTENDANCE: Not known
YEAR BUILT/OPENED: 1920s
CURRENT LEAGUE: Everards Brewery Leicestershire Senior League Premier Division

CLUB FOUNDED: 1920s as Ibstock Penistone Rovers
PREVIOUS GROUNDS: None

The Ibstock Welfare club formed out of the ashes of a moderately successful club called Ibstock Penistone Rovers who were Leicestershire Senior League Division Two champions in 1951 and 1968. They also took the Leicestershire Senior Cup on a couple of occasions. Rovers disbanded and the local colliery welfare took over the Leicester Road ground. This has been their ground since the early 1920s when it was nothing more than an open field. Nowadays the pitch has a post and rail pitch surround and a modest covered stand that sits on top of a couple of steps of terrace. The stand is a concrete-block construction with a flat steel roof. However, the decision to paint the walls white has meant the stand looks in permanent need of repainting.

ILKESTON TOWN
GROUND: New Manor Ground, Awsworth Road, Ilkeston, Derbyshire
CURRENT CAPACITY: 3,500
RECORD ATTENDANCE: 2,504 v. Boston United (FA Cup) 15/11/97
YEAR BUILT/OPENED: 1992
CURRENT LEAGUE: Dr Marten's (Southern) League Premier Division
CLUB FOUNDED: 1945
PREVIOUS GROUNDS: Manor Ground (1945–92)

In 1992 Ilkeston Town left their historic Manor Ground, home to the club since their formation in 1945, and home to a dynasty of various Ilkeston clubs since its opening in 1893. It boasted a classic brick and timber-pitched roof main stand dating from 1957. Sadly, like many grounds

Welfare Ground, Ibstock Welfare

of its era it was on prime town centre land and when the moneymen came knocking, the offer was too good to turn down. The large ground, which held 9,800 at its peak, now lies under a supermarket. The club moved to an out-of-town site that has plenty of room and was formerly a rubbish dump. One side of the ground houses the changing rooms and office blocks and the two end stands are terraced with roofs just bolted onto the perimeter walls, no end panels or back walls needed here! There is a functional seated main stand that was built in 1992, but eight years later it was joined on that side by the club's pride and joy, the Clocktower Stand. It represents a modern classic, in terms of originality, functionality and just plain old good looks. The stand is highly elevated, giving an excellent view and on the corner there is a superb clocktower topped with a weather vane. The illuminated clocktower has a viewing gallery and the stand

itself is set off nicely, with ITFC being picked out in different coloured brick. Attention to detail has set this modern ground apart from the numerous clone grounds around the country. For that, the committee at this fine Derbyshire venue should stand up and take a bow.

K

KENDAL TOWN
GROUND: Parkside Road, Kendal, Cumbria
CURRENT CAPACITY: 2,500
RECORD ATTENDANCE: 5,184 v. Grimsby Town (FA Cup) 19/11/55
YEAR BUILT/OPENED: 1919
CURRENT LEAGUE: Unibond (Northern Premier) League Division One
CLUB FOUNDED: 1919 as Netherfield
PREVIOUS GROUNDS: None

New Manor Ground, Ilkeston Town

The Netherfield area of this very pleasant Lake District town has a long history of shoemaking. In 1919 Netherfield were formed by workers from the local shoe factory called Somerville Brothers (now K Shoes). The club have always played at Parkside Road and their first set of goalposts were acquired second hand from the Kendal Amateurs club. The players had use of the factory facilities until changing rooms were opened on the ground in 1928. The present timber stand was opened two years later and extended in 1955. The two areas of cover on the opposite side were also erected before World War Two. The visit of Grimsby in the FA Cup in 1955 saw the record gate at Parkside and for the game a scaffold pole cover was erected over the terracing. This temporary cover remained until 1990, when it was badly damaged in a storm. The cover has since been replaced. Floodlights came to Parkside in 1965 and three years later they became founder members of the Northern Premier League. The club changed their name to Netherfield Kendal in 1998 before changing again a year later to Kendal Town, to more closely identify with the whole town. It is unusual these days to find a ground with all three original stands intact and still doing excellent service.

KETTERING TOWN
GROUND: Rockingham Road, Kettering, Northamptonshire
CURRENT CAPACITY: 6,170
RECORD ATTENDANCE: 11,536 v. Peterborough United
YEAR BUILT/OPENED: 1897
CURRENT LEAGUE: Nationwide Football Conference
CLUB FOUNDED: 1872 as Kettering FC
PREVIOUS GROUNDS: Green Lane (1872–94); North Park (1894–97)

One of the best-known clubs in non-League football, Kettering lost their continuous membership of the

Parkside Road, Kendal Town

Conference following relegation at the end of the 2000/01 campaign. They were one of only three surviving founder members from 1979 with Northwich Victoria and Telford being the others. To their credit The Poppies bounced back at the first attempt, bringing top-flight football back to their superb Rockingham Road ground. The club have played at the ground since 1897, although the modern-day ground is vastly different to the original. The most striking feature of the modern ground is the fantastic obstruction-free can-tilevered main stand, built in 1972, which is strangely situated on one half of the pitch. The clubhouse and dressing rooms occupy the other half of this side. The Cowper Street end is open ter-racing, as is the Rockingham Road end, although this end is fairly narrow, with an ugly chipboard rear fence. The side opposite the main stand has a sizeable, pitch-length covered terrace, slightly wonky due to the considerable slope that once existed. The rapid elevation of near neighbours Rushden & Diamonds to Football League status must irk Kettering the most, considering their applications for League status were turned down on no less than 15 occa-sions between 1900 and 1979.

KIDSGROVE ATHLETIC
GROUND: Clough Hall, Hollinswood Road, Kidsgrove, Stoke-on-Trent, Staffordshire
CURRENT CAPACITY: 4,500
RECORD ATTENDANCE: 1,903 v. Tiverton Town (FA Vase) 1998
YEAR BUILT/OPENED: 1958
CURRENT LEAGUE: Unibond (Northern Premier League) Division One
CLUB FOUNDED: 1952
PREVIOUS GROUNDS: Bathpool Park; Vickers & Goodwin Ground

Rockingham Road, Kettering Town

Formed as recently as 1952 when members of the existing Kidsgrove Town club broke away to form their own club. The club started off in the Burslem & Tunstall League but started to make real progress when they moved into Clough Hall in the summer of 1958. The council land was enclosed with corrugated iron fencing and a pavilion was erected. The main stand, known as the Ernest Langford Stand, replaced an older stand destroyed in a storm. There is also a smaller stand adjacent to this. Floodlights were erected in 1991 as the club were promoted to the North West Counties League. The championship win in this competition at the end of 2001/02 saw Kidsgove promoted to the Northern Premier League for the first time, bringing the highest standard of football to this corner of Staffordshire. Clough Hall was also briefly home to the ill-fated Eastwood Hanley club for several seasons during the 1990s.

KINGSBURY TOWN
GROUND: Silver Jubilee Park, Townsend Lane, Kingsbury, London NW9
CURRENT CAPACITY: 2,500
RECORD ATTENDANCE: 1,500 v. Tottenham Hotspur (Friendly) 1980
YEAR BUILT/OPENED: 1943
CURRENT LEAGUE: Ryman (Isthmian) League Division Two
CLUB FOUNDED: 1919 as Kingsbury FC
PREVIOUS GROUNDS: Numerous pitches

In the heart of a massive urban sprawl, Silver Jubilee Park is a semi-rural, tree-lined oasis of a ground. The ground itself is an enclosed part of a much larger park and has been home to Kingsbury Town since 1943. The majority of the arena is grass banking with all the facilities occupying one side of the ground. The main stand was built in 1978, replacing one damaged in a storm. The clubhouse dates from the mid-1960s and is a rather fore-boding looking edifice. The present changing rooms are far more salubrious compared to their predecessors, which were old Nissen huts. The most recent changes to this fairly basic ground are the pitch surround and floodlights, both nec-essary for the club's elevation to the Isthmian League in the competition's expansion in 1984.

KINGS LYNN

GROUND: The Walks, Tennyson Road, Kings Lynn, Norfolk
CURRENT CAPACITY: 8,200
RECORD ATTENDANCE: 12,931 v. Exeter City (FA Cup) 24/11/50
YEAR BUILT/OPENED: 1879
CURRENT LEAGUE: Dr Marten's (Southern) League Eastern Division
CLUB FOUNDED: 1879 as Lynn Town
PREVIOUS GROUNDS: None

The long trek for a visitor to this remote part of North Norfolk will be rewarded with a truly classic venue. The Walks has been home to the club since its forma-tion in 1879 as Lynn Town. The vast main stand was built in 1956 and replaced an older wooden stand. As well as seating 1,200 people, the stand also houses the clubhouse, dressing rooms and club offices. Opposite the main stand is a long covered terrace, although originally this had additional seating. The seats were disposed with in 1968, but still live on at Hereford United's Edgar Street ground. The rest of the ground has ample terrac-ing. The club's heyday was undoubtedly the 1950s and '60s when large crowds thronged to The Walks, including nearly 13,000 for a 1951 FA Cup tie with Exeter. Between 1956 and 1962 the club made seven successive, but ultimately unsuc-cessful, applications for Football League membership. Another run in 1962 culmi-

The Walks, Kings Lynn

nated in a third round tie at Everton where a 45,366 gate secured a share of gate receipts of £4,341, which cleared all debts and paid up mortgages for houses owned by the club. Even with today's stringent safety guidelines, The Walks has a capacity of 8,200 and with Kings Lynn having a potential catchment area of 150,000 people, you can't help but think that the club really should have achieved so much more.

KINGSTONIAN
GROUND: Kingsmeadow Stadium, Kingston Road, Kingston-on-Thames, Surrey
CURRENT CAPACITY: 9,000
RECORD ATTENDANCE: 4,582 v. Chelsea (Friendly) 22/07/95
YEAR BUILT/OPENED: 1989
CURRENT LEAGUE: Ryman (Isthmian) League Premier Division
CLUB FOUNDED: 1885 as Kingston & Surbiton YMCA
PREVIOUS GROUNDS: Three different grounds all in Richmond Road; Hampton FC

The loss of Kingstonian's cherished Richmond Road ground in 1988 was a savage blow. It was a magnificent ground with huge terracing and a vast wooden grandstand built in 1922. The club were very well supported, particularly in their heyday of the 1950s and '60s and the ground held 11,000 for a famous Amateur Cup tie against Bishop Auckland in 1955. By 1988 the club were looking to secure their future and cashed in on the commercial value of the site. The old ground was duly demolished and Kingstonian spent the 1988/89 campaign at their close neighbours Hampton. The new ground was built on an existing sports ground

and was ready for the first game 1989/90. Unfortunately, as with the majority of new stadia, Kingsmeadow is constructed in modular form, which means it looks like countless other modern grounds. It has all the social and corporate facilities and all the plastic seating you could possibly wish for, but has no sense of history or character.

L

LANCASTER CITY
GROUND: The Giant Axe, West Road, Lancaster, Lancashire
CURRENT CAPACITY: 2,500
RECORD ATTENDANCE: 7,509 v. Carlisle United 1936
YEAR BUILT/OPENED: 1902
CURRENT LEAGUE: Unibond (Northern Premier) League Premier Division
CLUB FOUNDED: 1902 as Lancaster Town
PREVIOUS GROUNDS: Quay Meadow

Lancaster Town's first two games were at a field adjacent to the current ground, which was known as Quay Meadow. Since then home has always been the unusually named Giant Axe Ground. Now 100 years old, The Giant Axe has undergone numerous changes over its lifetime, most recently in November 1976 when two wooden grandstands were gutted by fire. The ground now has amazingly fortified retaining walls to try and put off would-be vandals. The old clubhouse was also left as charred remains after an arson attack. The impressive main stand was built on the site of the burned-out stands.

153

The Giant Axe, Lancaster City

There is also ample covered accommodation, all of recent vintage, to give The Giant Axe a thoroughly modern outlook. The oldest remaining part of the ground is the wooden pavilion that serves as the changing rooms, just about the only part of the ground that has survived the attention of the local delinquents.

LANCING
GROUND: Culver Road, Lancing, West Sussex
CURRENT CAPACITY: 2,500
RECORD ATTENDANCE: 2,340 v. Worthing 25/10/52
YEAR BUILT/OPENED: 1952
CURRENT LEAGUE: Rich City Sussex County League Division Two
CLUB FOUNDED: 1941
PREVIOUS GROUNDS: Crowshaw Recreation Ground

Lancing played in the Brighton League until 1948 when they were elected to the Sussex County League in place of Worthing, who were promoted to the Corinthian League. At the time the club played on the Crowshaw Recreation Ground, but it would soon become apparent that a more suitable ground would be needed for senior football. A field off Culver Road was acquired and completely enclosed. The modest main stand is the original and was erected during their first season. Little changed until 1981 when the Sussex County FA purchased the ground from the struggling club and made it their headquarters. The redevelopment of the ground saw a plush new clubhouse and floodlights go up at Culver Road. However, the construction of the new clubhouse was poorly considered and blocks the view of the pitch from many of the seats in the dear old stand. Still, without the timely intervention of the County FA, Culver Road would almost certainly have been sold off, so for that we should be grateful.

Culver Road, Lancing

LEATHERHEAD

GROUND: Fetcham Grove, Guildford
Road, Leatherhead, Surrey
CURRENT CAPACITY: 3,500
RECORD ATTENDANCE: 5,500 v.
Wimbledon (FA Cup) 11/12/76
YEAR BUILT/OPENED: 1924
CURRENT LEAGUE: Ryman (Isthmian)
League Division One (South)
CLUB FOUNDED: 1946 merger of
Leatherhead Rose (1907) and
Leatherhead United (1920)
PREVIOUS GROUNDS: United:
Fortyfoot Road. Rose: Kingston Road;
Barnett Wood Lane

The present club were founded after
Leatherhead United and Leatherhead
Rose joined forces after the war and
elected to play at United's home ground,
Fetcham Grove. The club had moved
there in 1924, but after the ground was
commandeered by the military during
World War Two, the newly merged club
had a considerable amount of work to do
to make the ground useable once again.
The new stand and dressing rooms were
completed by 1948, although the stand
was extended eight years later. The clubhouse was erected in 1954 and terracing
laid around the same time. Floodlights
were opened in 1963, with an inauguration match against Fulham. The club hit
the headlines in 1974 when they had a
tremendous FA Cup run, reaching the
fourth Round. In 1976 the FA Cup saw a
record gate of 5,500 come to Fetcham
Grove for a tie against Wimbledon.
However, the glory years of 'The
Leatherhead Lip' Chris Kelly *et al*, did not
last and the club have been in something
of a 20-odd year coma.

LEEK TOWN

GROUND: Harrison Park, Macclesfield
Road, Leek, Staffordshire
CURRENT CAPACITY: 3,600
RECORD ATTENDANCE: 5,312 v.

Macclesfield Town (FA Cup) 06/10/73
YEAR BUILT/OPENED: 1948
CURRENT LEAGUE: Unibond
(Northern Premier) League Division One
CLUB FOUNDED: 1946 as Abbey Green
Rovers
PREVIOUS GROUNDS: White Lion
Ground; Millwards Field

Harrison Park has been home to Leek Town since 1948 when it was bought for £1,250. At that time it was called Hamil Park and eventually changed its name in the early 1970s in honour of their deceased chairman, Geoff Harrison. The older, seated stand dates from 1972 and predates the larger, modern cantilevered stand by some 20 years. The club's floodlights are second hand, having previously seen service at the defunct Rugby Town's Oakfield ground. The club covered both end terraces during 1994 as the Northern Premier League was successfully captured. However, in highly controversial circumstances Leek were denied their rightful place in the Conference due to alleged financial problems. However, the club finally achieved top-flight football in 1997, although their tenure was ultimately to prove somewhat brief. Since relegation, in 1999, a slump has set in but hopefully the club can get back on an even keel. They certainly possess a fine stadium.

LEIGH RMI (RAILWAY MECHANICS INSTITUTE)
GROUND: Leigh RLFC, Hilton Park, Kirkhall Lane, Leigh, Lancashire
CURRENT CAPACITY: 10,000
RECORD ATTENDANCE: 7,125 v. Fulham (FA Cup) 24/11/99
YEAR BUILT/OPENED: 1947

CURRENT LEAGUE: Nationwide Football Conference
CLUB FOUNDED: 1896 as Lancashire & Yorkshire Railway FC
PREVIOUS GROUNDS: Horwich RMI: Grundy Hill (1990–1994)

It is quite unusual for clubs to move lock, stock and barrel from one town to another, but such is the case with the RMI club that played in the town of Horwich for exactly 100 years. The rot had set in when Horwich RMI lost their classic, but crumbling, Grundy Hill to a housing development in 1994. There was no alternative venue available in Horwich, so the club took up the option to move 15 miles south to ground-share at Leigh RLFC. The Hilton Park ground was opened in August 1947 and once held 31,326 spectators for Leigh against St Helens in a Challenge Cup tie in 1953. It remains a vast ground with large open terraces, both laid in 1964, at either end. Both sides have large, seated stands, the larger of which has been re-roofed and reclad in recent years. The addition of rugby grounds to the football scene in recent years has been a welcome innovation as these invariably large venues are seemingly immune to the push for modernity.

LEIGHTON TOWN
GROUND: Bell Close, Lake Street, Leighton Buzzard, Bedfordshire
CURRENT CAPACITY: 2,800
RECORD ATTENDANCE: 1,522 v. Aldershot Town (League) 30/01/93
YEAR BUILT/OPENED: Not recorded
CURRENT LEAGUE: Ryman (Isthmian) League Division Two
CLUB FOUNDED: 1885 as Leighton FC
PREVIOUS GROUNDS: Wayside Ground

Hilton Park, Leigh RMI

The Bell Close ground was originally part of a sports association complex that also catered for cricket, hockey and tennis. The present ground was only enclosed in 1984 as the club attained senior status in the South Midlands League. At the same time the club erected the current modest main stand. After a period of relative success, promotion to the Isthmian League was achieved in 1992. The club were accepted on the proviso that floodlights, terracing and new dressing rooms were built and all have been duly provided. Although by Ryman League standards Bell Close is a somewhat humble venue, much work has been put in to transform a virtual park pitch into a proper football ground.

LETCHWORTH
GROUND: Jackman's Meadow, Baldock Road, Letchworth, Hertfordshire
CURRENT CAPACITY: 3,200
RECORD ATTENDANCE: Not Known

YEAR BUILT/OPENED: 1924
CURRENT LEAGUE: Minerva Spartan South Midlands League Premier Division
CLUB FOUNDED: 1906
PREVIOUS GROUNDS: Letchworth Corner; Garth Road; Cashio Lane

The Jackman's Meadow ground has undergone a total transformation since 1999 when the venue was chosen to be the new headquarters of the Hertfordshire Football Association. The old main stand, with a quite remarkable extended pitched roof, was cleared away to be replaced by a new, bog-standard seated stand, and a state-of-the-art administration block. The long derelict turnstiles were also spruced up and returned to working order after a considerable period of disuse. The club's early years were fairly nomadic before securing the freehold on Baldock Road in 1924, the grandstand being erected three years later. The club

Jackman's Meadow, Letchworth

have also gone through a host of name changes, most recently when Letchworth Garden City, then of the Isthmian League, collapsed and reformed as Letchworth FC, joining the South Midlands League. Although a very mundane ground has been transformed, the loss of a unique, but worn out and aged stand was indeed a fearful body blow to enthusiasts of stadium architecture.

LEWES
GROUND: The Dripping Pan, Mountfield Road, Lewes, East Sussex
CURRENT CAPACITY: 2,500
RECORD ATTENDANCE: 2,500 v. Newhaven (Sussex County League) 26/12/47
YEAR BUILT/OPENED: 1885
CURRENT LEAGUE: Ryman (Isthmian) League Division One (South)
CLUB FOUNDED: 1885

PREVIOUS GROUNDS: None

This is a classic and ancient venue, as old as the club, which was formed at a meeting in the Royal Oak in 1885. The first item passed that night was to secure the use of a bowl-shaped field adjacent to the Old Priory. The field was steeply banked on all sides and was known as The Dripping Pan. It is believed that monks at the medieval Priory once panned river water for salt, hence the name of the field located on the flood plain of the River Ouse. The main stand is a long wooden stand perched awkwardly on top of the steep banks. The stand has recovered well from a major battering sustained during the terrible storms of 1987. The dressing room and clubhouse are situated at the car-park end. The ground's steepest bank on the town side of the ground is undeveloped, save for a few

The Dripping Pan, Lewes

scattered wooden benches. These afford the best view of the ground on a beautifully sunny day, with the glorious outlook of the South Downs rolling hills looming invitingly behind the stand. There are few finer places to be.

LEYTON
GROUND: The Hare & Hounds Ground, Lea Bridge Road, Leyton, London E10
CURRENT CAPACITY: 2,500
RECORD ATTENDANCE: Not Known
YEAR BUILT/OPENED: 1892
CURRENT LEAGUE: Ryman (Isthmian) League Division Two
CLUB FOUNDED: 1999 reformation of a club formed in 1868
PREVIOUS GROUNDS: Brisbane Road (1905–37)

This is the reincarnated version of the ancient Leyton club formed in 1999. The new club successfully petitioned their right to be recognized as a direct relative of the original club. This meant that Leyton Pennant, a club formed out of a 1995 merger between Leyton FC (a de-merged section of the former Leyton-Wingate club) and Walthamstow Pennant, were officially a separate entity. The original Leyton club were one of the great amateur clubs, winning the FA Amateur Cup two years running in 1927 and 1928. At that time they were playing at the present Leyton Orient ground, Brisbane Road, although it was better known as Osborne Road in those days. The club were booted off that ground in 1937 due to unpaid rent. Since then the club have played at the Hare & Hounds Ground in Lea Bridge Road although since the merger with Wingate FC in 1975 the ground was known as the Wingate-Leyton Stadium. The ground has two

The Hare & Hounds Ground, Leyton

seated stands and two small areas of covered standing on the Lea Bridge Road side of the ground. The Seymour Road end and the side opposite the main stand has shallow uncovered terracing. The ground was deemed unsuitable for Isthmian League football in the early 1990s and precluded the 1995 merger and move to Walthamstow Pennant's Wadham Lodge ground. The Hare & Hounds grounds was due to be sold for development but plans fell through until the newly formed version of Leyton FC took up the lease on the disused ground.

LEYTON PENNANT

GROUND: Wadham Lodge, Kitchener Road, Walthamstow, London E17
CURRENT CAPACITY: 2,000
RECORD ATTENDANCE: 676 v. Aldershot Town (League) 10/02/96
YEAR BUILT/OPENED: 1995

CURRENT LEAGUE: Ryman (Isthmian) League Division One (North)
CLUB FOUNDED: 1995 merger of Leyton (1868) and Walthamstow Pennant (1964)
PREVIOUS GROUNDS: Leyton: Brisbane Road; Hare & Hounds Ground. Pennant: A second pitch at Wadham Lodge

The history of Leyton Football Club must rank as one of the most complex. In 1999 a brand new club called Leyton FC, playing at the Hare and Hounds Ground, successfully petitioned that they were the rightful owners of the original club's history. This meant that Leyton Pennant, a 1992 merger of the original Leyton club and Walthamstow Pennant, should consider themselves to have a totally different ancestry! The merger had come about due to Leyton's Hare & Hounds

Ground being considered inadequate for senior football. To perpetuate the name of this ancient club, a relocation to Walthamstow Pennant's Wadham Lodge ground was a matter of survival. Leyton FC were formed in 1868 and were the original tenants of Brisbane Road before Clapton Orient. However, they were thrown off in 1937 due to unpaid rent. The O's subsequently took their place at the ground. Leyton relocated to the historic Hare & Hounds Ground, located in nearby Lea Bridge Road, which had been used for football since at least 1892 when amateur outfit Newportonians had started playing there. Leyton developed into one of the most renowned amateur clubs, taking the FA Amateur Cup on two occasions. Walthamstow Pennant had formed in 1964 as Pennant FC and had worked their way up from the junior ranks up to the Spartan League in 1984. The club played on a different pitch at Wadham Lodge until the merger saw a ground enclosed off at the top end of the complex. The ground, of course, is a thoroughly modern and functional affair, with all the necessary seats and covered stands. Ironically the boardroom contains many artefacts and photos of the original Leyton club. Who rightfully owns that proud history? Leyton Pennant and the new Leyton club will probably never reach an amicable settlement.

LINCOLN UNITED
GROUND: Ashby Avenue, Hartsholme, Lincoln, Lincolnshire
CURRENT CAPACITY: 2,700
RECORD ATTENDANCE: 2,000 v. Crook Town (FA Amateur Cup) 1968
YEAR BUILT/OPENED: 1982
CURRENT LEAGUE: Unibond (Northern Premier) League Division One

CLUB FOUNDED: 1938 as Lincoln Amateurs
PREVIOUS GROUNDS: Skew Bridge; Co-op Ground; Hartsholme Cricket Ground

In the post-World War Two years the club had lengthy spells at the Co-operative Ground and on the outfield of the cricket ground at Hartsholme. Their 15-year tenure at the latter saw them have first refusal on a basic council pitch adjacent to the cricket club. Terms were agreed in 1982 and they dismantled their small cover from the cricket ground and re-erected it at one end of the new venue. The site was also enclosed and soon the club gained permission for floodlights and the erection of a small brick-built stand. The early 1990s were highly successful and funds raised from their 1991 FA Cup run saw the new dressing rooms erected. The impressive development of the ground continued and in 1993 the present main stand was erected in accordance to Northern Premier League criteria. The plans worked and Northern Premier League status was duly achieved in 1995. The old wooden cricket club stand was replaced by a pitch-wide covered terrace to complete the transformation of the ground . So much has been achieved at Ashby Avenue in just 20 years, that Lincoln United are much admired throughout football.

LITTLEHAMPTON TOWN
GROUND: Sportsfield, St Flora's Road, Littlehampton, West Sussex
CURRENT CAPACITY: 4,000
RECORD ATTENDANCE: 4,000 v. Northampton Town (FA Cup) 17/11/90
YEAR BUILT/OPENED: 1920
CURRENT LEAGUE: Rich City Sussex

Littlehampton Town

County League Division One
CLUB FOUNDED: 1894
PREVIOUS GROUNDS: Lobb's Wood
(1894–1914)

St Flora's Road has been home to Littlehampton Town and the cricket club since it was laid out just after World War One. The present seated main stand was erected in 1930 and retains a certain charm and looks better when the club's yellow and black colours are touched up. On either side of the stand are two covered stands with shallow concrete steps, both of which are now more than 50 years old. The only blot on the landscape is the more modern sports centre/clubhouse, which is ugly in the extreme and contrasts starkly with the old stands and the far more pleasing cricket pavilion. The ground, however, must have been heav-

ing when 4,000 congregated for a FA Cup tie in 1990 against Northampton, which was broadcast live on television.

LOWESTOFT TOWN
GROUND: Crown Meadow, Love Road, Lowestoft, Suffolk
CURRENT CAPACITY: 3,000
RECORD ATTENDANCE: 5,432 v. Watford (FA Cup) 09/12/67
YEAR BUILT/OPENED: 1894
CURRENT LEAGUE: Jewson Eastern Counties League Premier Division
CLUB FOUNDED: 1885 as East Suffolk FC
PREVIOUS GROUNDS: Gunton Deanes and two other Crown Meadows

The club's first ground was called Gunton Deanes, part of the vast North Deanes that ran along the North Sea coast. The pitch is now part of a caravan park. They then played on two pitches on Crown Meadow, a vast tract of land that ran along the length of Beccles Road, now known as St Peters Street. The club moved to the present Crown Meadow site in 1894, this ground being on the same land as the other two, but in between Beresford Road and a foot-path east of the later Yeovil Road. The present grandstand on the east side was built in 1985. The old grandstand, a beau-tifully dilapidated wooden stand built in1896, stood on the other side until completely destroyed by fire in July 1979. The small covered terrace on that same side survived unscathed but now looks very lonely, stranded alone in the south-west corner. The old wooden pavilion, acquired from the Royal Norfolk and Suffolk Yacht Club, survived until replaced by the present clubhouse/ changing room complex in1988. At the north end of the ground is a floodlit hard court training surface, but much of that end and the site of the old grandstand has been sold off and is now used for storing new cars. The east side of the ground is a small area of covered terrace adjacent to the grandstand and just to the right of the turnstiles at the Love Street end.

LYE TOWN
GROUND: Sports Ground, Stourbridge Road, Lye, West Midlands
CURRENT CAPACITY: 5,000
RECORD ATTENDANCE: 6,000 v. Brierley Hill Alliance
YEAR BUILT/OPENED: 1930
CURRENT LEAGUE: Express & Star West Midlands League Premier Division
CLUB FOUNDED: 1930
PREVIOUS GROUNDS: None

The Sports Ground in Stourbridge Road has been home to Lye Town since their formation in 1930 and shares its northern boundary with Lye Cricket Club, the two sports separated on match days by a removable rope cordon. Originally the pitch was oriented at a right angle to its current axis. The main stand was built in 1971 and has seating that was previously operational in the stand that once stood at the Stourbridge Road end. The ground's most remarkable feature is the barrel-roofed 'barn' stand at the club-house end. When built, this was literally a roof on support poles, but the erection of a rear retaining wall gives the structure a more enclosed feel. The east end of the ground has a steep grass bank but no cov-ered accommodation. The clubhouse was opened in 1975, and occupies the site of the old dressing rooms. The main entrance to the ground is on Stourbridge Road, but an indication of the ground's past size and seniority is the presence of two disused gatehouses on the Cemetery Road end and Pedmore Road side. Stourbridge Road remains one of the largest grounds in the West Midlands.

M

MAIDENHEAD UNITED
GROUND: York Road, Maidenhead, Berkshire
CURRENT CAPACITY: 4,000
RECORD ATTENDANCE: 7,920 v. Southall (FA Amateur Cup) 07/03/36
YEAR BUILT/OPENED: 1871
CURRENT LEAGUE: Ryman (Isthmian) League Premier Division

Sports Ground, Lye Town

CLUB FOUNDED: 1870 as Maidenhead FC
PREVIOUS GROUNDS: Kidwells Park

York Road is one of the oldest grounds in the country, having first staged Maidenhead's matches as early as 1871. However the ground really began taking shape after World War One, when the club took the present name, following a merger with Maidenhead Norfolkians. A wooden main stand was erected in 1922 and stood until gutted by fire in 1986. It was most unusual and featured a large gabled roof and has, sadly, never been replaced. The stand on the railway side of the ground was built in 1935 and now serves as the main stand following the addition of plastic seating, much of which came from Millwall's former ground at The Den. The Town End has a large cov-

ered terrace that has a unique mural of events from the club's history, an unusual touch to an otherwise bland wall. The terrace sweeps around the north side of the ground and suddenly stops where it formerly abutted the old stand. The far end of the ground has a modern covered section of shallow terrace. The north side of the ground is completed by the presence of the shell of a new clubhouse, now abandoned, that nearly led to the club's financial ruin in the mid-1990s. Although York Road has certainly seen better days, the club have done well to maintain its essential character in the face of extreme adversity. It remains one of the most historic venues of our national game.

MALDON TOWN
GROUND: Wallace Binder Ground, Park Drive, Maldon, Essex

York Road, Maidenhead United

CURRENT CAPACITY: 2,500
RECORD ATTENDANCE: 1,033 v.
Millwall (Friendly) July 2000
YEAR BUILT/OPENED: 1994
CURRENT LEAGUE: Jewson Eastern
Counties League Premier Division
CLUB FOUNDED: 1946
PREVIOUS GROUNDS: Sadd's Ground
(1946–48); Fambridge Road (1948–94)

Maldon Town had played at the wholly
inadequate Fambridge Road ground
from 1948 and, although it boasted a
small stand, the club's future would be
best served at a new venue. The club
finally secured a new site in 1994 on the
southern edge of town. The clubhouse
on the car-park side of the ground is quite
magnificent and has a covered walkway
leading to the pitch and dugouts. There
is flat, hard standing for spectators on this
side of the ground. The main stand is
opposite at the foot of a large grass bank.
It has a smart fascia board and MTFC
picked out in white seats around blue
seats. At the training-pitch end there is a
small covered terrace. The superb facilities at the Wallace Binder ground meant
promotion from the Essex Senior League
to the Eastern Counties League was a for-
mality. Should the club wish to climb
further in the future, to the Dr Marten's
League, there would be minimal
improvements required to bring the
ground up to scratch. What's more is that
this splendid new ground is situated in a
historic and pretty little maritime town.
Well worth a day out.

MALTBY MAIN
GROUND: Welfare Ground, Muglet
Lane, Maltby, South Yorkshire

Wallace Binder Ground, Maldon Town

CURRENT CAPACITY: 2,000
RECORD ATTENDANCE: 1,500 v.
Sheffield Wednesday (Friendly) June
1991
YEAR BUILT/OPENED: 1970
CURRENT LEAGUE: Northern Counties
East League Division One
CLUB FOUNDED: 1970 as Maltby
Miners Welfare
PREVIOUS GROUNDS: Adjacent pitch

Maltby Main's Welfare Ground is an enclosed part of a huge area devoted to sport. There is a cricket pitch and another full size football pitch, on which the club first played. The move to the lower pitch came so the club could fully enclose the ground with a concrete wall and not get in the way of the cricketers. The separated venue meant the club could also play at a higher level, reaching the Northern Counties East League in 1982 after nine seasons in the Yorkshire League. The ground now has floodlighting courtesy of disused pylons at the colliery and a post and rail fence around the pitch. There are two areas of cover on the Muglet Lane side, the first opened in the mid-1980s and the larger, taller area is a more recent structure, having been erected in 1997. Interestingly the new stand has the same diamond-shaped steelwork as nearby Worsborough Bridge. The floodlight bulbs were replaced in 1997 after the original set was the victim of bulb rustlers. However, the Welfare Ground has recently hit financial trouble and could not find the £6,000 needed to lay hard standing around the ground. Unfortunately this led to the club being demoted from the Premier Division at the end of 1999/2000.

MANGOTSFIELD UNITED
GROUND: Cossham Street,
Mangotsfield, Bristol, Avon

Welfare Ground, Maltby Main

CURRENT CAPACITY: 2,500
RECORD ATTENDANCE: 2,386 v. Bath
City (FA Cup) 19/10/74
YEAR BUILT/OPENED: 1940s
CURRENT LEAGUE: Dr Marten's
(Southern) League Western Division
CLUB FOUNDED: 1950
PREVIOUS GROUNDS: None

The Cossham Street ground has always
been used for sport even before the current club was formed in 1950. The club
dawdled along for a number of years in
the Bristol & District and Avon Premier
Combination before biting the bullet and
joining the Western League in 1972.
Shortly afterwards, the football ground
was enclosed off from the adjacent field
to comply with senior football requirements. The ground has gradually been
developed, with a clubhouse, changing
rooms and a smart 300-seater stand.
However, the pace of developments was

deemed too slow to satisfy the Southern
League committee when the Western
league title was won in 1990/01.
Promotion was denied due to the facilities at Cossham Street and it was almost
10 years before the club were in a position to re-apply for elevated status. This
time the facilities were given the thumbs
up from the Dr Marten's League and the
club were welcomed with open arms.
The record gate at Cossham Street
remains at 2,386 for the visit of near
neighbours, Bath City, in an FA Cup 3rd
qualifying round tie in October 1974.

MARCH TOWN UNITED
GROUND: GER Sports Ground, Robin
Goodfellows Lane, March,
Cambridgeshire
CURRENT CAPACITY: 4,000
RECORD ATTENDANCE: 7,500 v. Kings
Lynn (FA Cup) 06/10/56
YEAR BUILT/OPENED: 1923

M

CURRENT LEAGUE: Jewson Eastern
Counties League Division One
CLUB FOUNDED: 1885 as March Town
PREVIOUS GROUNDS: The Avenue
Ground; Estover Road; Gaul Drove;
Burromoor Road

The obvious focal point of the GER sports
ground is the brightly coloured main
stand, liberally striped in club colours
with an intensity straight out of a Warhol
painting. The ground was originally
opened in 1923 when it was home to GER
United. However, this club did not reap-
pear after the shutdown of football
during World War Two and March Town,
who had lead a nomadic life before the
hostilities, took over the venue. The
ground was originally called
Shepperson's Field and was owned by
the March Grammar school before GER
bought the site. Although the pitched
roof wooden stand is certainly impressive
to look at, the view from within is hampered by the presence of no less than 12
roof-supporting struts, a floodlight pylon
and the modern two-story administration
block that obstructs the view of the goal
areas for many of the seats. On the opposite side is a covered terrace erected in
1950. There was originally a greyhound
track around the pitch but this has long
been grassed over and the pitch widened
slightly to bring the action nearer to the
stands. A truly diverse sporting venue,
the ground has played host to a large
number of sports over the years including cricket until 1960.

MARGATE

GROUND: Hartsdown Park, Hartsdown
Road, Margate, Kent
CURRENT CAPACITY: 4,800
RECORD ATTENDANCE: 14,169 v.

Tottenham Hotspur (FA Cup) 13/01/73
YEAR BUILT/OPENED: 1929
CURRENT LEAGUE: Nationwide
Football Conference
CLUB FOUNDED: 1929
PREVIOUS GROUNDS: None

The present club were formed in 1929
out of the ashes of the professional
Margate Town who had been formed in
1896 and spent their last four seasons
playing in Dreamland! The Dreamland
ground was a pitch laid out within the
amusement park of the same name. It
was a most unusual, if not quite unique
football ground. Southend United's
ground at the time, The Kursaal, was in a
similar vein. However, Margate Town
folded with crippling debts in 1928. The
present club decided to find a new venue
and found a suitable site when a patch of
land was made available within the
grounds of Hartsdown Hall. The wooden
stand was built in time for the first match
in August 1929 and had to be re-erected
in 1952 when it blew down. The stand has
been modernized in recent years but if
current plans for Hartsdown Park pro-
ceed the ground will be turned into a £6
million, 10,000 capacity stadium with
conference and banqueting facilities as
well as a hotel and casino. The club's pro-
gression in the last five years has been
nothing sort of remarkable; gates have
risen from an average of 200 to 1,500 and
if all goes well Margate stand a very good
chance of being Kent's second Football
League club. Five years ago that state-
ment would have been denounced as
living in, well, Dreamland!

MARINE

GROUND: Rossett Park, College Road,
Crosby, Merseyside

Hartsdown Park, Margate

CURRENT CAPACITY: 2,800
RECORD ATTENDANCE: 4,000 v.
Nigeria (Friendly) 1949
YEAR BUILT/OPENED: 1903
CURRENT LEAGUE: Unibond (Northern
Premier) League Premier Division
CLUB FOUNDED: 1894
PREVIOUS GROUNDS: Waterloo Park
(1894–1903)

Marine have played at Rossett Park since
1903 and despite tremendous success,
including winning the Northern Premier
League in 1994/95, the ground has been
a major bugbear for the club. The title win
should have entitled the club to a place
in the Conference but promotion was
denied due to the ground only having
three sides. One side of the ground is so
close to neighbours' houses that it is inac-
cessible to spectators. Originally the old
grandstand stood at the Crossender Road
end, with a covered terrace known as The
Shed at the College Road end. One side
has a narrow covered terrace. The old
grandstand and Shed were demolished in
the summer of 1999 to make way for
£215,000 worth of redevelopments. The
new grandstand, dubbed the 'Millennium
Stand' was sited at the College Road end
and provides seating for 400. It has an
unobstructed view thanks to a magnificent cantilevered roof that extends over
the shallow terracing in front of the
stand. The Crossender Road end now
boasts a pitch-width section of covered
terrace. The new grandstand was officially opened by Cherie Blair on 22
October 1999 as Marine entered the new
millennium with renewed vigour.

MARLOW
GROUND: Alfred Davis Memorial
Ground, Oak Tree Road, Marlow,

Buckinghamshire
CURRENT CAPACITY: 3,000
RECORD ATTENDANCE: 3,000 v.
Oxford United (FA Cup) 13/11/94
YEAR BUILT/OPENED: 1924
CURRENT LEAGUE: Ryman (Isthmian)
League Division One (North)
CLUB FOUNDED: 1870 as Great Marlow
PREVIOUS GROUNDS: Aldermeadow
(1870–98); Crown Ground (1898–1914);
Star Meadow (1919–24)

Arguably the finest of all Isthmian League
venues, the Alfred Davis Memorial
ground has been home to Marlow since
1924. Marlow were formed in 1870 and
were one of the 15 clubs in the very first
FA Cup competition. The club's ground
at Crown Meadow had been sold during
World War One and after five years at the
basic and unsatisfactory Star Meadow,
the club secured the use of a field just off
Oak Tree Road. The finances had been
organized by club secretary Alfred Davis,
who sadly passed away before the
ground was opened. Fittingly the committee named the new venue in his
memory. The wonderful main stand was
built in 1930 and looks as good now as it
has ever done. Lovingly kept and with
only the slightly unsightly addition of
steel fire escapes in recent years, the
stand is a masterpiece of construction.
The cover opposite was opened in 1950
and was joined behind the goal by one
of a modern design in 1992. The top goal
has a shallow open terrace behind which
is an all-weather surface opened in 1991.
The club has gained an extra source of
revenue by turning over one corner of
the ground to a small electricity genera-
tor. However, the ground remains
picturesque and a more than fitting trib-
ute to Alfred Davis.

MATLOCK TOWN

GROUND: Causeway Lane, Matlock,
Derbyshire
CURRENT CAPACITY: 7,500
RECORD ATTENDANCE: 5,123 v.
Burton Albion (FA Trophy) 1975
YEAR BUILT/OPENED: 1895
CURRENT LEAGUE: Unibond
(Northern Premier) League Division One
CLUB FOUNDED: 1885
PREVIOUS GROUNDS: Hall Leys
(1885–95)

This is another ground that has now
passed its centenary having been home
to Matlock Town since 1895. The
Causeway Lane ground is set in one of
the most picturesque towns in the Peak
District. It has a splendid setting with
panoramic views of the Matlock Dales,
with Riber Castle perched on high overlooking the ground. The focal point of
the ground is the ramshackle wooden
stand, the Cyril Harrison Stand, on the
Causeway Lane side of the ground. This
was erected in 1920 and had sadly
reached the end of its serviceable life. A
£300,000 redevelopment programme
will see a new modern stand taking its
place, with provision for 500 seats. The
opposite side of the ground has a small
wooden seated stand, which was built in
1959 and the adjacent building houses
the changing rooms. The Castle end of
the ground has temporary railings as this
forms part of the cricket club's outfield
during the summer. Without a doubt the
new stand will bring the ground kicking
and screaming into the twenty-first century, although the ultimate veto lies with
the Derbyshire Dales District Council
who have yet to pass the ambitious
plans.

Causeway Lane, Matlock Town

MERTHYR TYDFIL
GROUND: Pennydarren Park, Pen-y-Darren Road, Merthyr Tydfil, Mid Glamorgan
CURRENT CAPACITY: 10,000
RECORD ATTENDANCE: 21,000 v. Reading (FA Cup) 04/12/46 21,686 Merthyr Town v. Millwall (FA Cup) 27/12/21
YEAR BUILT/OPENED: 1908
CURRENT LEAGUE: Dr Marten's (Southern) League Western Division
CLUB FOUNDED: 1945
PREVIOUS GROUNDS: None

There cannot be many grounds that are more hidden from view than Merthyr Tydfil's Pennydarren Park. This sizeable ground is in the middle of a much larger park and cannot be seen from the main road. It can only be accessed by a narrow entrance off Park Terrace, a small back street. The ground had been built in 1908 to house the newly formed Merthyr Town side. That club progressed through the Southern League and spent 10 seasons in the Football League Division Three (South) between 1920 and 1930. However, with desperate unemployment in the area leading to poor support, the club folded with insurmountable debts in June 1934. The current club were formed after World War Two and took over at Pennydarren Park. The large oval ground once held greyhound racing and indeed cycling even further back in time, and hence there is quite a gap between pitch and stands. The large 1,500-seater grandstand is a modern structure that replaced a far smaller stand lost in a fire. There is a large covered terrace opposite and as a result of their Conference days between 1989 and 1995, large sections of uncovered terrace has been laid in the former

Imber Court, Metropolitan Police

grass banks. Ironically in modern times with much sensitivity over the construction of football stadia, Pennydarren Park would never be allowed nowadays as the ground lies right on top of an ancient Roman fort.

METROPOLITAN POLICE
GROUND: Imber Court, Imber Road, East Molesey, Surrey
CURRENT CAPACITY: 3,000
RECORD ATTENDANCE: 4,500 v. Kingstonian (FA Cup) 14/11/31
YEAR BUILT/OPENED: 1919
CURRENT LEAGUE: Ryman (Isthmian) League Division One (South)
CLUB FOUNDED: 1919
PREVIOUS GROUNDS: None

The whole of the Imber Court complex is first class and immaculately kept. It was acquired for recreation for the Metropolitan Police in 1919. The impressive clubhouse was much smaller when built in 1920, but numerous additions have turned it into the plush facility it is today. The football ground was not separated off until the late 1960s, although it shared a boundary with a cricket pitch until 1983. The old stand was constructed in 1923 from steel and timber, but was deemed unsafe in the wake of the Bradford fire disaster and was demolished and replaced with the present stand. The large cover behind the goal was erected in 1988 and, unusually for a covered terrace, has a strut-free cantilevered roof. Floodlights went up in 1971, although the fourth pylon could not be added until the cricket square was moved. The pitch, as should be expected, has few rivals and completes a truly excellent venue.

Mill Park, Millbrook

MILLBROOK

GROUND: Mill Park, Sandown Road, Millbrook, Cornwall
CURRENT CAPACITY: 2,000
RECORD ATTENDANCE: 496 v. St Blazey (League) 21/04/99
YEAR BUILT/OPENED: 1977
CURRENT LEAGUE: Carlsberg South-Western League
CLUB FOUNDED: 1973
PREVIOUS GROUNDS: Insworke Park (1973–77)

A relatively new club, Millbrook suffered an unusual problem at their original ground. There were low-level telephone wires criss-crossing the pitch that would get in the way of the ball. The problem was so bad that when the club vacated the ground in 1977, the Insworke Park pitch fell into disuse. The new ground at Mill Park, with a picturesque backdrop of rolling green fields, has a wooden club-house that was formerly a mess room at HMS Raleigh. The small but perfectly adequate stand was erected in 1990.

MILNTHORPE CORINTHIANS

GROUND: Strands Lane, Milnthorpe, Cumbria
CURRENT CAPACITY: 1,000
RECORD ATTENDANCE: Not Known
YEAR BUILT/OPENED: Not Recorded
CURRENT LEAGUE: Asda Logic West Lancashire League Premier Division
CLUB FOUNDED: 1919
PREVIOUS GROUNDS: None

I must confess to knowing very little about Milnthorpe Corinthians, but their endearing Recreation Ground, with its rickety covered stand, is the epitome of village football in this beautiful area of England. Playing so far down the pyra-

Walton Road, Molesey

mid, Strands Lane will never have any pretensions to greatness and its earthy and uncomplicated appearance is part of its charm. One thing for certain is that in an area renowned for it generous quantities of precipitation, rarely will a humble little stand be more welcomed by drenched supporters.

MOLESEY
GROUND: Walton Road, West Molesey, Surrey
CURRENT CAPACITY: 4,000
RECORD ATTENDANCE: 1,255 v. Sutton United (Surrey Senior Cup) 1966
YEAR BUILT/OPENED: 1950
CURRENT LEAGUE: Ryman (Isthmian) League Division One (South)
CLUB FOUNDED: 1953 as Molesey St Pauls
PREVIOUS GROUNDS: None

The Walton Road ground was already in use when Molesey St Pauls took over the lease in 1953. By 1960 a small stand had been erected but the club decided to rotate the pitch at right angles after acquiring land that had been in use as an orchard. The covered stand was resited and the high, unusual clubhouse and main stand were opened. The clubhouse has a large, glazed viewing area fronted by an elevated seated section, accessed from a metal staircase from ground level. The stand is set off by a splendid fascia bearing the club's name. Floodlights were erected in 1971 as the club progressed to the Isthmian League. The club nearly went bankrupt in 1988, but were saved and enjoyed great success in the 1990s, culminating with promotion to the Premier Division in 1993. By now the main stand had been furnished with the requisite plastic tip-up seating. The

The Moorlands, Moor Green

ground has been extensively terraced and a new turnstile block installed. However in recent seasons the club have slipped back down the divisions.

MOOR GREEN
GROUND: The Moorlands, Sherwood Road, Hall Green, Birmingham, West Midlands
CURRENT CAPACITY: 3,250
RECORD ATTENDANCE: 5,000 v. Romford (FA Amateur Cup) 1951
YEAR BUILT/OPENED: 1930
CURRENT LEAGUE: Dr Marten's (Southern) League Premier Division
CLUB FOUNDED: 1901
PREVIOUS GROUNDS: Moor Green Lane; Russel Road; Windermere Road

Few grounds have sacrificed so much to appease a planning committee. In order to obtain permission to erect floodlights at The Moorlands in 1983, the club had to rotate the pitch through 90 degrees. This meant the classic 1930 wooden main stand and dressing rooms contained within, were left stranded behind one of the resited goals at the Delamere Road end. The two extensive open terraces that previously stood behind either goal were demolished. Also, the second pitch, which was rented to Highgate United was also lost. Even with all the work done, the council only granted permission for pylons that could be winched down and out of sight when not in use. Not only were these considerably more expensive than conventional pylons, but they require a good deal of manual labour to erect before every evening game. Both sides now have flat, hard standing, but in recent years the Petersfield Road end has had a shallow terrace laid along the entire dead-ball line. This has now been covered to give the ground a more enclosed feel. With the general havoc caused in the

Christie Park, Morecambe

last 20 years at The Moorlands, I suppose we should be grateful that the superb grandstand stood defiantly untouched.

MORECAMBE
GROUND: Christie Park, Lancaster Road, Morecambe, Lancashire
CURRENT CAPACITY: 6,300
RECORD ATTENDANCE: 9,324 v. Weymouth (FA Cup) 04/01/62
YEAR BUILT/OPENED: 1921
CURRENT LEAGUE: Nationwide Football Conference
CLUB FOUNDED: 1920
PREVIOUS GROUNDS: Woodhill Lane(1920–21)

The club first played at this ground in 1921 when it was known as Roseberry Park, although it was renamed four years later when a local benefactor bought the site and gave it to the club in perpetuity. From humble beginnings it developed into today's magnificent venue. The main stand was built in 1962 and is a reverential copy of the identical stand at Cheltenham Town's Whaddon Road ground. The opposite side has a large length of uncovered terracing that replaced a former grassed bank. The covered stand behind the far goal dates from the late 1960s and replaced one destroyed by a gale. The floodlights were erected in 1960, although the lighting system and bulbs were replaced in 1993. The most recent addition to Christie Park has been the stand at the north end of the ground. This magnificent structure (surely there is not a better covered terrace outside of the Football League) has seen the capacity of the ground rise to more than 6,000, providing standing room for 2,000 people alone. Morecambe have achieved considerable success in the last decade and their admirable modernization of the ground is a real credit to them.

Seel Park, Mossley

MOSSLEY

GROUND: Seel Park, Market Street,
Mossley, Lancashire
CURRENT CAPACITY: 4,500
RECORD ATTENDANCE: 7,145 v.
Stalybridge Celtic (Cheshire League)
1950
YEAR BUILT/OPENED: 1920s
CURRENT LEAGUE: North West
Counties League Division One
CLUB FOUNDED: 1903 as Park Villa
PREVIOUS GROUNDS: Luzley Field

Seel Park has been the home of Mossley
since the early 1920s and over the years
has seen some considerable crowds
including 7,000 for a Cheshire League
game against near neighbours,
Stalybridge Celtic, in 1950. The ground
used to have extensive banking but in
more recent times this has been levelled.
Only the main stand, built in 1968, has
the benefit of the sole remaining banking. In 1980 the Park End covered terrace
was erected and three years later a smart
brick-built cover was erected opposite
the main stand. The extensive ground
developments were a direct result of a
sustained period of success for the club
which culminated in a Wembley appearance for the 1980 FA Trophy Final.
However, the glory days faded and relegation from the Northern Premier
League was suffered at the end of the
1994/95 campaign.

MURTON

GROUND: Murton Park, Church Lane,
Murton, County Durham
CURRENT CAPACITY: 3,500
RECORD ATTENDANCE: 3,500 v.
Spennymoor United (Durham Cup)
1951
YEAR BUILT/OPENED: 1928
CURRENT LEAGUE: Albany Northern
League Division Two

Murton Park, Murton

CLUB FOUNDED: 1904
PREVIOUS GROUNDS: Fatten Pasture
(1904–28)

Poor old Murton have the dubious honour of owning one of the unluckiest, and most vandalized, grounds in the country. In recent years the 70-odd-year-old ground has suffered the ignominy of arson, graffiti and downright criminal damage. Even Mother Nature has left her mark when in 2002, part of the pitch collapsed into an underground chasm. It is a far cry from its early years as one of the finest Colliery Welfare grounds in the country. The present main stand was built in 1928 although it was resited four years later to its present position. However, though it is still standing it cannot be used as the insides were removed due to safety concerns. A new stand was erected in 1982 at the opposite side of the

ground. The Colliery and Welfare closed for good in 1976 and the ground became council property. The club, however, retained the Colliery Welfare name until joining the Northern League in 1988 when they reverted to plain Murton FC. Your heart goes out to the tireless club officials who wage a constant war against the local youths who seem to delight in destroying a facility that is intended for their benefit. It is a strange world we live in.

NANPEAN ROVERS
GROUND: Victoria Park, Victoria Bottoms, Nanpean, Cornwall
CURRENT CAPACITY: 2,000

Victoria Park, Nanpean Rovers

RECORD ATTENDANCE: Not Known
YEAR BUILT/OPENED: 1936
CURRENT LEAGUE: Cornwall Guardian
East Cornwall Premier League
CLUB FOUNDED: Not Recorded
PREVIOUS GROUNDS: None

Victoria Park has gained cult status among ground aficionados over the last decade. It was carved out of a clay quarry in 1936 and the resulting banking has created a unique footballing venue. The banks are covered in grass, trees and bushes and are criss-crossed by numerous pathways. Behind both goals are white shelters, useful in inclement weather, but the regular followers of The Rovers could choose a different vantage point for every home game during a season and would still have plenty more to try out! The attractive pavilion also doubles as a memorial to lads from the village killed in World War Two. Victoria Park is a football watcher's paradise, with plenty to look at around the ground if the on-pitch action is not too great!

NANTWICH TOWN
GROUND: Jackson Avenue, Nantwich, Cheshire
CURRENT CAPACITY: 1,500
RECORD ATTENDANCE: 2,700 v. Altrincham (Cheshire Senior Cup) 1967
YEAR BUILT/OPENED: 1884
CURRENT LEAGUE: North West Counties League Division One
CLUB FOUNDED: 1884 as Nantwich FC
PREVIOUS GROUNDS: Kingsley Fields; Barony Park

More than 100 years of football at the Jackson Avenue ground, or London Road as it was originally known, will shortly come to an end as The Dabbers are in the process of building a new ground at Kingsley Fields. Ironically the new venue

Jackson Avenue, Nantwich Town

will be very close to the site of one of their former grounds. Nantwich were a well-supported club at the turn of the twentieth century and in 1902 the club constructed a large wooden grandstand that stood for 70 years until the construction of the present brick-built main stand. There is a sizeable covered stand opposite the main stand. After both wars Nantwich were forced to temporarily relocate to other, less satisfactory venues. However, in the late 1940s an agreement was reached with the landowner to buy the London Road ground outright for £750. The club funded the erection of new dressing rooms replacing the derelict ones at the top end of the ground. A new canteen replaced the old supporters' hut and in 1989 the clubhouse was opened. Floodlights came two years later and completed the gradual transformation of the ground. However,

with housing springing up all around the ground in recent years, the club have taken the decision to secure their future by cashing in their most valuable asset. The new ground should be ready by the summer of 2003.

NEWCASTLE TOWN
GROUND: Lyme Valley Parkway Stadium, Lilleshall Road, Newcastle-under-Lyme, Staffordshire
CURRENT CAPACITY: 4,000
RECORD ATTENDANCE: 3,586 v. Stoke City (Friendly) August 1991
YEAR BUILT/OPENED: 1955
CURRENT LEAGUE: North West Counties League Division One
CLUB FOUNDED: 1986 merger of Parkway Clayton (1964) and Newcastle Town (1980)
PREVIOUS GROUNDS: Hanley Park; Northwood Lane; Lilleshall Road

Lyme Valley Parkway Stadium, Newcastle Town

The Lyme Valley Parkway Stadium is something of a rarity in this country as it still sports a velodrome. The whole sports complex was opened in 1955 and was, for many years, Stoke City's training ground. As well as cycling, the complex also catered for rugby and cricket. The ground was regenerated when two local clubs merged in 1986 and departed their existing grounds in favour of the velo-drome. There is fine 200-seater stand adjacent to the old wooden clubhouse and, more recently, a large covered stand has been erected on the other side of the ground. Even the cycling track has been bought back to life and is once again in regular use. The club have played a 'home' game in front of a larger crowd when 3,948 watched an FA Cup tie with Notts County in November 1996 although the tie was actually staged at Stoke City's former home at Victoria Park.

NEWMARKET TOWN
GROUND: Town Ground, Cricketfield Road, Newmarket, Cambridgeshire
CURRENT CAPACITY: 1,750
RECORD ATTENDANCE: 2,701 v. Abbey United (FA Cup) 01/10/47
YEAR BUILT/OPENED: 1885
CURRENT LEAGUE: Jewson Eastern Counties League Premier Division
CLUB FOUNDED: 1877
PREVIOUS GROUNDS: The Severals (1877–78); Sefton Lodge (1878–85)

The Town Ground is now well over 100 years old, having been opened in 1885, although since the club's centenary, all facilities at the ground have been replaced. The first change in 1985 was the completion of the pitch railing, which was only three-sided due to the long-time presence of the cricket club. Strangely Newmarket Cricket Club had owned the

Town Ground, Newmarket Town

ground until 1959 when it was sold to the football club for a bargain £800. However, the cricket club stayed sharing the venue until their departure in 1985. Newmarket's centenary year was a remarkably busy one as the club also opened the new clubhouse with an adjacent covered terrace, as well as switching on their first set of floodlights. The most recent development at the Town Ground has seen the replacement of the elderly, but charismatic, wooden main stand, which had stood on the railway side of the ground since 1930. Arguments for the siting of the new stand on the training pitch side of the ground opposite the old stand were weighed up, rejected, and the old stand met its maker in the summer of 1996. In its place rose a modern cantilevered stand in an unusual dark red colour. This accommodates 120 seats and is set off by the club's name smartly picked out on the fascia board.

NEWPORT COUNTY

GROUND: Newport Stadium, Spyty Park, Langland Way, Newport, Gwent
CURRENT CAPACITY: 3,300
RECORD ATTENDANCE: 2,475 v. Redditch United (League) 24/08/94
YEAR BUILT/OPENED: 1993
CURRENT LEAGUE: Dr Marten's (Southern) League Premier Division
CLUB FOUNDED: 1989 as Newport AFC
PREVIOUS GROUNDS: Moreton Town FC(1989-90); Somerton Park(1990–92); Gloucester City (1992–94)

There is surely no club in existence that can have had the problems and heartache suffered by poor old Newport County in the last 15 years or so. The old Football League club lost their League status at the end of the 1987/88 campaign and due to huge debts, failed to complete their first season as a non-League club. Their old Somerton Park

St George's Park, Newport, Isle of Wight

home was stripped of fixtures and fittings and was eventually demolished in 1993. Following the demise of the old club, a new club, initially called Newport AFC, was formed. However, a bitter and contentious dispute with the FA of Wales, which saw Welsh clubs refusing to join the League of Wales in favour of remaining in English competitions, meant the newly formed club were forced to play 'home' games at Moreton Town's London Road ground some 80 miles away in Gloucestershire. Following an injunction against the League of Wales, the club briefly returned to Somerton Park, before its protracted death in 1993. The League of Wales row resurfaced and two more seasons were spent playing in England, this time at Gloucester City's ground. The club finally returned to Wales in 1994. The newly built Newport Stadium, albeit an athletics stadium, has a huge main stand and flat standing on one side and a shallow uncovered terrace on the other. The club readopted the name of Newport County and have the nickname of 'The Exiles'. This is technically inappropriate now they are 'back home', but a pointed and permanent reminder of the bitter, and ultimately futile, row with the FAW.

NEWPORT (IOW)
GROUND: St George's Park, St George's Way, Newport, Isle of Wight
CURRENT CAPACITY: 5,000
RECORD ATTENDANCE: 2,217 v. Aylesbury United (FA Cup) 12/11/94
YEAR BUILT/OPENED: 1988
CURRENT LEAGUE: Dr Marten's (Southern) League Eastern Division
CLUB FOUNDED: 1888
PREVIOUS GROUNDS: Church Litten (1888–1988)

Of many grounds now lying under supermarkets, the addition of Newport's delightfully rural-looking Church Litten ground was a savage blow. The old ground was within touching distance of its centenary when the club was offered a substantial sum of money, believed to be £2.5 million. In a harsh financial climate they could ill afford to turn it down. The club had always played there and the revenue generated represented a sound return on the outlay of £3,000 the club made to make the venue their own back in 1924. The new ground was built well away from the town centre and is perfectly adequate in every way. The main stand affords a fine view of the match and the two-story building behind it houses all the official and social facilities needed for modern-day senior football. The neat ground is completed by the presence of three modest covered terraces on the remaining three sides of the ground. The large site also provides ample car-parking facilities. In short it provides everything that was found wanting with Church Litten but to many its loss remains a bitter pill to swallow.

NORTH FERRIBY UNITED
GROUND: Grange Lane, Church Road, North Ferriby, Humberside
CURRENT CAPACITY: 3,000
RECORD ATTENDANCE: 1,800 v. Tamworth (FA Vase) 1989
YEAR BUILT/OPENED: 1970
CURRENT LEAGUE: Unibond (Northern Premier) League Division One
CLUB FOUNDED: 1934
PREVIOUS GROUNDS: Various pitches

North Ferriby United joined senior football in 1969 when they gained election to the Yorkshire League. However, a year's hard slog went by before their new Grange Lane ground was ready for use.

The Drill Field, Northwich Victoria

Northwood Park, Northwood

The whole site was levelled and the pitch laid, a post and rail fence was acquired cheaply second hand from Sutton Ings, the home of the defunct Hull Brunswick club. A pair of prefabricated buildings were removed from the village and were eventually put in place for use as changing rooms. The present main stand was built in 1993 replacing the original stand. In 1984, on the dressing-room side, the club built a small stand with a pitch roof to serve as accommodation for dignitaries and club officials. The club's elevation to the Northern Premier League in 2000 has seen the provision of a clubhouse, floodlights and more suitable changing facilities. The most recent addition has been the laying down of flat hard standing around the perimeter of the pitch. Grange Lane has become very much a blue print for a small town ground, and very nice it is too.

NORTHWICH VICTORIA
GROUND: The Drill Field, Drill Field Road, Northwich, Cheshire
CURRENT CAPACITY: 6,000
RECORD ATTENDANCE: 11,290 v. Witton Albion (Cheshire League) 15/04/49
YEAR BUILT/OPENED: 1875
CURRENT LEAGUE: Nationwide Football Conference
CLUB FOUNDED: 1874
PREVIOUS GROUNDS: Stumper's Field

A truly historic venue, certified by the FA as the oldest continuously used senior football ground in the world. The Drill Field, so called as it was previously a military training ground, has been used for football since 1875. It was even a Football League venue for two seasons between 1892 and 1894. Due to its incredible age, the Drill Field has been built and rebuilt

185

several times. The main stand dates from 1968 and the huge sweep of terrace called the Dane Bank was completely relaid and re-covered in 1999. The flood-lights were replaced in 1979, taking the place of an older set that was purchased from Crewe Alexandra in 1965. In 1992 the club nearly lost the ground to devel-opers, but at the 11th hour a rescue package saved the day. The club played their last game at the ground in April 2002, when massive debts forced the club into selling their ancient ground. The club hope to build a brand new ground in Wincham in the near future, and in the meantime look likely to ground-share with bitter rivals, Witton Albion.

NORTHWOOD

GROUND: Northwood Park, Chestnut Avenue, Northwood, Middlesex
CURRENT CAPACITY: 2,500
RECORD ATTENDANCE: 1,642 v.

Chelsea (Friendly) July 1997
YEAR BUILT/OPENED: 1946
CURRENT LEAGUE: Ryman (Isthmian) League Division One (North)
CLUB FOUNDED: 1899
PREVIOUS GROUNDS: Numerous pitches

Although they have a long history, mainly in local football in the Harrow & Wembley League, Northwood only really arrived in 1981 when senior status was obtained. The real climb to their present position started in 1984 with a move from the Hellenic League to the Spartan League. The club have played at Chestnut Avenue since World War Two, but have used various pitches within the large sporting complex. The present ground was enclosed in the late 1970s and, with financial assistance from the local Hillingdon council, floodlights were erected in May 1981. During their

Manor Park, Nuneaton Borough

successful spell in the Spartan League the main stand and covered terrace were erected, which meant little was needed in the way of ground improvements when they successfully applied for Isthmian League membership in 1992. Since then only minor improvements, such as extra turnstiles and hard standing, have been needed to keep Chestnut Avenue up to scratch.

NUNEATON BOROUGH

GROUND: Manor Park, Beaumont Road, Nuneaton, Warwickshire
CURRENT CAPACITY: 6,500
RECORD ATTENDANCE: 22,114 v. Rotherham United (FA Cup) 28/01/67
YEAR BUILT/OPENED: 1919
CURRENT LEAGUE: Nationwide Football Conference
CLUB FOUNDED: 1937
PREVIOUS GROUNDS: None

The defunct Nuneaton Town initially developed Manor Park after acquiring the site for £2,300 just after World War One. However, after a relative period of success, which included a couple of applications for Football League membership, Town disbanded at the end of 1936/37. In recent times, however, Nuneaton Borough's rapid progress has seen most vestiges of the old ground replaced. The oldest remaining part of the stadium, dating from 1962, is the superb, highly elevated covered terrace at the east end of the ground. On the far side of the ground, which is penned in by the Ashby Canal, is a smart new covered terrace, finished in time for the club's promotion to the Conference in 1999. This replaced a barrel-roof stand that was pulled down after the storms of 1987. There is a shallow open terrace at the other end of the ground, although any

Invicta Park, Oadby Town

The Cricketts, Oldbury United

future development has been hampered by the proximity of neighbouring housing. The main stand is another modern structure that has recently been reclad externally and fitted with new seating. Borough now possess an impressive and thoroughly modern home, a far cry from Manor Park's early years when a public footpath bisected the pitch.

O

OADBY TOWN

GROUND: Invicta Park, Wigston Road, Oadby, Leicestershire
CURRENT CAPACITY: 2,000
RECORD ATTENDANCE: 1,100 v. Newcastle United (Friendly) 1990

YEAR BUILT/OPENED: 1948
CURRENT LEAGUE: Midland Alliance
CLUB FOUNDED: 1939
PREVIOUS GROUNDS: Various pitches

Despite the presence of the modern clubhouse, built in 1990, Invicta Park gives off the general appearance of being far older than its birthdate of 1948. Maybe it's the rickety old corrugated iron cover that gives off this impression. The club used various fields around the town until the Wigston Road site was initially leased and then purchased from a local landowner. The club spent many years in the Leicestershire Senior League before gaining promotion to the Midlands Alliance in 1999. Apart from the old stand, the only covered accommodation is provided by a narrow overhanging roof from the clubhouse.

OLDBURY UNITED
GROUND: The Cricketts, York Road, Rowley Regis, Warley, West Midlands
CURRENT CAPACITY: 3,000
RECORD ATTENDANCE: 2,200 v. Walsall Wood (Walsall Senior Cup) 1982
YEAR BUILT/OPENED: 1978
CURRENT LEAGUE: Midland Alliance
CLUB FOUNDED: 1958
PREVIOUS GROUNDS: Britannia Park (1961–63); Newbury Lane (1963–78)

The relatively flat nature of The Cricketts belies the fact that the ground was fashioned from a disused clay quarry. Such grounds normally benefit from natural banking, but not so at the York Road venue. The club bought the ground from the council in 1978 for a bargain price of £3,000. The Oldbury committee has subsequently developed the ground to an impressive degree. There are five areas of cover, two on each side of the ground and a pitch-length cover at one end. The clubhouse side covers are equipped with wooden-bench seating. The most noticeable aspect of Oldbury United's ground is the tremendous noise, generated by the fact that it is separated from the M5 by just a vast wooden fence. Despite the unglamorous location, Oldbury have a venue that highlights what can be achieved by sheer hard work.

OSSETT ALBION
GROUND: Dimple Wells, Queens Terrace, Ossett, West Yorkshire
CURRENT CAPACITY: 3,000
RECORD ATTENDANCE: 1,200 v. Leeds United (Floodlight Opener) 1986
YEAR BUILT/OPENED: 1955
CURRENT LEAGUE: North West Counties League Premier Division
CLUB FOUNDED: 1944
PREVIOUS GROUNDS: Church Street; Beck Lane; Kingsway; Fern House

The club acquired an old rubbish tip that was part of Ossett Cricket Club's ground in 1950. However there was considerable work needed to prepare the site and Albion shared Ossett Town's Fern House ground for five seasons before everything was ready. A small grandstand was built and this remains, although substantially updated in the mid-1990s. Most of the developments have come since the club joined the newly formed Northern Counties East League in 1983. The ground was completely enclosed with a new perimeter wall. This was followed by floodlights, turnstiles and new dressing rooms. Covered areas also sprung up behind both goals. Albion then won the Northern Counties East League during the 1998/99 season but were denied promotion to the Northern Premier League having just failed to complete required ground improvements in the allotted time. This allowed the runners up to leapfrog them to gain promotion. To Albion's chagrin it was rivals Ossett Town that took their place. However, Albion's deserved elevation was only postponed by one more season. After only two seasons, though, Albion were relegated from the Unibond League.

OSSETT TOWN
GROUND: Ingfield, Prospect Road, Ossett, West Yorkshire
CURRENT CAPACITY: 4,000
RECORD ATTENDANCE: 2,600 v. Manchester United (Friendly) 1988
YEAR BUILT/OPENED: 1957
CURRENT LEAGUE: Unibond (Northern Premier) League Division One
CLUB FOUNDED: 1936

Washbrook Meadow, Ottery St Mary

PREVIOUS GROUNDS: Fern House; Back Lane

Despite being formed as recently as 1936, Ossett Town are the elder of the two Ossett teams by eight years. Their first home was behind Fern House Working Men's Club, which was also later used by Ossett Albion, but this was inadequate for senior football. The club sold a couple of high-quality players – Ron Liversedge to Bradford City and Derek Blackburn to Swansea Town – and the funds generated meant that in 1957 the club could afford to buy the site known as Ingfield, off the Prospect Road. The Ingfield ground has only really been developed since the club moved from the Yorkshire League to the Northern Counties East League in 1983. A cover was erected behind one goal, although this has since been replaced by a larger cover on top of a few steps of ter-

racing. Floodlights arrived in 1987 and two years later the modest main stand was erected. The ground developments were rewarded with promotion to the Northern Premier League at the end of the 1998/99 campaign.

OTTERY ST MARY
GROUND: Washbrook Meadow, Butts Road, Ottery St Mary, Devon
CURRENT CAPACITY: 2,000
RECORD ATTENDANCE: 2,000 v. Nottingham Forest (Friendly) 1985
YEAR BUILT/OPENED: 1946
CURRENT LEAGUE: Firewatch Devon League
CLUB FOUNDED: 1911
PREVIOUS GROUNDS: Shoot's Mead; Slade Road; Kings School

Although Washbrook Meadow is a post-war venue, the delightful pitch roof stand with glazed end panels lends the impression of far greater antiquity. The club has fallen on hard times in recent years, slipping from the Western League, the top competition in the area, down to the County League, but this has not stopped the club modernizing the ground with a new clubhouse and dressing-room block. Fortunately the ground's crowning glory, the corrugated main stand, has remained untouched.

OXFORD CITY
GROUND: Court Place Farm, Marsh Lane, Marston, Oxford, Oxfordshire
CURRENT CAPACITY: 3,000
RECORD ATTENDANCE: 1,760 v. Belper Town (FA Vase) 25/03/95
YEAR BUILT/OPENED: 1993
CURRENT LEAGUE: Ryman (Isthmian) League Division One (North)
CLUB FOUNDED:1882
PREVIOUS GROUNDS: The White House (1882–1988); Cuttleslow Park (1990–91); Roman Way (1991–93)

Much has been chronicled about the sad demise of Oxford City's classic ground, The White House, which was an impressive 106 years old at its untimely death in 1988. With no advanced warning, the landlords sold the site from under the club for property development and the club were homeless as the 1988/89 season approached. The club had no choice but to carry on in youth football for two seasons before using grounds at Cuttleslow Park and Headington Amateurs' Roman Way venue when senior football was rejoined in 1990. Ironically the old grandstand at The White House remained intact until 1992 although the rest of the ground was redeveloped almost overnight. The club eventually secured a site for a new stadium just off the A40 in Marston. The new

Nyetimber Lane, Pagham

Athletic Ground, Paulton Rovers

ground has been developed into a first-class arena, perfect for their current Ryman League status. It has excellent social facilities, extensive seating and covered accommodation. Oxford City have gained much respect for their efforts in recent years, recovering admirably from what for many clubs would have almost certainly been a death knell.

P

PAGHAM
GROUND: Nyetimber Lane, Pagham, West Sussex
CURRENT CAPACITY: 2,000
RECORD ATTENDANCE: 1,200 v. Bognor Regis Town 1971
YEAR BUILT/OPENED: 1950

CURRENT LEAGUE: Rich City Sussex County League Division One
CLUB FOUNDED: 1903
PREVIOUS GROUNDS: Various pitches

Pagham were a junior club until 1950, when a move to a new ground coincided with a step up to the West Sussex League. The new ground was adjacent to Pagham Cricket Club in Nyetimber Lane and was not enclosed from the cricket outfield until as recently as 1988. The club's rise to the Sussex County League in 1970 saw a number of developments at the ground, including the current clubhouse and dressing rooms. The current stand, of basic breeze-block construction, also dates from this time, although the provision of seats is a more recent addition. The club laid shallow terracing on the side opposite the stand and at one end, but have yet to follow

Southend Road, Penrith

through on their plans to erect covers over these tracts of terrace. In 1988 the current floodlights were opened and replaced a storm-damaged set that were only used for training sessions. A trip to this remote section of West Sussex will be rewarded by the sight of this particularly attractive venue.

PAULTON ROVERS
GROUND: Athletic Ground, Winterstoke Road, Paulton, Somerset
CURRENT CAPACITY: 5,000
RECORD ATTENDANCE: 2,000 v. Crewe Alexandra (FA Cup) 08/12/1906
YEAR BUILT/OPENED: 1967
CURRENT LEAGUE: Screwfix Direct Western League Premier Division
CLUB FOUNDED: 1881
PREVIOUS GROUNDS: Chapel Field; Paulton Cricket Club; Recreation Ground

A lovely little ground built up from an undeveloped field since the late 1960s. The stand is a 1990s erection, replacing an old cover, and this side of the ground is completed by the clubhouse and dressing rooms. The ground is enclosed on the other side by tall hedges and has uncovered standing at the far end. The opposite side to the main stand and the car-park end of the ground has newly erected covered terracing. The club also plan to extend the main stand in the near future. The Athletic Ground's lofty location also affords an excellent view of the North Somerset coalfields with a disused colliery clearly visible on the horizon.

PENRITH
GROUND: Southend Road, Penrith, Cumbria
CURRENT CAPACITY: 4,000
RECORD ATTENDANCE: 2,100 v.

Penlee Park, Penzance

Chester 21/11/81
YEAR BUILT/OPENED: 1880s
CURRENT LEAGUE: Albany Northern League Division Two
CLUB FOUNDED: 1894
PREVIOUS GROUNDS: None

Originally known as Kilgour's Field, this ground was at first home to Carleton Rovers. This club seem to have disbanded and the site was not used until Penrith formed in September 1894. Southend Road was an open ground – indeed a public footpath crossed the pitch, and it was not properly enclosed until 1959. The main stand was built in the same year and complemented the covered stand on the opposite side. This was built in 1954 and replaced the original wooden stand. There is also some terracing at both ends of the ground. In 1975 a set of floodlights was erected at the ground, having been purchased from the Black & Decker factory at Spennymoor. These have given excellent service, although the bulbs were upgraded in 1989. However the club face a battle to keep their ground, which is a prime town-centre site. Developers have long coveted the land and the club have deep concerns over plans to relocate them to an out-of-town venue. Such a move would doubtless have a bad effect on their already modest support.

PENZANCE
GROUND: Penlee Park, Alexandra Place, Penzance, Cornwall
CURRENT CAPACITY: 4,000
RECORD ATTENDANCE: Not Known
YEAR BUILT/OPENED: 1952
CURRENT LEAGUE: Carlsberg South-Western League
CLUB FOUNDED: 1888

PREVIOUS GROUNDS: Trereife Farm; Sona Merg Park; St Clare Park

Another of Cornwall's many glorious grounds, and another like Falmouth and Bodmin that looks older than it really is. What makes Penlee Park special is the fact that it was built solely from volunteer labour. Many tonnes of soil were moved by hand as the pitch was levelled and drainage laid. Due to appalling weather, the workers would often return to find their previous day's toils washed away by torrential rain. The ground finally opened in time for the 1952/53 season and the club enjoyed their halcyon days at their new home. However in recent years the club has fallen on hard times and Penlee fell into a state of considerable disrepair not helped by the unwanted attention of local vandals. In the late 1990s the club under-took extensive repairs, fencing was reinstated, and the stand and the ground's ornate entrance were restored to their for-mer glory. The original builders, some of whom still attend matches, would have been proud as Penlee Park is once again a beautiful venue and a suitable monument to their endeavour.

PICKERING TOWN
GROUND: Mill Lane, off Malton Road, Pickering, North Yorkshire
CURRENT CAPACITY: 2,000
RECORD ATTENDANCE: 1,412 v. Notts County (Friendly) August 1991
YEAR BUILT/OPENED: 1920
CURRENT LEAGUE: Northern Counties East League Premier Division
CLUB FOUNDED: 1888
PREVIOUS GROUNDS: Westgate Beck

Pickering is a particularly attractive mar-ket town on the edge of the North

Yorkshire Moors and is also the terminus for the famous steam railway that takes you high on to the moors at Grosmont. What is really pleasing is that the town's football ground is equally attractive. The venue at Mill Lane has been home to the town's football, cricket and bowls clubs since 1920. The present clubhouse was opened in 1963 replacing the old wooden pavilion. Interestingly it was co-funded by all three sports clubs. The football club replaced the old stand in 1993, a year after the floodlights were erected. Unusually there are five pylons to cater for the overlap shared with the cricket outfield. A covered stand was then opened at the clubhouse end and in the summer of 2000, a smart seated stand went up behind the Town End goal. Although The Pikes have upgraded their ground to an impressive standard, future promotion will be hampered by the fact that Mill Lane remains a three-sided venue.

PONTEFRACT COLLIERIES
GROUND: Skinner Lane, Pontefract, West Yorkshire
CURRENT CAPACITY: 1,200
RECORD ATTENDANCE: 1,000 v. Manchester United (Floodlight Opener) 1985
YEAR BUILT/OPENED: 1958
CURRENT LEAGUE: Northern Counties East League Division One
CLUB FOUNDED: 1958
PREVIOUS GROUNDS: None

Pontefract Collieries have always lived in the shadow of their near neighbours at Frickley, however they have developed Skinner Lane into a perfectly functional ground. The club was formed in 1958, pretty much taking over from the defunct

Skinner Lane, Pontefract Collieries

Pontefract United club. The Colliers moved up through the West Yorkshire League and then the Yorkshire League until becoming founder members of the Northern Counties East League in 1982. Success on the field has not matched the progress off the field. The Skinner Lane ground now has a super clubhouse and floodlights were erected in 1985. The present seated stand was built in 1996 and has seating for 200.

PURFLEET

GROUND: Thurrock Hotel, Ship Lane, Grays, Essex
CURRENT CAPACITY: 4,500
RECORD ATTENDANCE: 2,572 v. West Ham United (Friendly) 1998
YEAR BUILT/OPENED: 1985
CURRENT LEAGUE: Ryman (Isthmian) League Premier Division
CLUB FOUNDED: 1985
PREVIOUS GROUNDS: None

The progress of Purfleet since their formation as recently as 1985 has been nothing short of remarkable. Within four years the club had left the Essex Senior League for the Isthmian League and had made it to the Premier Division by 1994. The club play at a ground behind the Thurrock Hotel that is clearly visible from Junction 30 of the M25, just before the Dartford Tunnel. The whole area was originally Aveley Technical College but the site was closed in the early 1980s until being developed as a leisure/hotel complex. The club's formation was the brainchild of Tommy and Harry South after whom the clubs impressive pitched roof main stand is named. Confusingly, therefore, the South Stand is actually on the east side of the ground! In 1994 the club erected a covered terrace at the dressing room end of the ground and this has since been joined by a large cover at the Tunnel End. The side opposite the

Ship Lane, Purfleet

main stand has a lengthy terrace but as yet this remains uncovered. The ground has been completed by the long-awaited opening, in 2001, of the clubhouse at the car-park end. Previously patrons had to use the hotel's facilities.

R

RACING CLUB WARWICK
GROUND: Townsend Meadow, Hampton Road, Warwick, Warwickshire
CURRENT CAPACITY: 1,000
RECORD ATTENDANCE: 1,000 v. Halesowen Town (FA Cup) 10/10/87
YEAR BUILT/OPENED: 1967
CURRENT LEAGUE: Dr Marten's (Southern) League Premier Division
CLUB FOUNDED: 1919 as Saltisford Rovers
PREVIOUS GROUNDS: Dun Cow Field; St Nicholas Park; Coventry Road

Townsend Meadow is one of the more modest venues in the Dr Marten's League. The ground was made available to the club in 1967 and was part of Warwick Racecourse. The first building on the site was a converted Nissen hut, acquired cheaply from RAF Gaydon, which served as changing rooms. Before the pitch was ready for use the club had to embark on the arduous task of levelling a considerable latitudinal slope. Later in the same year, the club unveiled a brand new clubhouse. Finally, existing stables were converted into a changing room for match officials. Little changed until 1985 when the existing small cover on the racecourse side was replaced with a simple seated stand made of breeze

197

Townsend Meadow, Racing Club Warwick

blocks with a corrugated iron roof. An identical stand was subsequently erected on the opposite side of the ground. The club were promoted to the Southern League in 1989 and a year later floodlights were erected at the ground. In 1997 the club announced redevelopment plans for Townsend Meadow, which included two new stands, although lack of funding has seen the plans left firmly on the drawing board.

RADCLIFFE BOROUGH
GROUND: Stainton Park, Pilkington Road, Radcliffe, Lancashire
CURRENT CAPACITY: 3,000
RECORD ATTENDANCE: 2,495 v. York City (FA Cup) 18/11/01
YEAR BUILT/OPENED: 1970
CURRENT LEAGUE: Unibond (Northern Premier) League Division One
CLUB FOUNDED: 1949

PREVIOUS GROUNDS: Bright Street (1949–68); Crumpsall (1968–70)

Radcliffe Borough's first ground was at Bright Street and was little more than an open field. The club was evicted from that ground in 1968 when the site was required for a housing estate. The club spent a couple of seasons using an unsatisfactory pitch at Crumpsall before moving back across town to an area of open land adjacent to Radcliffe Cricket Club. The club soon enclosed the ground and opened a modest stand. The ground was called Stainton Park in recognition of the efforts of a local builder in the early days of the new ground. The club rose rapidly through the Cheshire County and North West Counties League before gaining promotion to the Northern Premier League in 1987. The promotion saw floodlights erected at

Stainton Park, Radcliffe Borough

Stainton Park and also a smart new covered stand behind the Pilkington Road goal. In the summer of 1997 a new seated stand was opened behind the Coronation Road goal. It was furnished with 350 seats acquired from Bolton Wanderers' former ground at Burnden Park. The older main stand was also reclad and new sections of shallow terracing were built. The club's record attendance of 1,468 for a Championship decider against Caernarfon town in 1983 was comfortably beaten when the club hosted York City as they reached the first round Proper of the FA Cup in November 2001.

RADSTOCK TOWN
GROUND: Southfield Recreation Ground, Frome Hill, Radstock, Somerset
CURRENT CAPACITY: 2,000
RECORD ATTENDANCE: 2,000 v. Yeovil & Petters United (FA Cup) 13/11/37
YEAR BUILT/OPENED: 1895
CURRENT LEAGUE: Somerset County League Premier Division
CLUB FOUNDED: 1895
PREVIOUS GROUNDS: None

There are numerous football clubs situated in the villages that sprung up around the once-prosperous North Somerset coalfields. Peasedown, Clutton, Tunley and Timsbury all have long histories and great little grounds, but Radstock have one of the best. The former colliery ground at Southfield has seen better days, despite renovation of the small stand in recent years, but served the club well during their halcyon days as a major force in the Western League. In the lengthy period that Bristol Rovers played their home Football League games at Bath City's Twerton Park ground, Bath

Southfield Recreation Ground, Radstock Town

City's reserve team played their home games at Southfield, earning Radstock some welcome revenue. Now in reduced circumstances in county league football, Southfield seems a million miles away from getting the four-figure crowds that once gathered there. However with its prime views of the Mendips it is a very scenic place to watch a game of football.

REDDITCH UNITED

GROUND: Valley Stadium, Bromsgrove Road, Redditch, Worcestershire
CURRENT CAPACITY: 5,000
RECORD ATTENDANCE: 5,500 v. Bromsgrove Rovers (West Midlands League) 1955
YEAR BUILT/OPENED: 1948
CURRENT LEAGUE: Dr Marten's (Southern) League Western Division
CLUB FOUNDED: 1900 as Redditch Town

PREVIOUS GROUNDS: Millsborough Road (1900–48)

The Valley Stadium was derelict land after World War Two, so Redditch acquired the site cheaply and began to develop a new ground. Soon the Valley Stadium had a cover, turnstiles and a social club although all would eventually be replaced as the club stormed through the Southern League eventually becoming founder members of the Alliance Premier League (now the Football Conference) in 1979. The original stand was damaged in a storm and was replaced by the present stand. This unique stand remains visually stunning and incorporates all dressing-room, official and social facilities and includes a large glazed viewing area above the seats. The rest of the ground is extensively banked and has a large cover opposite the main stand and at the car

Caburn Pavilion, Ringmer

park end. At one time the club claimed a capacity of 9,000 but with stricter safety standards nowadays, 5,000 is a more realistic figure, although the Valley Stadium remains a very large arena.

RINGMER

GROUND: Caburn Pavilion, Anchor Field, Ringmer, East Sussex
CURRENT CAPACITY: 1,000
RECORD ATTENDANCE: 1,200 v. Maidstone United (FA Cup) 13/09/75
YEAR BUILT/OPENED: 1967
CURRENT LEAGUE: Rich City Sussex County League Division One
CLUB FOUNDED: 1906
PREVIOUS GROUNDS: None

Ringmer have developed the Caburn Pavilion into a very pleasant venue since the ground was officially opened in December 1967. Originally the club played on a field to the south of the present ground, close to the Anchor Inn. It was quite literally a working field with no facilities at all. Players changed in a storage room at the nearby inn. The present ground started to take shape in the mid-1960s, although after the club had built changing rooms, they were asked to move the pitch some 40 yards to allow for road widening. The newly built wooden changing rooms were replaced with a building acquired from Croydon Airport. The old clubhouse was resited to its present location and the club acquired the collapsible type of floodlight pylons to circumvent planning application problems. The resited ground was given some form of frontage when the local council opened the village car park. The most recent addition came in 1995 when the small seated stand was opened on the far side of the ground.

ROCESTER
GROUND: Rivers Field, Mill Street, Rocester, Staffordshire
CURRENT CAPACITY: 4,000
RECORD ATTENDANCE: 1,026 v. Halesowen Town (FA Vase) 1987
YEAR BUILT/OPENED: 1987
CURRENT LEAGUE: Dr Marten's (Southern) League Western Division
CLUB FOUNDED: 1876
PREVIOUS GROUNDS: Mill Street

The Rivers Field ground was opened in 1987 and the club's move across Mill Street was not without controversy. The new venue was found to be on the site of a Roman fort. However planning permission was eventually granted after local archaeologists had cleared the site of precious artefacts. The new venue was a vast improvement on their old Mill Street ground, which boasted an ageing wooden dressing room. The new ground was fully enclosed and the grandstand was built in time for the 1987/88 campaign. Floodlights were erected in 1989 and in the same year the club acquired a small covered stand from the demolished Walsall ground, Fellows Park. Rocester's ambition to provide the town with a senior football ground was rewarded with promotion to the Southern League in 1999. All the ground needs is a large crowd to gather to beat the club's attendance record, which was set at a 'home' game that was staged at Leek Town's Harrison Park ground.

ROCHE
GROUND: Trezaise Road, Roche, Cornwall
CURRENT CAPACITY: 1,500
RECORD ATTENDANCE: Not Known
YEAR BUILT/OPENED: 1988
CURRENT LEAGUE: Cornwall Guardian East Cornwall Premier League
CLUB FOUNDED: Not Recorded
PREVIOUS GROUNDS: Church Playing Field

An amazing ground due to the wonders of geology rather than the facilities on offer. Although there is nothing wrong with the ground – it provides ample parking and has a very acceptable clubhouse. The playing surface is excellent and there is also a floodlit all-weather training surface. There is a very small cover that bears the club's name and looks suspiciously like a converted dug-out. However, the most remarkable feature of this ground is the unmissable presence of the granite cliff outcrop known as Roche Rock. It is a stunning edifice topped with the ruins of a church believed to date from the fifteenth century. The rock is actually open for climbers and provides a stunningly lofty view of the ground and the surrounding Cornish clay hills.

ROMFORD
GROUND: Ford Sports Ground, Rush Green Road, Romford, Essex
CURRENT CAPACITY: 2,500
RECORD ATTENDANCE: 820 v. Leatherhead (League) 15/04/97
YEAR BUILT/OPENED: 1948
CURRENT LEAGUE: Foresters Essex Senior League
CLUB FOUNDED: 1992 re-formation of club in existence 1876–1977
PREVIOUS GROUNDS: Hornchurch FC (1992–95); Ford United FC (1995–96)

They say in life, 'what goes around, comes around' and this idiom can certainly be applied to Romford Football Club. The original Romford club were

Trezaise Road, Roche

one of the most respected clubs outside the Football League. Their revered home at Brooklands once held 18,237 for an FA Amateur Cup tie against Southall in 1951. The club actually applied to join the Football League no less than 12 times although all applications would be rejected with their best performance coming in 1967 when they were the highest placed of 15 applicants. However, the demise in the early 1970s of the Romford Bombers Speedway Club and resulting loss of ground rental saw the football club plunged into severe financial problems. In 1977 the club sold the Brooklands site to clear debts but the proposed move to a new ground at Oldchurch came to nothing. The club folded after playing 'home' games of the 1977/78 season on borrowed grounds. In 1992 a group of enthusiasts re-formed the club and secured a ground share at Hornchurch's ground. After playing the 1995/96 campaign at Ford United's ground, the club's new owners approached nearby Collier Row with a view to a merger. The merger happened amid rumours of strong-arm tactics by the Romford board. Within a year, the Collier Row name disappeared from the merged club's title as Romford took over Row's Sungate ground completely. However, since the club's dubious and controversial acquisition of Sungate, Romford have had a host of problems with the ground. The Isthmian League closed the ground on several occasions due to pitch and floodlight problems as well as safety concerns over the stand. This was an impressive stand that boasted comfortable seats acquired from the cinema that once stood at Butlins in Clacton. By December 2001, the ground had been closed yet again and the club quit for good, echoing the

Ford Sports Ground, Romford

1977/78 by finishing the campaign using borrowed grounds. The club have now secured the use of Ford United's former home ground at Rush Green Road.

ROSSENDALE UNITED
GROUND: Dark Lane, Staghills Road, Newchurch, Waterfoot, Lancashire
CURRENT CAPACITY: 2,500
RECORD ATTENDANCE: 3,450 v. Shrewsbury Town (FA Cup) 22/11/75
YEAR BUILT/OPENED: 1880s
CURRENT LEAGUE: Unibond (Northern Premier) League Division One
CLUB FOUNDED: 1898
PREVIOUS GROUNDS: None

Rossendale United were formed in 1898 after the demise of the area's two previously dominant sides Rawtenstall and Myrtle Grove – the latter having made an audacious attempt at Football League membership as Rossendale FC in 1894. The newly formed club took over at the Dark Lane ground that had previously been used for rugby union. The present main stand was opened in August 1928 but by the late 1970s it was decidedly worse for wear. However, extensive renovation and a smart blue and white paint job have seen the old stand returned to its former glory. The Dark Lane ground was first lit up with floodlights in 1959 although the present set date from 1972. The new set of pylons was funded by the club's tremendous run in the 1971 FA Cup. They were finally defeated by Bolton Wanderers in the second round in front of a 12,000 crowd in a match staged at Bury's Gigg Lane ground. An important event happened in 1982 when the club secured its long-term future when a 99-year lease was agreed with the grounds owners. The club's promotion to the

Northern Premier League in 1989 saw further ground improvements. In recent years the club has built an impressive gymnasium and the floodlights have once again been upgraded. The ground has certainly never looked better, with the classic main stand and impressive amounts of terracing.

ROTHWELL TOWN
GROUND: Cecil Street, Rothwell, Northamptonshire
CURRENT CAPACITY: 3,500
RECORD ATTENDANCE: 2,508 v. Irthlingborough Diamonds (League) 1971
YEAR BUILT/OPENED: 1896
CURRENT LEAGUE: Dr Marten's (Southern) League Eastern Division
CLUB FOUNDED: 1895 as Rothwell Town Swifts
PREVIOUS GROUNDS: Harrington Road; Castle Hill

Rothwell Town's Cecil Street ground quietly passed its centenary in 1996 although much has changed at the ground since The Bones' early days at the venue. Until 1960 the pitch's orientation was at right angles to its current position. However, when fire gutted the 1924 vintage main stand in 1959, the club took the opportunity to realign the pitch to give them more space to develop the ground. The charred remains of the stand were removed and an existing area of cover was resited. The present main stand was erected with a generous financial donation from near neighbours, Kettering Town. The main stand houses the changing rooms although the old sunken plunge bath from the original dressing rooms was incorporated into the design of the new structure. Little change at Cecil Street until 1982 when the club purchased six floodlight pylons from McAlpines. However, one of the pylons was sited right in front of the stand, obscuring the view from many of the seats. In 1994 the club erected an additional area of cover at the clubhouse end. Another interesting feature of Cecil Street is the building at the entrance, which is a converted railway carriage.

ROYSTON TOWN
GROUND: Garden Walk, Royston, Hertfordshire
CURRENT CAPACITY: 4,000
RECORD ATTENDANCE: 876 v. Aldershot Town 13/02/93
YEAR BUILT/OPENED: 1923
CURRENT LEAGUE: Minerva Spartan South Midlands League Premier Division
CLUB FOUNDED: 1875
PREVIOUS GROUNDS: Newmarket Road; Baldock Road; Mackerall Hall

Royston Town are one of the oldest clubs in the county, being able to trace their history back to 1875. They played at three grounds around the town, before settling in a field between Garden Walk and the cemetery. The Crows have risen from the humble surroundings of the Buntingford and District League through to the Isthmian League, which they graced between 1986 and 1995. The legacy of their stint in the Isthmian League is owning one of the best grounds in the South Midlands League. Although, ironically, it was the strict ground-grading policy of the Isthmian League that forced Royston into rejoining the South Midlands League in 1995. The ground boasts an excellent clubhouse, floodlights and a superb seated stand on the cemetery side of the ground. Although the venue is hemmed in on three sides by housing and a school, the Garden Walk ground is surprisingly capacious. However, the club are not blessed with large support, as the record attendance testifies.

RUGBY TOWN
GROUND: Rugby RFC, Webb Ellis Road, Rugby, Warwickshire
CURRENT CAPACITY: 4,000
RECORD ATTENDANCE: 826 v. Leamington (League) 16/04/01
YEAR BUILT/OPENED: c1880
CURRENT LEAGUE: Midland Combination Premier Division
CLUB FOUNDED: 2000 re-formation of club in existence 1945–73
PREVIOUS GROUNDS: Thorn field (1945–50); Oakfield (1950–73)

In 2000 it was interesting to see the re-formation of an old name when Rugby Town joined the Midland Combination. The original Rugby Town played in the Birmingham Combination until folding in 1934. A new club was formed in 1945, playing at a ground called Thornfield, and progressed to the United Counties League. In 1950 they merged with Oakfield and turned professional, eventually reaching the Southern League in 1958. However, by 1973 debts proved to be insurmountable and coupled with the sudden loss of their home ground, the club decided to call it a day. Many of the club's officials and players went to the nearby AP Leamington club, which coincided with a substantial period of success for that club. The third and latest incarnation of Rugby Town have chosen an interesting home venue, for they share Webb Ellis Road, the home of Rugby RUFC. It is a historic venue, generally accepted as the origin of the oval ball game, and is named after William Webb Ellis, synonymous with the development of the rugby union code. Nevertheless, apart from its luxurious clubhouse, the venue is more than a little disappointing, considering its wealth of history. The main stand on the clubhouse side is relatively small and a little worse for wear, and the opposite side has a sizeable, but characterless, covered terrace. However, considering the rise of Rugby United in the interim, it is an admirable decision to bring a second senior non-League side to this East Warwickshire town.

RUGBY UNITED
GROUND: Butlin Road, Rugby, Warwickshire
CURRENT CAPACITY: 6,000
RECORD ATTENDANCE: 3,961 v. Northampton Town (FA Cup) 21/11/84
YEAR BUILT/OPENED: 1973
CURRENT LEAGUE: Dr Marten's (Southern) League Western Division
CLUB FOUNDED: 1956 as Valley Sports
PREVIOUS GROUNDS: Various council pitches

Valley Sports Rugby, or Rugby United as they have been known since 2000, moved onto a pitch off Butlin Road in 1973 that was previously allotment land. The club have since upgraded the ground at a steady rate and Butlin Road is now an impressive Southern League venue. On the car park side of the ground there is a large and well-appointed clubhouse and sizeable sweeps of terracing, although the recent addition of an ugly mesh player's tunnel spoils the overall appearance. There is cover on the car-park side and at either end, but the main stand is on the far side of the pitch and was joined in 1991 by a pair of covered terraces on

Webb Ellis Road, Rugby Town

either side of the seated stand. However, the club's development of Butlin Road into an excellent and sizeable stadium has not come without cost. In early 1993 the club's perilous financial position put them on the brink of closure although, happily, the club was saved at the eleventh hour. Since those harrowing days the club have kept development to modest cosmetic changes and now face a much healthier future.

RUNCORN HALTON
GROUND: Widnes RLFC, Autoquest Stadium, Lowerhouse Lane, Widnes, Cheshire
CURRENT CAPACITY: 10,883
RECORD ATTENDANCE: 10,111 v. Preston (FA Cup) 07/01/39 at Canal Street
YEAR BUILT/OPENED: Ground-shared since 2001
CURRENT LEAGUE: Unibond (Northern Premier) League Premier Division
CLUB FOUNDED: 1918 as Runcorn FC
PREVIOUS GROUNDS: Canal Street (1918–2001)

Another historic venue was lost when Runcorn staged their last match at Canal Street in May 2001. Severe financial constraints had meant the club had little option but to relocate to the impressive home of Widnes RLFC. The club also changed its name to incorporate the district name of their new home. Ironically the move is something of a full circle move as Canal Street was originally a rugby venue as well. The club used the ground from their formation in 1918 and developed it sufficiently to accommodate a crowd of 10,111 for a 1939 FA Cup tie with Preston North End. However, the ground's exposed location on the windswept Mersey estuary saw storm damage to several generations of stands

Butlin Road, Rugby United

at the ground. The most severe damage was sustained in 1993, when storm damage de-roofed a covered terrace, a perimeter wall collapsed in an FA Cup tie against Hull, and to make matters worse, the old main stand was burnt to the ground in March 1993. The club finished the season staging home games at Northwich Victoria, Witton Albion and Chester City. The ground was closed and speculation began to emanate regarding a potential move to Widnes, but to their credit the club plugged away and restored the ground with the addition of a smart new main stand. However, these strenuous efforts proved to be in vain as the eventual move to Widnes meant the club lived to fight another day.

RUSHDEN RANGERS

GROUND: Hayden Road, Rushden, Northamptonshire

CURRENT CAPACITY: 6,000
RECORD ATTENDANCE: 5,600
Rushden Town v. Kettering Town 1949
YEAR BUILT/OPENED: 1922
CURRENT LEAGUE: Travis Perkins Northants Combination Division One
CLUB FOUNDED: 1990
PREVIOUS GROUNDS: None

The merger of Rushden Town and Irthlingborough Diamonds in 1992 and the subsequent redevelopment of Diamonds' Nene Park venue into a superb Football League stadium have been nothing short of remarkable. However, it remains a pleasant surprise that Rushden Town's former ground at Hayden Road remains intact and in use for Northampton Combination football by Rushden Rangers. The Hayden Road ground was opened in 1922 after the area was bequeathed to the town for sporting activ-

Hayden Road, Rushden Rangers

ity. The present main stand was erected in the same year and originally had an impressive pitched roof. However, by 1998 the old roof was deemed unsafe and was removed and replaced with a flat corrugated iron roof. There is also a covered terrace on the opposite side, a remnant of Town's Southern League days. The floodlights were erected in 1975, a year after the present clubhouse was opened, replacing a Nissen hut that had previously served as social facilities. Ironically it was Hayden Road's rejection by the Southern League ground-grading criteria that led to merger discussions. It is refreshing to see that Hayden Road has survived tremendous upheaval in this corner of Northamptonshire over the last decade.

RYDE SPORTS

GROUND: Smallbrook Stadium, Ashey Road, Ryde, Isle of Wight

CURRENT CAPACITY: 5,000
RECORD ATTENDANCE: 3,100 v. Aston Villa (Friendly) 17/12/90
YEAR BUILT/OPENED: 1990
CURRENT LEAGUE: Isle of Wight League
CLUB FOUNDED: 1888
PREVIOUS GROUNDS: College Ground (1888–92); Partlands (1892–1990)

In 1990 Ryde Sports took the decision to sell their centrally located, 98-year-old Partlands Stadium for the considerable sum of £400,000. The sale realized a remarkable return on the £2,000 outlay to secure ownership of the site in 1957. The Partlands ground had been developed considerably in the 1950s after being badly damaged during World War Two. However, the record gate at the ground remained at the figure set for a 1936 FA Cup with Gillingham when more than 5,000 people attended. The reloca-

S

tion of the club to the out-of-town Smallbrook Stadium was intended to usher in a new era of semi-professional football as Ryde joined the Wessex League. However, the dream was short lived as after only seven seasons the club dropped back down to the Island League in 1997. The Smallbrook Stadium also caters for athletics and has a smart, pitch-length, seated stand although the view from it is spoiled by the inconsiderate sit-ing of four floodlight pylons right in from of the stand. Despite the drawbacks of the new stadium, a day out to this very pleasant East island town is highly rec-ommended.

S

SAFFRON WALDEN TOWN
GROUND: Catons Lane, Saffron Walden, Essex
CURRENT CAPACITY: 5,000
RECORD ATTENDANCE: 1,500 v. Moor Green (AFA Senior Cup) 22/01/38
YEAR BUILT/OPENED: 1890
CURRENT LEAGUE: Foresters Essex Senior League
CLUB FOUNDED: 1872
PREVIOUS GROUNDS: Friends School; The Common

The Bloods were formed in 1872 and are the oldest club in Essex. They disbanded briefly in 1890 until revived later in the same year when Arthur Smith moved from East Dereham to become headmas-ter at the Castle Street school. The club immediately secured the use of a field owned by Lord Braybrooke in Catons Lane then known as Loft's Lane, for an

annual rent of £3. The ground was sig-nificantly developed during the 1920s when the enclosing fence, a covered stand and changing rooms were all erected, although all have subsequently been replaced. The present main stand was built in 1953 and renovated in the late 1970s. That decade saw the next major redevelopment of the ground when the clubhouse and floodlights were opened and the ground was extensively terraced. The club progressed to the Isthmian League in 1984 and remained there until falling foul of ground-grading issues in 1996. The club accepted volun-tary relegation back to the Essex Senior League. In recent years the club have undertaken the task of levelling the noto-rious slope that had foxed visiting teams to Catons Lane for more than a century.

SALFORD CITY
GROUND: Moor Lane, Kersal, Salford, Greater Manchester
CURRENT CAPACITY: 8,000
RECORD ATTENDANCE: 3,000 v. Whickham (FA Vase) 1981
YEAR BUILT/OPENED: 1940s
CURRENT LEAGUE: North West Counties League Division One
CLUB FOUNDED: 1940 as Salford Central
PREVIOUS GROUNDS: Littleton Road; White City Stadium; The Crescent

Salford City are football's original poor relations, staging home games in front of a handful of spectators, while the hulking mass of the North Stand of Old Trafford, home of the world's richest football club, can be clearly seen from all parts of Salford's humble home. Close proximity is not the only common factor between the two clubs. City's former home of the

Catons Lane, Saffron Walden Town

Littleton Road Recreation Ground is still used by Manchester United's junior sides. Salford City moved to Moor Lane in 1979 after the ground had lain derelict and vandalized for three years. The venue has an interesting history, having been almost exclusively a rugby stadium. The ground was used for a long time for rugby union by the Manchester Rugby Club. The Moor Lane ground then 'switched codes' to rugby league as the amateur Langwithy club used the ground before folding in 1976. Before City moved in, the ground had sustained considerable vandalism. The main stand had its roof destroyed and the dressing room had been burned out. Salford gradually restored the ground, re-roofing the stand, erecting an additional area of cover and new changing rooms, and in 1989 they opened a new set of floodlights. The regeneration of Moor Lane is something the committee of Salford City can be rightly proud of.

SALISBURY CITY
GROUND: Raymond McEnhill Stadium, Partridge Way, Old Sarum, Salisbury, Wiltshire
CURRENT CAPACITY: 4,000
RECORD ATTENDANCE: 2,570 v. Hull City (FA Cup) 14/11/98
YEAR BUILT/OPENED: 1997
CURRENT LEAGUE: Dr Marten's (Southern) League Eastern Division
CLUB FOUNDED: 1947
PREVIOUS GROUNDS: Hudson Field (1947–48); Victoria Park (1948–97)

For 49 post-World War Two years, Salisbury City played at the pleasant, tranquil setting of Victoria Park. The old ground, which itself was set in a public park, was owned by the local council.

Moor Lane, Salford City

Although it had extensive cover, the club's future was best served by a move to a ground of their own. When City were taken over by ambitious new owner Raymond McEnhill, the old ground's fate was sealed. The club removed the floodlights and two covered stands, but the council-owned main stand, and the classic clapboard pavilion, itself a listed building, remained intact. It is a shame that this classic old venue, used for football since the turn of the twentieth century, has been left a pale shadow of its former self. In its heyday the record gate at Victoria Park was an impressive 8,902 against Weymouth in a Western League match in 1948. The club moved to the new stadium in the Old Sarum area of the Wiltshire town for the start of the 1997/98 season. The move was planned to be a launchpad to bring Conference football to Salisbury. Although the new stadium is truly impressive, with all the requisite facilities, the team have not obliged and at the end of the 2001/02 season, the club were relegated from the Dr Marten's League Premier Division.

SALTS (SALTAIRE)
GROUND: Salts Playing Fields, Hirst Lane, Shipley, West Yorkshire
CURRENT CAPACITY: 1,500
RECORD ATTENDANCE: Not Known
YEAR BUILT/OPENED: 1923
CURRENT LEAGUE: Mumtaz West Riding County Amateur League Division Two
CLUB FOUNDED: 1923
PREVIOUS GROUNDS: None

If you cast your mind back far enough, you may recall the 1970s TV series *Ripping Yarns*. One episode told the story of Golden Gordon and his fictitious Yorkshire Premier League side,

Salts Playing Fields, Salts

Barnstoneworth United. The club played at the 'Sewage Works Ground', which was the far-from-fictitious home of Salts (Saltaire) FC. Saltaire itself has an interesting history, being the textile worker's town purpose-built between 1851 and 1872 by industrial philanthropist Sir Titus Salt. The Salts Playing Fields host all manner of sports and are in a beautiful setting. On one side is the flowing water of the River Aire and on the opposite side lies the more sedate water of the Leeds and Liverpool canal. The football pitch originally had its own dressing room block and canteen, but these were demolished some years ago. Still remaining are the two identical covered terraces. Originally the far cover was distinguishable by having the team's name emblazoned on it, although recently the letters have been removed as the ground has become slightly dilapidated in the last few years. However the Hirst Lane is still a fascinating and historical venue.

SANDIACRE TOWN
GROUND: St Giles Park, Stanton Road, Sandiacre, Nottinghamshire
CURRENT CAPACITY: 2,000
RECORD ATTENDANCE: Not Known
YEAR BUILT/OPENED: 1978
CURRENT LEAGUE: Central Midland League Supreme Division
CLUB FOUNDED: 1978
PREVIOUS GROUNDS: Kilburn Weflare (1993–94)

A relatively recently formed club, Sandiacre Town began as a youth team in 1978. The club played at St Giles Park until the 1993/94 season was spent in enforced exile at Kilburn Welfare as the lack of covered accommodation and other facilities was addressed and their place in the

St Giles Park, Sandiacre Town

Central Midland League was secured. In March 1984 the club opened their impressive clubhouse and dressing room facility built over two years at a cost of £40,000. Around this time they strengthened their playing staff by merging with Lace Web United. The club returned to St Giles Park in time for the 1994/95 campaign having satisfied ground-grading criteria by installing a post and rail pitch surround, hard standing and the essential section of covered accommodation. Although the stand is a somewhat ugly construction with oddly angular end panels, the leafy location of this ground makes it a very appealing venue.

SCARBOROUGH
GROUND: McCain Stadium, Seamer Road, Scarborough, North Yorkshire
CURRENT CAPACITY: 5,900
RECORD ATTENDANCE: 11,162 v. Luton Town (FA Cup) 08/01/38
YEAR BUILT/OPENED: 1898
CURRENT LEAGUE: Nationwide Football Conference
CLUB FOUNDED: 1879 as Scarborough Cricketers FC
PREVIOUS GROUNDS: North Marine Ground (1879–87); Recreation Ground (1887–98)

Scarborough's 12-year stint in the Football League, which ended in 1999, saw the elderly Athletic Ground (its unsponsored name) brought up to date without doing any real damage to its character. The main stand was built in 1979 at a cost of £150,000 with a shallow terrace to either side. Opposite the main stand is a long covered terrace known as The Shed. This is the oldest remaining part of the ground having been opened in 1953. Floodlights came to Seamer Road as

McCain Stadium, Scarborough

recently as September 1970. The two end stands are the modern additions to the ground as the club needed to provide more seated accommodation. The Seamer Road end was opened first, in March 1995, and is a smart cantilevered stand with SFC picked out in white seats among red. It is cleverly constructed jutting forward to keep the roof line low in order to appease neighbours in the adjacent row of houses. Its partner at the East end of the ground opened a year later. It was a little sad that the town never really rallied to support the club in the Football League with gates rarely over 2,000, but with its surprisingly rural views to Falsgrave Moors, Seamer Road remains a very pleasant venue.

SEAHAM RED STAR
GROUND: Town Park, Stockton Road, Seaham, County Durham

CURRENT CAPACITY: 4,000
RECORD ATTENDANCE: 1,500 v. Sunderland (Floodlight Opener) 1979
YEAR BUILT/OPENED: 1930
CURRENT LEAGUE: Albany Northern League Division Two
CLUB FOUNDED: 1973
PREVIOUS GROUNDS: Deneside Recreation Ground; Vane Tempest Welfare Ground

Seaham Red Star switched from Sunday football in 1975 and three years later moved onto the disused and heavily vandalized Seaham Welfare Ground. This ground was built in 1930 and was home to two senior sides, Seaham Colliery Welfare and Seaham United. However, when the new club took over the ground they not only had to adopt the cumbersome title of Seaham Colliery Welfare Red Star but they faced a colossal amount of work to make the venue usable again. The enclosing fence was badly damaged, allowing local vandals easy access to the ground. The elderly pavilion had an interesting view of the sky, so holey was the roof, the pitch was hopelessly overgrown and the existing terracing had deteriorated into a dangerous state. The old pavilion was patched up but eventually renovated totally in 1982. It now boasts a lurid bright blue and red tiled roof. Floodlights had come three years earlier when the club entered and won a competition sponsored by Phillips in which the prize was a brand new set of lights! The rebuilding programme was completed in 1984 when the stand was opened having cost £18,000. The club reverted to Seaham Red Star when the old Welfare collapsed and the ground was bought by Seaham Town Council.

SHEPSHED DYNAMO
GROUND: The Dovecote, Butthole Lane, Shepshed, Leicestershire
CURRENT CAPACITY: 5,000
RECORD ATTENDANCE: 2,500 v. Leicester City (Friendly) 1996
YEAR BUILT/OPENED: 1899
CURRENT LEAGUE: Dr Marten's (Southern) League Western Division
CLUB FOUNDED: 1994 re-formation of Shepshed Albion in existence 1890-1994
PREVIOUS GROUNDS: Ashby Road (1890–97); Little Haw Lane (1897–1908)

Football in the Leicestershire town of Shepshed has been a complicated affair with a mixture of clubs disbanding and reforming on numerous occasions. The present side, Shepshed Dynamo, date from as recently as 1994 following the demise of Shepshed Albion. The one constant in the town's footballing heritage is the presence of the ground, known since 1899 as the Dovecote, in the unfortunately named Butthole Lane. The ground originally had a large hump in the middle and its levelling in 1909 caused the ground's closure for a prolonged spell. The coming and goings of the various outfits, coupled with ongoing lease problems with the landlords meant The Dovecote was relatively undeveloped until modern times. At the time the ground was being used by Shepshed Charterhouse and their eventual rise to the Southern League saw the arrival of the unusual grandstand, floodlights and the excellent clubhouse. Since Dynamo took over the venue the only real work undertaken has been the replacement of the enclosing perimeter wall. Hopefully Dynamo can bring a welcome spell of stability to this troubled venue.

SHEPTON MALLET
GROUND: West Shepton Playing Fields, Old Wells Road, West Shepton, Somerset
CURRENT CAPACITY: 2,000
RECORD ATTENDANCE: Not Known
YEAR BUILT/OPENED: 1956
CURRENT LEAGUE: Screwfix Direct Western League Division One
CLUB FOUNDED: 1986
PREVIOUS GROUNDS: Whitstone Park

Although less than 50 years old, West Shepton gives the impression of being much older. This is undoubtedly due to the fact that the ground's main stand is much older, having been relocated from Street FC's old Victoria Field ground in the late 1960s. The ground's unusual covered standings are converted lorry trailers acquired from a haulage company. The original club went bankrupt in

The Dovecote, Shepshed Dynamo

the mid-1980s and the newly formed club sensibly started life in the County League. It was great to see that this beautiful ground regained its Western League place in 2001, a league the original club had graced for many years.

SHIFNAL TOWN
GROUND: Phoenix Park, Coppice Green Lane, Shifnal, Shropshire
CURRENT CAPACITY: 3,000
RECORD ATTENDANCE: 1,002 v. Bridgnorth Town (FA Vase) 1984 at Admirals Park
YEAR BUILT/OPENED: 1992
CURRENT LEAGUE: Midland Alliance
CLUB FOUNDED: 1964 at St Andrews Youth Club
PREVIOUS GROUNDS: Admirals Park

The original Shifnal Town folded in 1936, so the Shropshire town had been with-

out senior representation for nearly 30 years. The current club started as a youth team called St Andrews in 1964 before joining the good standard Wellington League as Shifnal Juniors. Promotion to the Shopshire League in 1969 saw the change to the current name. The club played at various local pitches until the Bridgnorth District Council offered the club the site known as Admirals Park. The club developed the ground with dressing rooms and a stand but by 1985 the council had reclaimed the venue for a housing development. The club were reduced to park pitches until acquiring a site in Coppice Green Lane in 1988. However, Phoenix Park, was not finally completed until 1992 but is well worth the wait with a plush clubhouse and modern grandstand, floodlights and a top-quality playing surface. After a turbulent history, senior football in Shifnal could not be

West Shepton Playing Fields, Shepton Mallet

housed in a more appropriately named venue.

SHORTWOOD UNITED
GROUND: Meadowbank, Shortwood, Nailsworth, Gloucestershire
CURRENT CAPACITY: 5,000
RECORD ATTENDANCE: 1,000 v. Forest Green Rovers (FA Vase) 1982
YEAR BUILT/OPENED: 1972
CURRENT LEAGUE: Cherry Red Records Hellenic League Premier Division
CLUB FOUNDED: 1900
PREVIOUS GROUNDS: Table Land; Wallow Green Field

Shortwood United's Meadowbank ground is a marvellous feet of engineering born out of sheer hard work. The club had played on two nearby fields until work was started on the new site in 1972,

the club having acquired the site from Stroud District Council. The pitch was cut into the side of a hill and a considerable amount of earth was moved to achieve a remarkably flat playing surface. Within a few years the present wooden stand was opened and has an unusual raised centre fascia board section. Next, in 1984, the club opened their new clubhouse with a celebration match against Bristol Rovers. The most recent addition came in 1989 when floodlights came to Meadowbank. The club seem happy in the Hellenic League although, in truth, promotion would need an awful amount of work. In particular the unbelievably narrow approach lane would need widening. Shortwood's ground offers a panoramic view over Nailsworth and the floodlights of neighbours, Forest Green Rovers, can clearly be seen.

Phoenix Park, Shifnal Town

SITTINGBOURNE

GROUND: Central Ground, Eurolink, Sittingbourne, Kent
CURRENT CAPACITY: 8,000
RECORD ATTENDANCE: 5,951 v. Tottenham Hotspur (Friendly) 26/01/93
YEAR BUILT/OPENED: 1990
CURRENT LEAGUE: Dr Marten's (Southern) League Eastern Division
CLUB FOUNDED: 1881 as Sittingbourne United
PREVIOUS GROUNDS: Recreation Ground (1881–90); Gore Court Cricket Ground (1890–92); The Bull Ground (1892–1990)

There was much controversy over the 1990 sale of Sittingbourne's classic, and greatly revered, 98-year-old Bull Ground. Supporters and ground aficionados were opposed to the sale of the prime centre site, but the board countered by saying the £6.5 million that the sale realized, would see the club provided with a state-of-the-art stadium and with it the possibility of joining near neighbours Gillingham as Kentish representation in the Football League. However the move to Central Park has proved to be a millstone around the club's neck as building costs spiralled and playing standards were nowhere near as successful as the board had predicted. Nowadays, the average crowds of 500 or so look lost in a vast stadium and Football League status looks further away than ever. Central Park's vast emptiness represents a monument to overstated ambition and egotism. Sittingbourne's crippling financial worries resulted in the club opting to move to the lower pitch at Central Park. A temporary stand at the pitch allows the staging of Dr Marten's League games. The club will share the lower pitch with Kent

Meadowbank, Shortwood United

League outfit Maidstone United who started playing there in July 2001.

SKELMERSDALE UNITED
GROUND: White Moss Park, White Moss Road, Skelmersdale, Lancashire
CURRENT CAPACITY: 10,000
RECORD ATTENDANCE: 7,000 v. Slough Town (FA Amateur Cup) 1967
YEAR BUILT/OPENED: 1958
CURRENT LEAGUE: North West Counties League Division One
CLUB FOUNDED: 1882
PREVIOUS GROUNDS: Sandy Lane

Skelmersdale United played at Sandy Lane for many years until the site was needed for offices for the New Town Corporation. The club took over White Moss Park from the Skelmersdale Shoe Company in 1958 and during the 1960s and '70s the club enjoyed unprecedented success. They were Amateur Cup runners-up in 1967, before defeating Dagenham in the 1971 final. During these heady days, White Moss Park was developed to a high standard. The existing dressing rooms were replaced and the main stand was erected on the same side. There was steep banking around the ground and both ends originally had covered terrace, although these were condemned and demolished in the late 1970s. This period coincided with the club's decline in fortunes, which saw them slide down to the Lancashire Combination, although the slump in fortunes has been redressed with the club clawing their way back up to the North West Counties League. White Moss Park remains a sizeable venue, although only the main stand and open terraces survive.

Central Ground, Sittingbourne

SLOUGH TOWN

GROUND: Wexham Park, Wexham Road, Slough, Berkshire
CURRENT CAPACITY: 5,000
RECORD ATTENDANCE: 8,000 Slough Schools v. Liverpools Schools 1976
YEAR BUILT/OPENED: 1974
CURRENT LEAGUE: Ryman (Isthmian) League Division One (North)
CLUB FOUNDED: 1890 merger of Slough Albion and Young Men's Friendly Society
PREVIOUS GROUNDS: Dolphin Playing Fields; Chalvey Road; Maidenhead United FC; Slough Centre Stadium; Dolphin Stadium

Slough Town's history is a heady mix of mergers, wrangles and ground moves, which to catalogue in its entirety would merit a book itself. The club's ground of most longevity was the Dolphin Ground, used in two distinct periods, before World War One and after World War Two, until its untimely demise in 1974, an early victim of the dreaded supermarket blight. The club gladly accepted the offer of a patch of land to the north of the town and set about turning Wexham Park into a first-class football stadium. The commodious car park leads to an awesome, and very plush, clubhouse and office areas. This backs on to the main stand, with the remainder of the ground having ample covered terracing. However, the 2001/02 season ended with news that the lease at Wexham Park would not be renewed when it expires in 2003. The club are actively looking for new sites and are also looking at ground-sharing possibilities.

White Moss Park, Skelmersdale United

SNOWDOWN COLLIERY WELFARE

GROUND: Spinney Lane, Aylesham, Kent
CURRENT CAPACITY: 2,000
RECORD ATTENDANCE: 4,000 v.
Folkestone Town (Kent Cup Final) 1956
YEAR BUILT/OPENED: 1927
CURRENT LEAGUE: British Energy
Kent County League Division One East
CLUB FOUNDED: 1927
PREVIOUS GROUNDS: None

When you think of the coal-mining industry in England, the county of Kent – the Garden of England – does not readily spring to mind. However, the coalfields of East Kent provided some powerful sides during the 1950s including Colliery Welfare clubs at Snowdown and Betteshanger, and to a lesser extent similar clubs at Chislet and Tilmanstone Collieries. Snowdown played in the then-professional Kent League during its

heyday, winning the title in 1954/55, before joining the Aetolian League in 1959. The Welfare club had been set up in 1927, when many miners migrated from the North East and the Welsh valleys after one of the world's deepest coal pits was sunk. The Colliery was closed in 1987 and a year later the football club accepted voluntary relegation from the Kent League. The club then joined the Kent County League, but since the formation, in 1992, of that competition's Premier Division, Snowdown have stubbornly remained in Division One. The club have always played at Spinney Lane and in its prime the ground had a sizeable wooden stand and covered terrace. The old stand was dismantled in the wake of the Bradford fire disaster and the cover had long gone but the terracing and rudimentary seating made from railway sleepers remained. In 1996 the ground

Spinney Lane, Snowdown Colliery Welfare

was done up, with improvements to the changing rooms and a new cover was also erected over the old bench seating. Despite this modest renaissance, the clubs intended return to the county's premiere competition, the Kent Premier League, still seems some way off.

SOHAM TOWN RANGERS
GROUND: Julius Martin Lane, Soham, Cambridgeshire
CURRENT CAPACITY: 2,000
RECORD ATTENDANCE: 3,000 v. Pegasus (FA Amateur Cup) 1963
YEAR BUILT/OPENED: 1920
CURRENT LEAGUE: Jewson Eastern Counties League Premier Division
CLUB FOUNDED: 1947 merger of Soham Town (1920) and Soham Rangers (1919)
PREVIOUS GROUNDS: Soham Rangers: Brook Street (1919–47)

Julius Martin Lane has been home to Soham Town since 1920, some 27 years before their merger with local rivals, Soham Rangers. The present main stand was erected in 1989 and replaced an earlier wooden stand that had stood since the club acquired it from Abbey United (now Cambridge United) in 1949. The modern structure affords a nicely elevated view of the proceedings. The light-coloured brick of the stand matches the dressing rooms and the clubhouse extension. In 1993 the club went to town by erecting covered accommodation at both ends of the ground and a small area of cover was added to the same side as the main stand. There is further covered accommodation in the shape of a lean-to cover attached to the clubhouse. The undeveloped side opposite the main stand has a training pitch. Julius Martin Lane is now a thoroughly modern venue

Julius Martin Lane, Soham Town Rangers

with an excellent clubhouse and copious spectator accommodation. It is now one of the best venues in the Jewson Eastern Counties League.

SOLIHULL BOROUGH

GROUND: Damson Park, Damson Parkway, Solihull, West Midlands
CURRENT CAPACITY: 4,000
RECORD ATTENDANCE: 2,135 v. Darlington (FA Cup) 26/11/97 at Moor Green
YEAR BUILT/OPENED: 2000
CURRENT LEAGUE: Dr Marten's (Southern) League Western Division
CLUB FOUNDED: 1953 as Lincoln FC
PREVIOUS GROUNDS: Widney Stadium; Moor Green FC; Redditch United FC

When Solihull Borough sold their old Widney Lane ground in 1989 they surely could not have anticipated that it would be 11 years before they would play a home game back in the borough of Solihull. The club spent their exile playing at Moor Green and Redditch United while the club developed a modest ground at Tanworth Lane in Shirley. This was mainly used by the reserves but could not be developed to any great degree as it was a green-belt site. The club tendered an incredible 36 planning applications to Solihull Council for sites within the borough but all were turned down. Finally, in 1999 an area was identified that was occupied by a disused nightclub and an adjacent golf driving range. To the club's delight the proposals were accepted and work began on the new £2 million stadium. The old nightclub was converted into a clubhouse and offices as well as function and conference facilities.

The main stand is attached to the clubhouse and provides 220 seats and will eventually house executive boxes. The old driving range has been cleverly converted in a covered terrace behind the south goal. The two sides currently have flat hard standing, which will eventually be turned into covered terraces. After years of rejection, Damson Park is a just reward for dogged persistence.

SOUTHEND MANOR
GROUND: Southchurch Park Arena, Lifstan Way, Southend-on-Sea, Essex
CURRENT CAPACITY: 2,000
RECORD ATTENDANCE: 1,521 v. Southend United (Floodlight Opener) 22/07/91
YEAR BUILT/OPENED: 1950s
CURRENT LEAGUE: Foresters Essex Senior League
CLUB FOUNDED: 1955
PREVIOUS GROUNDS: Oakwood Recreation Ground; Victory Sports Ground

Southend Manor were formed in 1955 as an offshoot of the respected Eton Manor club. They played local football for many years in the Southend Borough Combination and Southend and District Alliance, using council grounds at the Oakwood Recreation Ground and the Victory Sports Ground. In 1985 the club were elected, as an intermediate club, to the Essex Senior League Division One, which mainly contained reserve teams. Their election coincided with the council granting use of the Southchurch Park Arena, home for many years of Southend Athletics Club. The ground is equipped with a smart barrelled roof, something of a trademark in Essex as Southend United have two and Chelmsford's old ground

also sported one. The stand has benefited considerably since it was reclad in 1998. The impressive clubhouse was built behind the main stand and the club were granted senior status in 1988. The only real developments since then have been the erection of a gatehouse and a rather ugly mesh player's tunnel. The club's long-time cohabiters, Southend Athletics Club, folded in 1999 and the athletics track has been grassed over to give the impression of slightly less distance from the pitch to the stand.

SOUTHPORT
GROUND: Haig Avenue, Southport, Merseyside
CURRENT CAPACITY: 6,000
RECORD ATTENDANCE: 20,010 v. Newcastle United (FA Cup) 12/01/32
YEAR BUILT/OPENED: 1905
CURRENT LEAGUE: Nationwide Football Conference
CLUB FOUNDED: 1881 as Southport Central
PREVIOUS GROUNDS: Ash Lane (1881–1905)

Southport's Haig Avenue ground has been almost completely transformed since their Football League days, which ended in 1978, when they lost a re-election battle to Wigan Athletic. Only the 1967 grandstand remains, itself replacing the old stand, which had been badly damaged by a devastating fire. By the early 1990s the rest of the Haig Avenue ground had degenerated into a considerably dilapidated state. In 1993 the condemned covers and crumbling terraces were demolished and the club used money generated from a share issue to completely modernize the old ground. The ground now has smart

Southchurch Park Arena, Southend Manor

areas of elevated covered terrace that complement the existing grandstand. The floodlights and spectator facilities were also upgraded at a total cost of £350,000. The investment allowed the Sandgrounders promotion to the Conference for the 1993/94 season and they are now in a position, on and off the field, to attempt a return to the Football League, which they graced for some 57 years.

SOUTH SHIELDS
GROUND: Filtrona Park, Shaftesbury Avenue, Jarrow, Tyne & Wear
CURRENT CAPACITY: 2,500
RECORD ATTENDANCE: 1,500 v. Spennymoor (Durham Cup) 1995
YEAR BUILT/OPENED: 1992
CURRENT LEAGUE: Albany Northern League Division Two

CLUB FOUNDED: 1974
PREVIOUS GROUNDS: Jack Clarke Park (1974–92)

A modern incarnation of an old name, this version of South Shields was formed in 1974. The original South Shields club folded in 1902 but their successors enjoyed a lengthy spell in the Football League from 1919, playing at Horsley Hill, which once held 24,000 people. The club were merged into the Gateshead club in 1930 and the South Shields name lay dormant for six years until a new club emerged, also playing at Horsley Hill. The old ground was unusable after military use during World War Two and in December 1949 the club moved to a magnificent new ground at Simonside Hall, in the grounds of an eighteenth-century manor house. The new ground held

18,000 and remained home until the club expressed a wish to return the old Horsley Hill ground to football use in the late 1960s. However, in 1972 Simonside Hall was sold to a property developer and South Shields were left homeless. A fruitless search for a new ground ended with the club controversially moving once again to Gateshead, keeping their place in the Northern Premier League, but changing their name to Gateshead United. The latest South Shields club played on a council pitch until a long search for a ground ended with a site being found in Jarrow. Some £400,000 has been spent on the 4.7-acre site, providing a splendid clubhouse and grandstand. The ground has plenty of scope for expansion, but after a torrid history perhaps a period of stability in the Northern League is in the Mariners' best interests.

SPALDING UNITED
GROUND: Sir Halley Stewart Playing Fields, Winfrey Avenue, Spalding, Lincolnshire
CURRENT CAPACITY: 7,000
RECORD ATTENDANCE: 6,972 v. Peterborough United (FA Cup) 11/10/52
YEAR BUILT/OPENED: 1921
CURRENT LEAGUE: Dr Marten's (Southern) League Eastern Division
CLUB FOUNDED: 1921
PREVIOUS GROUNDS: None

Spalding United emerged from the ashes of the defunct Spalding Thursdays club in 1921. They played at the current ground, although it was then known as the Black Swan Field, being behind the hostelry of the same name. The ground went into council ownership in the 1930s – indeed the ugly-looking Town Hall is just behind the ground. In fairness the council main-

Filtrona Park, South Shields

Sir Halley Stewart Playing Fields, Spalding United

tain the ground well and it is impeccably kept. The ground was given to the club on a permanent basis in 1954, having been named in recognition of an esteemed local MP, Sir Halley Stewart. The main stand is a sturdy brick-built structure, with a smart double wooden centre staircase being an attractive feature. Behind one goal is a large covered area of flat standing, partially fenced off for storage purposes. The opposite end has the 'Tulips 2000' social club, which has a brick-built extension to a portakabin clubhouse.

SPENNYMOOR UNITED
GROUND: Brewery Field, Durham Road, Spennymoor, County Durham
CURRENT CAPACITY: 7,500
RECORD ATTENDANCE: 7,202 v. Bishop Auckland (Durham Cup) 03/03/57

YEAR BUILT/OPENED: 1904
CURRENT LEAGUE: Unibond (Northern Premier) League Division One
CLUB FOUNDED: 1904 merger of Spennymoor Town and Weardale Ironopolis
PREVIOUS GROUNDS: Wood Vue

The Brewery Field ground had been in use for rugby by Tudhoe Rugby Club for several years until a merger of the two senior town football clubs occurred in 1904 and the lease for the Brewery Field was secured. For many years the ground's only covered accommodation was a small wooden enclosure. However, in 1932 the club secured the purchase of the splendid wooden stand from Catterick Racecourse for the considerable sum of £300. The old stand gave magnificent service until its ageing timber construction

Brewery Field, Spennymoor United

fell foul of the Safety of Sports Grounds Act, passed in the wake of the Bradford City fire disaster. This was joined in the post-war years by a huge covered terrace opposite, known as the Cow Shed, which was funded by the supporters club. This too was demolished in the mid-1980s to make way for the new grandstand. The Racecourse stand was removed and reduced to an area of hard standing. The rest of the ground was extensively terraced in the 1950s and in more recent years a large covered terrace has been erected at one end. Although many miss the classic old stands, the Brewery Field has undoubtedly seen a carefully and thoughtfully planned renaissance.

ST ALBANS CITY
GROUND: Clarence Park, York Road, St Albans, Hertfordshire

CURRENT CAPACITY: 6,000
RECORD ATTENDANCE: 9,757 v. Ferryhill Athletic (FA Amateur Cup) 27/02/26
YEAR BUILT/OPENED: 1894
CURRENT LEAGUE: Ryman (Isthmian) League Premier Division
CLUB FOUNDED: 1908
PREVIOUS GROUNDS: None

Clarence Park is a truly classic sporting arena, also catering for cricket and hockey. It faces an uncertain future as their resident club, St Albans City, has spent most of 2002 battling impending bankruptcy. Originally the recreation ground was donated to the city in 1894 for sporting activity. It had a cricket square and cycling track and the first football pitch was laid out on the cricket outfield and was used for several years by

Clarence Park, St Albans City

Old Albanians FC. St Albans City were formed in the summer of 1908 and purchased a set of goalposts from the defunct St Albans Abbey club. Eventually the ground was enclosed and the impressive pitch-length main stand was erected in 1922 at the considerable cost of £1,400. The remainder of the ground was steeply banked and had railway sleepers for terracing. The ground has remained unchanged since the six year period between 1958 and 1964 that saw the modern concrete terrace laid all around the stadium. This included a substantial covered section on the opposite side of the main stand. Floodlights also went up during this hectic period. The ground's most famous feature, sadly, is no longer with us. Out of the York Street terrace protruded an ancient Oak tree, which had a preservation order placed on it. The order prevented the club's promotion to the Conference in 1993.

However, in 1999 the old tree had become severely diseased, some say in suspicious circumstances, and was pulled down. Strangely since the removal of the tree, the clubs fortunes have waned considerably and tremendous financial hardship has been endured. It should be hoped that this glorious venue will somehow be secured for the enjoyment of future generations.

ST AUSTELL
GROUND: Poltair Park, Poltair Road, St Austell, Cornwall
CURRENT CAPACITY: 8,000
RECORD ATTENDANCE: 15,000 v. Penzance (Cornwall Senior Cup Final) 1949
YEAR BUILT/OPENED: c1934
CURRENT LEAGUE: Carlsberg South-Western League
CLUB FOUNDED: 1890
PREVIOUS GROUNDS: Rocky Park

Poltair Park, St Austell

St Austell's spectacular stand is certainly unusual and now has that weather-beaten patina that only comes with advancing age. The vast pitched roof extends down so far and, coupled with the double staircase, it leaves the viewing area somewhat restricted. From the outside it looks dark and foreboding but once inside it's surprisingly capacious. The rest of the ground has extensive grass banking and it comes as no surprise that 15,000 people were once accommodated for a match at Poltair Park. This was the largest gathering for any match ever staged in Cornwall. Despite some newer touches such as a 1980s clubhouse, Poltair Park is essentially untouched from the day it was opened.

ST LEONARDS
GROUND: The Firs, Elphinstone Road, Hastings, East Sussex

CURRENT CAPACITY: 3,768
RECORD ATTENDANCE: 1,798 v. Tiverton Town (FA Vase) 15/01/95
YEAR BUILT/OPENED: 1920
CURRENT LEAGUE: Dr Marten's (Southern) League Eastern Division
CLUB FOUNDED: 1971 as Stamco FC
PREVIOUS GROUNDS: Council pitches (1971–73); Pannel Lane (1973–93)

The 'upper pitch' at Elphinstone Road was opened in 1920 when the Rock-A-Nore club were the first tenants. This club merged with Hastings All Saints to become Hastings and St Leonards. In 1976 this club eventually became Hastings Town who now play at the adjacent Pilot Field ground. Town left for the lower ground in 1985 and The Firs remained relatively unused until the works side Stamco (Sussex Turnery and Moulding Company) took over the ground in 1993 on their elevation to senior football in the Sussex County League. The club enjoyed major success that culminated in promotion to the Southern League in 1996. The club had to change their name to St Leonards Stamcroft as works teams are not allowed in the Southern League. The club's rise in status was in part due to the brief involvement at the club of Mark Gardiner, a local man who was one of the first big winners of the National Lottery. The Firs has been greatly improved in recent times and now boasts considerable covered accommodation. This has been no mean feat of building work as The Firs has undulating banking all around the ground. However, to have two senior clubs in such close proximity to each other is most unusual, and provides the most local of local derbies.

STAFFORD RANGERS
GROUND: Marston Road, Stafford, Staffordshire
CURRENT CAPACITY: 3,000
RECORD ATTENDANCE: 8,536 v. Rotherham United (FA Cup) 04/01/75
YEAR BUILT/OPENED: 1896
CURRENT LEAGUE: Dr Marten's (Southern) League Premier Division
CLUB FOUNDED: 1876
PREVIOUS GROUNDS: Lammascotes; Stone Road; Newtown

Yet another late Victorian ground that has now passed its centenary. The modern version of the ground took shape in the 1970s when the old grandstand was replaced by the Bass Stand on the Marston Road side of the ground. The superbly elevated cantilever-roofed stand was opened in time for the 1975/76 season. A new dressing room complex

followed in 1977. The floodlights date from 1969, when Port Vale did the inauguration honours. The oldest part of the ground is the covered terrace opposite the main stand, which is believed to be the original stand from 1920, although it has been renovated several times since. The two ends of the ground are somewhat shallow uncovered terraces.

STAINES TOWN
GROUND: Wheatsheaf Park, Wheatsheaf Lane, Staines, Middlesex
CURRENT CAPACITY: 2,500
RECORD ATTENDANCE: 2,750 v. Banco Di Roma (Barassi Cup) 1975
YEAR BUILT/OPENED: 1951
CURRENT LEAGUE: Ryman (Isthmian) League Division One (South)
CLUB FOUNDED: 1892
PREVIOUS GROUNDS: The Lammas; Shortwood Common; Mill Mead; Shepperton Road; Chertsey Town FC

Football in Staines has an interesting history, with the coming and going of such clubs as Staines Lammas, Staines Lagonda, Staines Projectile and Staines Linoleum. The present club can trace its history back to 1892 when Staines Albion briefly hit the scene before disbanding then re-emerging after being strengthened following a merger with the St Peters club. The club played on a variety of grounds and under a variety of guises, including Staines Vale, until moving into Wheatsheaf Park in 1951. It was the answer to their prayers as, after leaving Mill Mead in 1935, games were either staged away from home or at an unsatisfactory venue in Shepperton Road, Lalham. In a remarkable reversal of the normal procedure a proposed housing development made way for the construction of the new ground! Geological studies revealed that deep foundations needed for the houses could not be built and therefore a modest-sized football ground was just the ticket. The main stand was built in 1961 and was totally refurbished in 1997. The cover behind the goal was taken down in 1981 when the land it used was sold off. However, despite its relatively young age, Wheatsheaf Park needed a substantial overhaul to remain within the ground-grading criteria for the Isthmian League and the club were forced to spend two years at Chertsey Town before returning to their newly modernized home for the 1998/99 campaign.

STALYBRIDGE CELTIC
GROUND: Bower Fold, Mottram Road, Stalybridge, Cheshire
CURRENT CAPACITY: 6,150
RECORD ATTENDANCE: 9,753 v. West Bromwich Albion (FA Cup) 13/01/23
YEAR BUILT/OPENED: 1909
CURRENT LEAGUE: Unibond (Northern Premier League) Premier Division
CLUB FOUNDED: 1906
PREVIOUS GROUNDS: None

It is a somewhat overlooked fact that Stalybridge Celtic spent a brief two-season spell in the Football League during the first two campaigns of Division Three North in 1921/22 and 1922/23. However, they failed to attract the desired crowds and resigned in May 1923. Celtic joined the Cheshire League, a competition in which they had quite a spectacular lack of success until the Championship was won in 1979/80. This was a catalyst for a rise in status that culminated in promotion to the Conference in 1992. However, the 2001/02 season ended in relegation back to the Northern Premier League after just one season back in the top flight after their first stint ended in 1998. Even though their spell in the Football League was nearly 80 years ago Celtic, like Gainsborough and Ashington, remain at their original Football League ground. Indeed the Bower Fold has been in use since the club's first competitive match in September 1909, the team having only previously played friendlies against local teams on mainly neutral venues. The ground lies in a surprisingly rural area and the splendid wooden grandstand from the Football League days stood until replaced in September 1996 by the modern cantilevered roof structure, built at a cost of £270,000, much of which came from grants. The rest of the ground is modern terracing, with large covers at one end and on the side opposite the new stand. The far end has a sizeable uncovered terrace.

STAMFORD
GROUND: Kettering Road, Stamford, Lincolnshire
CURRENT CAPACITY: 5,000
RECORD ATTENDANCE: 4,200 v. Kettering Town (FA Cup) 24/10/53
YEAR BUILT/OPENED: 1896
CURRENT LEAGUE: Dr Marten's (Southern) League Eastern Division
CLUB FOUNDED: 1896
PREVIOUS GROUNDS: None

Stamford have always played at the Wothorpe Road ground. However, when the entrance was recently changed, the renaming of the ground to the more correct Kettering Road suddenly caught people unaware and some thought the club had knocked up a new venue without anyone knowing! Pleasingly, however,

Bower Fold, Stalybridge Celtic

despite elevation to the Dr Marten's League in 1998, the club have kept hold of their delightfully old-fashioned ground. The old wooden main stand, the original dating from the clubs' earliest years, has stood the test of time and was extended in the mid-1970s with the club doing well to preserve its essential character. The dressing rooms are also the original buildings. Opposite the dear old stand is an area of covered terrace that originally ran the entire length of the pitch, although safety concerns saw it halved in length. Development on this side has always been hampered by the presence of the adjacent railway line. The most recent developments were the clubhouse, in 1975, and floodlights six years later. Interestingly the pylons are painted to blend in with the sand-coloured Georgian buildings so

prevalent in this historic market town. The club's nickname, The Daniels, stems from the town's fame as home at one time, to England's fattest man, Daniel Lambert.

STANLEY UNITED
GROUND: Hill Top Ground, High Road, Stanley, County Durham
CURRENT CAPACITY: 3,000
RECORD ATTENDANCE: 5,000 v. Leytonstone (FA Amateur Cup) 1920
YEAR BUILT/OPENED: 1919
CURRENT LEAGUE: Wearside League
CLUB FOUNDED: 1890 merger of Stanley Nops and Stanley Albion
PREVIOUS GROUNDS: Various pitches

The home of Stanley United has been nicknamed the Hill Top ground, which is something of an understatement as a drive

Kettering Road, Stamford

to the ground involves a climb through the Stockley Fells to the small mining village of Stanley that sits high above the Durham town of Crook. The two sides were bitter rivals in the 1930s and, indeed, Stanley lost their Northern League place to Crook in 1936. However, the club were re-elected to that prestigious competition in 1945. They remained in the Northern League until the end of 1973/74 when they resigned due to a lack of volunteers to run the club. They dropped down to the Durham City and District League before moving to the Wearside League. The High Road ground has been home since the end of World War One and is a remarkably atmospheric ground. On the far side is a large covered stand that provides very welcome refuge from biting winds. The ground's most well-known feature is on the opposite side where, within the ground itself, there is an old two-up, two-down house. This provides changing facilities and upstairs is the tea bar with amazingly wonky floorboards. The Hill Top ground remains a beguiling 'must-do' venue.

STEVENAGE BOROUGH
GROUND: Broadhall Way, Stevenage, Hertfordshire
CURRENT CAPACITY: 6,546
RECORD ATTENDANCE: 8,040 v. Newcastle United (FA Cup) 24/01/98
YEAR BUILT/OPENED: 1961
CURRENT LEAGUE: Nationwide Football Conference
CLUB FOUNDED: 1976
PREVIOUS GROUNDS: King George V Playing Field (1976–80)

Hill Top Ground, Stanley United

The Stadium in Broadhall Way has had a chequered history since its opening in 1961. The first tenants at the ground were Stevenage Town who moved from their London Road ground, bringing the covered terrace with them. This stand is still in use, although several miles away at Dunstable's Creasey Park. The area of Broadhall Way was farmland but, as the New Town expanded, it was soon surrounded by housing. The first main stand was opened in 1964 and stood until replaced by a more modern stand in 1994. This stand itself was extended to cover the entire pitch length in 1998. Stevenage Town collapsed with massive debts in 1968 and were replaced at Broadhall Way by Stevenage Athletic. Sadly Athletic's tenure was even shorter and they disbanded in 1976. Stevenage

Borough were formed in 1978 and took over the near-derelict ground. The club rose to the Conference in 1994 and have developed Broadhall Way into a fantastically modern arena, with the South Stand being the most recent addition, opened in 2001. Sadly for the club, they missed out on the chance of promotion to the Football League in 1996 when they failed to complete building work in the time stipulated by League inspectors. Torquay United retained their League status by this most dubious of technicalities.

STOCKSBRIDGE PARK STEELS
GROUND: Bracken Moor Lane, Stocksbridge, Sheffield, South Yorkshire
CURRENT CAPACITY: 3,500
RECORD ATTENDANCE: 2,000 v. Sheffield Wednesday (Floodlight

Broadhall Way, Stevenage Borough

Opener) 1991
YEAR BUILT/OPENED: 1900s
CURRENT LEAGUE: Unibond (Northern Premier) League Division One
CLUB FOUNDED: 1986 merger of Stocksbridge Works and Oxley Park
PREVIOUS GROUNDS: Stonemoor (1949–51 & 1952–53)

Of all the three-sided grounds still in use at a high level, Bracken Moor is arguably the best. Situated high above Sheffield, the football club share one side of the pitch with Stocksbridge Works Cricket Club. Until 1950, the whole ground had a steep slope, but with considerable effort, the pitches were levelled and the earth removed created banking around the ground. The excellent stand and adjacent dressing rooms were cut into the

banking when erected during the summer of 1964. Floodlights came in 1990 and the Bracken Moor Lane end was covered. Promotion was finally secured in 1996, having been denied two years earlier when improvements had not been completed. Just how long three-sided grounds such as Stocksbridge and Matlock remain in the Northern Premier League is open to question, but to all intents and purposes there is absolutely nothing wrong with them.

STONEHOUSE FREEWAY
GROUND: Oldends Lane, Stonehouse, Gloucestershire
CURRENT CAPACITY: 1,500
RECORD ATTENDANCE: 5,500 v. Gloucester City (FA Cup) 29/09/51
YEAR BUILT/OPENED: 1949

CURRENT LEAGUE: Gloucestershire Northern Senior League Division Two
CLUB FOUNDED: 1919 as Stonehouse FC
PREVIOUS GROUNDS: Various fields

Of the many glorious grounds in Gloucestershire, Oldends Lane remains my personal favourite. It positively reeks of atmosphere and cries out for a large crowd to gather. A large crowd did gather in September 1951, when 5,500 packed in to Oldends Lane, then two years old, as the FA Cup brought Gloucester City to Stonehouse. The ground is essentially the same now, except for a few coats of paint, as it was when it was opened by Wolves and England captain Billy Wright in August 1949. The ground has a magnificent seated stand on one side and a large covered stand on top of a grass bank at the car-park end of the ground. The club enjoyed some heady days in the Somerset Senior League, but fell into decline due to loss of revenue incurred when the clubhouse was sold off. Some would say the ground is past its best, but to me it is a splendid reminder of how village football used to be.

STOURBRIDGE
GROUND: War Memorial Athletic Ground, High Street, Amblecote, West Midlands
CURRENT CAPACITY: 2,000
RECORD ATTENDANCE: 5,726 v. Cardiff City (Welsh Cup) 1974
YEAR BUILT/OPENED: 1888
CURRENT LEAGUE: Midland Alliance
CLUB FOUNDED: 1876
PREVIOUS GROUNDS: Various fields

During the 2001/02 season, Stourbridge announced their relocation for first-team matches to the Dell Stadium, former home of Brierley Hill Town. However, after a late change of heart, their 114-year-old ground at Amblecote will remain home for the time being. The problem with the War Memorial Athletic Ground is that it shares one side with the cricket club and has never been able to reach an agreement to lay the mandatory hard standing down the shared boundary. It is a great shame because the old ground is most unusual, but has suffered from the loss in 1990 of the old High-Street-end wooden stand during its centenary year. At the opposite end of the ground is a large cavernous covered terrace that has stood since before World War Two. At the same time the unusually roofed seated main stand was also built, but was joined after the war by its less aesthetically pleasing wing extensions. The most recent developments at the ground came in the 1960s when floodlights, as well as a new clubhouse and changing rooms, were provided. The club still harbour thoughts of a return to the Dr Marten's League so the Amblecote ground should be visited soon before it disappears altogether from the non-League circuit.

STOURPORT SWIFTS
GROUND: Walshes Meadow, Harold Davis Drive, Stourport-on-Severn, Worcestershire
CURRENT CAPACITY: 2,000
RECORD ATTENDANCE: 4,000 v. Birmingham City (Charity Match)
YEAR BUILT/OPENED: 1946
CURRENT LEAGUE: Dr Marten's (Southern) League Western Division
CLUB FOUNDED: 1882
PREVIOUS GROUNDS: Bewdley Road; Moor Hall Park; Feathers Farm; Olive Grove; The Hawthorns

Oldends Lane, Stonehouse Freeway

Walshes Meadow is a very attractive ground on the banks of the River Stour and has been home to Stourport Swifts since the war. It ended a lengthy period of nomadism since their formation in 1882. The rickety old wooden stand, which had been opened against Aston Villa in 1950, has been replaced by a modern plastic-seated stand. This new facility allowed the club promotion to the Dr Marten's League when they won the Midland Alliance Championship in the 2000/01 season. The clubhouse was opened in 1972, although extended 11 years later. The ground's proximity to the river has always been a worry although, surprisingly, the last flood at Walshes Meadow was as long ago as 1949. It remains a very rural venue and development will be limited due to the affluent housing that overlooks the ground.

STREET
GROUND: Tannery Field, Middlebrooks, Street, Somerset
CURRENT CAPACITY: 2,000
RECORD ATTENDANCE: 4,300 v. Yeovil (FA Cup) 17/11/47 at Victoria Field
YEAR BUILT/OPENED: 1975
CURRENT LEAGUE: Screwfix Direct Western League Division One
CLUB FOUNDED: 1880
PREVIOUS GROUNDS: Victoria Field (1900–69); The Turnpike Ground (1969–75)

Many observers were pleased when Street regained their place in the Western League in 1997 after an absence of 31 years. They have had a hard time since losing their ancient Victoria Field home in 1969. They relocated to The Turnpike Ground, only to lose that ground six

Tannery Field, Street

years later when it was swallowed up in the building of the town's bypass. The council offered to lease the club an undeveloped playing field they had been given by the Co-op Tannery. The club moved to the Tannery Field and bought the small concrete and corrugated iron cover with them from The Turnpike Ground. The club have upgraded the ground ever since and actually have a lot of space to develop further, despite being enclosed on all sides by housing. A nice little historical touch sees one of the old stands at their much-missed Victoria Field ground still doing a sterling job of keeping spectators dry at the ground of Shepton Mallet.

AFC SUDBURY
GROUND: Brundon Lane, Sudbury, Suffolk

CURRENT CAPACITY: 3,000
RECORD ATTENDANCE: 1,342 v. Tiptree United (FA Vase) 23/03/02
YEAR BUILT/OPENED: 1976
CURRENT LEAGUE: Jewson Eastern Counties League Premier Division
CLUB FOUNDED: 1999 merger of Sudbury Town (1885); Sudbury Wanderers (1958)
PREVIOUS GROUNDS: Town: Friars Street; Priory Stadium. Wanderers: People's Park

Sudbury United were always the senior side in this pleasant border town but in 1999 huge debts saw them lose their pretty home at Priory Lane. The stadium was to be sold for housing although ironically developers have struggled to obtain planning consent and the old ground remains intact. The root of Town's financial troubles was put down to debts accrued in hefty travelling expenses during their spell in the Southern League between 1991 and 1997. In June 1999 the town's two sides, who were both now competing at the same level in the Eastern Counties League, decided to pool resources and use Sudbury Wanderers' well appointed Brundon Lane ground. There is a smart main stand, erected in 1993, as well as two identical areas of wooden cover on the opposite side of the pitch. The most recent improvement saw a large area of covered accommodation built at the car-park end. The club look to have a bright future with the burden of debts a distant memory.

SUTTON COLDFIELD TOWN
GROUND: Central Ground, Coles Lane, Sutton Coldfield, West Midlands
CURRENT CAPACITY: 4,500
RECORD ATTENDANCE: 2,029 v. Doncaster Rovers (FA Cup) 22/11/80
YEAR BUILT/OPENED: 1920
CURRENT LEAGUE: Dr Marten's (Southern) League Western Division
CLUB FOUNDED: 1897 as Sutton Coldfield
PREVIOUS GROUNDS: Meadow Plat (1879–89); Coles Lane (1890–1919)

Coles Lane has been home to Sutton Coldfield Town since 1920 although, in truth, their previous ground was just a bit further along the same road. Originally the ground had a wooden grandstand, but this was lost when a fire caused by a stray firework in October 1955 destroyed the structure. The present grandstand was something of a quick fix at the time and was a bank of seating, with a roof, attached to the existing changing rooms. It gives a marvellously elevated view, if

slightly off-centre from the halfway line. There is a lengthy section of covered terrace on the opposite side and shallow terracing all around the ground that replaced some shale banking. The magnificent clubhouse was officially opened in 1973. Recently the club announced plans to replace the main stand with a more modern structure, although planning restraints will only allow a building of the same size to be erected. Perhaps the club will stick with what they have got as it is a most unusual grandstand.

SUTTON UNITED
GROUND: Borough Sports Ground, Gander Green Lane, Sutton, Surrey
CURRENT CAPACITY: 7,000
RECORD ATTENDANCE: 14,000 v. Leeds United (FA Cup) 24/01/70
YEAR BUILT/OPENED: 1912
CURRENT LEAGUE: Ryman (Isthmian) League Premier Division
CLUB FOUNDED: 1898 merger of Sutton Association and Sutton Guild Rovers
PREVIOUS GROUNDS: Western Road; Manor Lane; London Road; The Find

The ground was opened in 1912 as the Adult School Sports Ground and did not become Sutton United's home until 1919. The dark, forbidding grandstand, which is surprisingly capacious, was built in 1953, but suffers from the presence of a view-blocking floodlight pylon. Around the same time the co-tenant athletic club moved out, enabling new terracing to be laid nearer the pitch over the now-disused running track. The covered terrace opposite the main stand was built in 1986 in time for the club's promotion to the Conference. Both ends have modern terracing. Although Gander Green Lane

Brundon Lane, AFC Sudbury

remains a sizeable venue, with a healthy 7,000 capacity, the days of a 14,000 gate for a Cup tie against Leeds seem a lifetime ago.

SWINDON SUPERMARINE

GROUND: Hunts Copse, Highworth Road, South Marston, Swindon, Wiltshire

CURRENT CAPACITY: 3,000

RECORD ATTENDANCE: 498 v. Highworth Town 2000

YEAR BUILT/OPENED: 1966

CURRENT LEAGUE: Dr Marten's (Southern) League Western Division

CLUB FOUNDED: 1992 merger of Supermarine (1946) and Swindon Athletic (1970)

PREVIOUS GROUNDS: Supermarine: Vickers Airfield. Swindon: Merton Park; Southbrook

By Dr Marten's League standards, Hunts Copse is a modest ground but has been home to Supermarine, or Vickers FC as they originally were, since 1966. A large sporting complex, the team at first played on a different pitch although the present site was fenced off as the club rose to the Hellenic League from the Wiltshire League. The modest little stand was also moved down to the new pitch. Success in the Hellenic League during the mid-1990s saw floodlights and a clubhouse erected and when the club won their second Hellenic League title in 2000/01, the Dr Marten's League beckoned. Promotion was sealed when £40,000 was spent on the provision of a new 300-seater stand plus one or two other minor improvements. Despite their rise in status, Hunts Copse remains a pleasantly rural venue.

Central Ground, Sutton Coldfield Town

T

TADCASTER ALBION

GROUND: The Park, Ings Lane, Tadcaster, North Yorkshire
CURRENT CAPACITY: 1,500
RECORD ATTENDANCE: 1,200 v. Winterton Rangers (FA Vase) 1978
YEAR BUILT/OPENED: 1936
CURRENT LEAGUE: Northern Counties East League Division One
CLUB FOUNDED: 1936
PREVIOUS GROUNDS: None

The club play in the shadow of the famous John Smith's brewery in Ings Lane and are unsurprisingly nicknamed 'The Brewers'. The ground has all the requisite features, floodlights, clubhouse and a smart covered stand that looks tiny hiding under the vast brewery. Albion have attempted to give their stand a bit of individuality by alternately painting each roof support in the club's red and blue colours. The club have been in the Northern Counties East League since regaining their position in that competition in 1991. However promotion to the Premier Division will only come about when seating is provided at Ings Lane, a task the committee plan to rectify in the near future. The club have, however, come a long way since their early days in the Harrogate and District League.

TAMWORTH

GROUND: The Lamb Ground, Kettlebrook, Tamworth, Staffordshire
CURRENT CAPACITY: 3,410

Ings Lane, Tadcaster Albion

RECORD ATTENDANCE: 4,920 v.
Atherstone Town (Birmingham League)
1948
YEAR BUILT/OPENED: 1934
CURRENT LEAGUE: Dr Marten's
(Southern) League Premier Division
CLUB FOUNDED: 1933
PREVIOUS GROUNDS: Jolly Sailor
Ground (1933–34)

The present Tamworth club were formed
relatively recently in 1933 and have
always played at The Lamb Ground save
for their inaugural season spent at a field
behind the Jolly Sailor public house. The
Lamb Ground was a fairly rural location
at the time, and although much expansion and road building have gone on in
the intervening years, the Kettlebrook
venue has a surprising amount of room

for possible future expansion. The club
have modernized their home in recent
years and the sleek, modern main stand
on the car-park side replaced an older
wooden stand built before World War
Two. The clubhouse was extended in
1993 and incorporated new changing-
room facilities. The old covered terrace,
the oldest structure on the ground, has
also been re-roofed in recent years. The
floodlights came from Scarborough's
Seamer Road ground and have given sterling service. The Lamb Ground has been
gradually modernized into a fine venue.

TAUNTON TOWN
GROUND: Wordsworth Drive, Taunton,
Somerset
CURRENT CAPACITY: 4,000
RECORD ATTENDANCE: 2,960 v.

The Lamb Ground, Tamworth

Torquay United Reserves (League) 1958
YEAR BUILT/OPENED: 1955
CURRENT LEAGUE: Dr Marten's
(Southern) League Western Division
CLUB FOUNDED: 1947
PREVIOUS GROUNDS: Mountfields;
Ash Meadow; Rose Meadows; Victoria
Park; Denman's Park

Another ground that appears to be older
than it actually is. The club was re-
formed in 1947 and played on several
grounds before setting up home at
Wordsworth Drive. The covered terrace
on the Main Road side of the ground is
fairly modern, replacing the original
structure, and the terrace, which is now
in a poor state of repair also once had a
cover on it. The small but comfortable
main stand was only erected in 1960.
After dominating the Western League

since Tiverton's departure, Taunton have
followed their long time rivals into the
Dr Marten's League following a successful appraisal of the facilities at
Wordsworth Drive.

TELFORD UNITED
GROUND: New Bucks Head , Bucks
Way, Telford, Shropshire
CURRENT CAPACITY: 4,268 (under
revision)
RECORD ATTENDANCE: 13,000 v.
Shrewsbury Town (Birmingham League)
10/04/36
YEAR BUILT/OPENED: 1887
CURRENT LEAGUE: Nationwide
Football Conference
CLUB FOUNDED: 1876
PREVIOUS GROUNDS: Barnfield Farm;
Haygate Admaston; Red Lion Ground;
Spraggs Recreation Ground

Wordsworth Drive, Taunton Town

The Bucks Head ground has been in use since 1887 and is currently undergoing a major rebuild that started in April 2000. Current owner, property developer Andy Shaw, has totally dismantled the old ground and has begun developing a futuristic-looking new stadium. The two end stands have been built – both covered terraces with interestingly continental-style curved roof covers. Almost as an indication of the owners' ambition, a new fully equipped crowd-control room has also been erected in the north-west corner. A small temporary stand was erected on the East side terrace for use in the 2001/02 campaign, although some of the early games were staged at Worcester City's ground. The season ended with little work having been started on the proposed 2,500-seater west stand. There have been concerns raised over the pace of construction and spiralling costs, now quoted at £12 million. When it is completed, the Bucks Head ground will have a 6,800 capacity as well as an 89-bedroom hotel and plush conference facilities. To join neighbours, Shrewsbury Town, in the Football League is the ultimate goal although the club have struggled on the playing front in recent years. However, Telford remain one of only two clubs, Northwich Victoria being the other, to have continuous membership of the Conference since its inception as the Alliance Premier League in 1979.

THAME UNITED
GROUND: Windmill Lane, Thame, Oxfordshire
CURRENT CAPACITY: 3,600
RECORD ATTENDANCE: 1,035 v. Aldershot Town (League) 04/04/94

YEAR BUILT/OPENED: 1883
CURRENT LEAGUE: Ryman (Isthmian)
League Division One (North)
CLUB FOUNDED: 1883 as Thame FC
PREVIOUS GROUNDS: None

Although the Windmill Ground has been home to Thame United since their formation in 1883, promotion to the Isthmian League in 1991 has seen the ground totally rebuilt and casting off all vestiges of its past history. Originally the ground was not enclosed and until land behind one goal was sold for housing in 1981, horses and ponies regularly grazed behind the goal! The adjacent training pitch was also sold for housing. Floodlights were erected in 1980 and much of the ground has terracing with varying amounts of cover. The old stand and clubhouse were demolished in 1995 and have been replaced by an impressive cantilevered stand with dressing rooms and social facilities incorporated. The development also allowed for the provision of ample car parking for the club's current requirements. The total cost of the project was £750,000, but it was money well spent as Thame now have one of the best stadiums in Oxfordshire.

THETFORD TOWN

GROUND: Recreation Ground,
Mundford Road, Thetford, Norfolk
CURRENT CAPACITY: 2,000
RECORD ATTENDANCE: 394 v. Diss Town (Norfolk Senior Cup) 1991
YEAR BUILT/OPENED: 1905
CURRENT LEAGUE: Jewson Eastern Counties League Division One
CLUB FOUNDED: 1883
PREVIOUS GROUNDS: Abbey Heath (1883–1900);Meadowland (1900–05)

The Recreation Ground is fast approaching its centenary, having been home to Thetford Town since 1905. The enclosed ground is part of a large sports complex and until the 1960s was shared with the cricket club. Most of the ground's facilities are on the Mundford Road side. The main stand, a strange concrete and timber affair, was erected in 1946. To either side of the stand are a few steps of open terrace. Behind the stand is a modest clubhouse and adjacent to the pay hut is a small boardroom. The club erected eight floodlight pylons in time for the 1988/89 season. However, the ground's major talking point is on the far side of the ground. There is a long rickety old cover built of corrugated iron with wooden-bench seating. The wooden dog-tooth stand ends have many missing slots and it is a wonder the whole thing still stands or, indeed, survives condemnation from the council. However, while it remains standing it should be enjoyed for its eccentricities.

THORNE COLLIERY

GROUND: Recreation Ground, Grange Road, Moorends, Thorne, South Yorkshire
CURRENT CAPACITY: 1,000
RECORD ATTENDANCE: Not Known
YEAR BUILT/OPENED: 1920s
CURRENT LEAGUE: Central Midland League Premier Division
CLUB FOUNDED: 1919
PREVIOUS GROUNDS: None

The club's heyday was the immediate post-World War Two years, when they won the Yorkshire League in 1946/47, having been runners-up to Wombwell Athletic the previous campaign. However the club declined and their time in the fledgling

Windmill Lane, Thame United

Northern Counties (East) League ended after the 1984/85 season. The club took the dramatic decision to drop back down to local football in the Doncaster Senior League. The club regrouped and after five successive Championships, they stepped up to the Central Midlands League. The Miner's Welfare Ground has been home since the early 1920s and is surprisingly open. The huge stand was built before World War Two and somehow has survived the attention of local youths in this depressed area of South Yorkshire. The Grange Road ground is something of an anomaly in modern senior football, having no enclosing walls, floodlights or a clubhouse.

TILBURY
GROUND: Chadfields, St Chad's Road, Tilbury, Essex

CURRENT CAPACITY: 4,000
RECORD ATTENDANCE: 5,500 v. Gorleston (FA Cup) 19/11/49
YEAR BUILT/OPENED: 1945
CURRENT LEAGUE: Ryman (Isthmian) League Division One (North)
CLUB FOUNDED: 1900
PREVIOUS GROUNDS: Green & Siley Weir Ground (1900–11); Orient Field (1919–38)

Tilbury originally played at a ground owned by the Green & Siley Weir Company and later on a field adjacent to the current ground, known as the Orient Field. This was so called because its owner was a director of Leyton Orient Football Club. With Tilbury being a strategic dock town, the Orient Field and the current ground were seconded by the MoD for anti-aircraft gun emplacements.

Recreation Ground, Thetford Town

After the war, Tilbury looked to re-use the Orient Field, but the owner insisted on the fact that the club would do so under the proviso that Tilbury would become Orient's nursery club. The club declined, moved next door and Orient took over Chase of Chertsey as their nursery club. The adjacent field, known as Chadfields, had been used for greyhound racing before World War Two, but had been badly damaged during the conflict. The club erected a small wooden stand and laid rudimentary terracing opposite. The club's amazing FA Cup run of 1949 and the sale of goalkeeper Tommy Scannell to Southend United meant the club were in a position to buy out their new ground. In the 1950s and '60s the ground was extensively developed, including a boardroom, clubhouse and floodlights. The present main stand, a rather austere concrete edifice, was opened in 1970. The 1970s saw a new clubhouse and an extension to the dressing rooms. However, the end of that decade saw the club in severe financial difficulties that, after a prolonged struggle, thankfully were overcome. No new developments happened until 1995, when a new seated stand was opened on the west side with two additional areas of cover. Chadfields joined the new millennium looking better than it had done for a number of years, and the club look to have a bright future.

TIVERTON TOWN
GROUND: Ladysmead, Bolham Road, Tiverton, Devon
CURRENT CAPACITY: 3,500

Recreation Ground, Thorne Colliery

RECORD ATTENDANCE: 3,000 v. Leyton Orient (FA Cup) 12/11/94
YEAR BUILT/OPENED: 1939
CURRENT LEAGUE: Dr Marten's (Southern) League Premier Division
CLUB FOUNDED: 1913
PREVIOUS GROUNDS: Athletic Ground (1913–20); The Elms (1920–39)

Tiverton Town regrouped after World War Two and needed a new venue to play at because their pre-war ground at The Elms was no longer useable for football. It had been requisitioned by the military authorities as a storage dump and the existing grandstand was badly damaged. The club received £10 in compensation and were allowed to salvage any useable material from the old ground. The new site at Ladysmead was very basic, with the teams having to change at the Cross Keys public house. A stand was cobbled together from the old Elms stand, but was soon replaced by a new stand. In the 1990s the club had considerable success and it was reflected in the development at the ground when new stands, changing rooms and covered terracing went up all round the ground. They won the Western League four times and were runners up three times in seven years. They also won the FA Vase in 1998 and 1999. Ladysmead by then was a first-class venue and the club took their rightful place in the Southern League for the 1999/2000 campaign. During the summer of 2002 the club installed an additional 200 seats in the main stand that should see Ladysmead upgraded to Conference standard. However, the club's rapid rise up the non-League pyramid has ended one of the most interesting rivalries in recent non-League football history, with perennial challengers Taunton Town.

TONBRIDGE ANGELS
GROUND: Longmead Stadium, Darenth Avenue, Tonbridge, Kent
CURRENT CAPACITY: 5,000
RECORD ATTENDANCE: 1,463 v. Yeovil Town (FA Cup) 26/10/91
YEAR BUILT/OPENED: 1980
CURRENT LEAGUE: Dr Marten's (Southern) League Eastern Division
CLUB FOUNDED: 1948
PREVIOUS GROUNDS: The Angel Ground (1948–80)

Tonbridge left The Angel Ground in 1980 after the council made provision for a new site at Longmead. The Angel Ground had been a cricket venue since before the turn of the last century. However, it had only been used for football from when the new Tonbridge club had been formed just after the war. Longmead had been an empty field, but within months was converted into a serviceable ground in time for the start of the 1980/81 campaign. The conversion process was made easier as the pitch-length covered enclosure that ran down the High Street side of The Angel Ground was transported to Longmead and re-erected in all its glory. The Angels have steadily improved the Longmead site and now have a home more than adequate for their current needs.

TOOTING & MITCHAM UNITED
GROUND: Imperial Fields, Bishopsford Road, Mitcham, Surrey
CURRENT CAPACITY: 3,500
RECORD ATTENDANCE: 17,500 v. QPR (FA Cup) 08/12/56 (at Sandy Lane)
YEAR BUILT/OPENED: 1932
CURRENT LEAGUE: Ryman (Isthmian) League Division One (South)
CLUB FOUNDED: 1932 merger of Tooting Town (1919) and Mitcham Wanderers (1912)
PREVIOUS GROUNDS: Sandy Lane (1932-2002)

By the time this book is published, Tooting & Mitcham United will be safely ensconced in their brand new Bishopsford Road ground. The new facility has been taking shape over the last year and will undoubtedly serve the club's future well. However, the considerable down side is that the club have abandoned the last large-scale venue left in the London area. Sandy Lane was built in 1932 with all the flamboyance of that era. The huge grandstand, built in 1958, stretches along the majority of the near side of the ground and replaced the original gable-roofed wooden stand, itself extended in 1932. The rest of the ground has large sections of now crumbling terrace. The clubhouse is behind the stand and shows many fading photos of Tooting & Mitcham's glory years when cup runs and five-figure crowds were not unusual at Sandy Lane. However, with the 2,000 capacity grandstand having wooden-bench seating rather than the more politically-correct plastic tip-up seats, Sandy Lane was becoming something of an albatross around the club's neck. It is a terrible shame that this leviathan of a ground has no place in the modern game. If you never visited Sandy Lane, you missed out on an integral part of British football history. The new ground has been built on the site of an existing sports ground, used as a training facility by the likes of Crystal Palace, Chelsea and

Longmead Stadium, Tonbridge Angels

Brentford over the years. Initially Bishopsford Road will have a 3,500 capacity with a 600-seater cantilever grandstand and plenty of scope for expansion if required.

TORPOINT ATHLETIC
GROUND: The Mill Field, Mill Lane, Torpoint, Cornwall
CURRENT CAPACITY: 2,500
RECORD ATTENDANCE: Not Known
YEAR BUILT/OPENED: 1940's
CURRENT LEAGUE: Carlsberg South-Western League
CLUB FOUNDED: 1887
PREVIOUS GROUNDS: HMS Defiant Ground (1960–71)

An interesting ground that leaves you in no doubt of its coastal location, with an impressive backdrop of maritime cranes and lighting towers. Strangely the football club were unceremoniously booted off The Mill Field for an 11-year period when St Columbus RUFC forced their way into occupancy. However, after Torpoint reclaimed their rights to the ground in 1971, they started to develop the ground with a new clubhouse and dressing rooms and the current small stand on the River Tamar side of the ground. It is now a perfectly acceptable and unpretentious venue.

TORRINGTON
GROUND: Vicarage Field, School Lane, Great Torrington, Devon
CURRENT CAPACITY: 4,000
RECORD ATTENDANCE: Not Known
YEAR BUILT/OPENED: 1908

Sandy Lane, Tooting & Mitcham United

CURRENT LEAGUE: Screwfix Direct Western League Division One
CLUB FOUNDED: 1908
PREVIOUS GROUNDS: None

An elderly ground situated just off the main road in this attractive market town. A large church provides an imposing backdrop and it is on the field behind the vicarage that Torrington have always called home. It was little more than an open field for 50 years until the stand on the south side of the ground was erected, although seats did not arrive until 1994. An additional cover was erected opposite the main stand in 1984. The clubhouse was erected in 1978 and has twice been extended. Interestingly, in 1983 the club discovered that their pitch was actually too short for senior football and a hasty lengthening of the turf was arranged. You will need to be quite observant to spot the most unusual feature of the Vicarage Field. It comes in the shape of a small plaque on one of the goals commemorating Sid Trickett's eleven headed goals in an 18-0 defeat of Ilfracombe in 1948.

TOW LAW TOWN
GROUND: Ironworks Road, Tow Law, County Durham
CURRENT CAPACITY: 6,000
RECORD ATTENDANCE: 5,500 v. Mansfield Town (FA Cup) 09/12/67
YEAR BUILT/OPENED: 1892
CURRENT LEAGUE: Albany Northern League Division One
CLUB FOUNDED: 1890
PREVIOUS GROUNDS: Various pitches

The Mill Field, Torpoint Athletic

The Ironworks Ground rivals Buxton's Silverlands as Britain's highest ground. Tow Law is one of those places that always seems to be freezing cold. On my visit I was dressed up like the Michelin man and was still shivering, and I swear the gateman was wearing a vest t-shirt! They breed them tough up in the Durham coalfields. The ground was built by striking coal miners, and used the banking of the adjacent, now-closed, railway to good effect. The current main stand replaced an old wooden one in 1970. Soon afterwards, the cover behind the goal was erected, which offered some resistance from the bitter winds that howl across the pitch from the hills all around. The most recent development at the Ironworks Ground came in 1992 when the club acquired their first set of floodlights. It is a truly unique footballing experience at Tow Law, so wrap up warm and take a flask of something reviving to thaw yourself out!

TRAFFORD

GROUND: Shawe View, Pennybridge Lane, Urmston, Greater Manchester
CURRENT CAPACITY: 2,500
RECORD ATTENDANCE: 803 v. Flixton (League) 27/12/97
YEAR BUILT/OPENED: 1946
CURRENT LEAGUE: Unibond (Northern Premier) League Division One
CLUB FOUNDED: 1990 as North Trafford
PREVIOUS GROUNDS: None

Shawe View has an interesting history, although its incumbent side, Trafford, have only been in existence for little

Vicarage Field, Torrington

more than a decade. The ground was acquired in 1946 by Manchester City as their new training ground and was used for many years by their junior sides. In those days it had a modest floodlighting system in the shape of halogen lamps on telegraph poles. Since City acquired a more modern training ground, Shawe View has been used by Altrincham's reserve side and also staged rugby league by hosting games for both Trafford Borough and Salford. More recently the ground was used by now-defunct North West Counties League side Urmston. However, after Urmston's departure, Shawe View had lain unkempt and derelict until rescued in 1990 by a newly formed club, North Trafford. The ambitious committee set about reinstating perimeter fencing, laid hard standing and erected a main stand and two additional areas of covered terrace. The local council funded new dressing rooms. The main stand was seated with the acquisition of nearly 200 seats from Huddersfield Town's former home at Leeds Road. Trafford's tremendous work ethic and drive was justly rewarded with promotion to the Northern Premier League in 1997.

TRING TOWN
GROUND: Pendley Sports Ground, Cow Lane, Tring, Hertfordshire
CURRENT CAPACITY: 2,500
RECORD ATTENDANCE: 3,500 v. West Ham United (Floodlight Opener) 1975
YEAR BUILT/OPENED: 1948
CURRENT LEAGUE: Ryman (Isthmian) League Division Two

Ironworks Road, Tow Law Town

CLUB FOUNDED: 1889
PREVIOUS GROUNDS: Tring Cricket Club

A rural venue, some way from the centre of this commuter town, the Cow Lane ground was opened in 1948 after the show jumping broadcaster, Dorian Williams, donated land to the town for sporting activities. There is now also a superb rugby union ground next to the football venue. The new venue was a great improvement on Tring Town's previous home, on the outfield of Tring Cricket Club! The Pendley Sports Ground boasts a most unusual main stand, built in 1968 – a sheet metal and timber construction with a highly elevated seated section, accessed from the side by a metal staircase. There is a large section of cov-

ered terrace behind the north goal. The clubhouse and changing facilities are in fact portakabins that once served as classrooms at the Rothschild School until the club acquired them in 1974. A year later the club turned on the floodlights for the first time in a match against West Ham, which remains the record gate at Cow Lane. In recent years fellow Ryman League clubs have ground-shared at Tring, these being Slough Town and Southall.

Moor Lane, Tring Town

U

UXBRIDGE

GROUND: Honeycroft, Horton Road,
West Drayton, Middlesex
CURRENT CAPACITY: 3,770
RECORD ATTENDANCE: 1,000 v.
Arsenal (Floodlight Opener) 1981
YEAR BUILT/OPENED: 1978
CURRENT LEAGUE: Ryman (Isthmian)
League Division One (North)
CLUB FOUNDED: 1871
PREVIOUS GROUNDS: The Common;
Colne Farm; Hillingdon House Farm;
Cowley Road; RAF Uxbridge Stadium;
Cleveland Road

A very old club, formed in 1871, Uxbridge played on several grounds before using the fine stadium at RAF Uxbridge for several years. In 1948 the club acquired a ground of their own in Cleveland Road. The club, then in the Corinthian League, rapidly developed the new venue, which was known as Honeycroft. At its peak it boasted a capacity of 6,000, with a wooden grandstand, covered terrace and ample banking around the ground. However, by 1969 the ground was owned by an investment company and the club were served notice to quit. After an exhaustive search, the club acquired the former ground of Drayreg FC in 1978 for £100,000. Their old ground was then flattened and became an extension of the Brunel University campus. The new ground in Horton Road was also called

Honeycroft as club officials were so fond of their old home. The only problem with the new Honeycroft ground was that it is located in West Drayton, several miles from Uxbridge. Since 1978 the ground has been developed into one of the best-kept Ryman League venues. There are two covered terraces at each end and, on one side, a small, seated stand with an unusual roof. The main stand is compact and does have roof supports obstructing the view, but is immaculately kept nonetheless.

V

VAUXHALL MOTORS
GROUND: Rivacre Park, Rivacre Road, Hooton, Wirral
CURRENT CAPACITY: 2,000

RECORD ATTENDANCE: 1,019 v. Northwich Victoria (FA Cup) February 2002
YEAR BUILT/OPENED: 1997
CURRENT LEAGUE: Unibond (Northern Premier) League Premier Division
CLUB FOUNDED: 1995 re-formation of club formed in 1963
PREVIOUS GROUNDS: Vauxhall Motors Sports Ground

Since the club were re-formed in 1995, having disbanded in 1992, they have risen from the humble West Cheshire League to the Unibond League with a remarkable four promotions in six seasons, which has included three Championships. The real catalyst for the spectacular rise was the move to a new ground, Rivacre Park, in 1997. The ground is a splendid facility with a clubhouse, smart, seated stand and a pitch the envy of many. It is an

Honetcroft, Uxbridge

amazing success story that could bear fruit if Everton carry through plans to have their youth academy centred at Rivacre Park. The club have, however, suffered from low attendances and a name change to either Wirral FC or Ellesmere Port has been mooted. The club are not tied to the car company and are fully owned by the sports and social club committee, so a name change to more fully represent the area is a distinct possibility.

WAKEFIELD & EMLEY

GROUND: Wakefield RLFC, Belle Vue, Doncaster Road, Wakefield, South Yorkshire
CURRENT CAPACITY: 11,000
RECORD ATTENDANCE: 5,134 v. Barking (FA Amateur Cup) 01/02/69
YEAR BUILT/OPENED: Ground-shared since 2000
CURRENT LEAGUE: Unibond (Northern Premier) League Premier Division
CLUB FOUNDED: 1903 as Emley Clarence Association
PREVIOUS GROUNDS: Albert Hills; Chapel Lane; Chapel House Farm; Out Lane; Welfare Ground

It was in many ways a shame that this progressive club found it necessary to quit their homely Welfare Ground towards the end of the 1999/2000 season. The club decided that promotion to the Conference was an achievable target, but their existing ground could well hold them back. So an agreement was reached with Wakefield Wildcats RLFC to share their historic Belle Vue Ground, some

eight miles away from the tiny former mining village. The Welfare Ground itself was first used, ironically for rugby, in 1884, but Belle Vue is senior in age by five years. The main stand is vintage 1924, but the rest of the ground has been gradually modernized since the mid-1980s – developments that have seen Belle Vue's capacity slashed to a still sizeable 11,000. However, this is still some way from the ground's halcyon days, most notably the 1930s, when the record gate of 37,906 congregated for a rugby league Challenge Cup semi-final. The club elected to incorporate their new home town into the football club's name during the summer of 2002.

WALTON & HERSHAM

GROUND: Sports Ground, Stompond Lane, Walton-on-Thames, Surrey
CURRENT CAPACITY: 6,000
RECORD ATTENDANCE: 6,500 v. Brighton & Hove Albion (FA Cup) 1973
YEAR BUILT/OPENED: 1933
CURRENT LEAGUE: Ryman (Isthmian) League Division One (South)
CLUB FOUNDED: 1896 as Walton FC
PREVIOUS GROUNDS: Various pitches

The ground was acquired in 1933 at a cost of £7,000, although Kerry Miller's excellent club history tells us that it had been offered to the club as early as 1908. It is arguably the best of several non-League grounds that share with athletics tracks, for Stompond Lane has been home to Walton Athletics Club since 1942. This is perhaps due to the track having only six lanes, rather than the more usual eight. The large brick-built main stand dates from the late 1960s and replaced a much older and dilapidated wooden structure. The new stand also provided new changing room facilities, with the existing structure being converted into a clubhouse. Opposite the main stand is a long, covered terrace erected by the supporters club in the immediate post-World War Two years. Terracing was later laid behind the goal and in 1967 floodlights were erected. The most recent change at the ground has seen the council replace the old cinder running track with an all-weather surface.

WANTAGE TOWN

GROUND: Alfredian Park, Manor Road, Wantage, Oxfordshire
CURRENT CAPACITY: 1,500
RECORD ATTENDANCE: 500 v. Newport AFC 1989
YEAR BUILT/OPENED: 1922
CURRENT LEAGUE: Cherry Red Records Hellenic League Premier Division

CLUB FOUNDED: 1892
PREVIOUS GROUNDS: Challow Park (1892–1922)

Alfredian Park is an endearing venue with an eclectic mix of covered accommodation. The club acquired the site in 1922 for a princely £400, which was only possible after club officials went cap-in-hand to local tradesman and shopkeepers. Its unusual name came from a local football tournament, The Alfredian Shield, which had been organized by the club for several years. The changing rooms were opened in 1987, replacing the old pavilion, itself erected in 1933. There are now two sections of cover, the smaller being the elder. This was erected in 1938 and quite honestly looks its age, suffering the brunt of storms. The larger structure was opened in 1954, but was originally slightly

Stompond Lane, Walton & Hersham

larger, a section being dismantled after storm damage. The clubhouse dates from 1969 and the floodlights are a much more recent addition in 1984. Alfredian Park is a beautiful tree-lined venue and the Ridgeway Hills falling away to the distance complete an idyllic venue.

WARE

GROUND: Wodson Park, Wadesmill Road, Ware, Hertfordshire
CURRENT CAPACITY: 3,300
RECORD ATTENDANCE: 3,800 v. Hendon 1957 at Buryfield
YEAR BUILT/OPENED: 1995
CURRENT LEAGUE: Ryman (Isthmian) League Division Two
CLUB FOUNDED: 1892 as Ware Town
PREVIOUS GROUNDS: Presdales; Highfields; Canons Park; London Road; Lower Park; Page's Field; Buryfield

Ware played on six pitches around the town in their early years, one of which is still a sporting venue. This ground is Hoe Lane, which has been used for many years by Hertford RUFC. In 1926 they moved to a pitch previously used by Ware Engineers. It was situated to the north of the town's two medicine companies Allen and Hanburys, who would later be bought out by Glaxo. The ground became erroneously known as Buryfields, although it should have been called the Recreation Ground as the true Buryfields was the adjacent field. The old ground had a brick and timber main stand built in 1948 and an older covered terrace resited on the opposite side to the main stand in 1961. The club played their last game there in May 1995 when the landowners, Glaxo-Wellcome, relocated the club to the north of the town

Alfredian Park, Wantage Town

with a new purpose-built £1 million stadium. The old ground was levelled in September 1995 and became an extension to Glaxo's car park. The new site, called Wodson Park, was sited next to the existing leisure centre. The new venue staged its first match in November 1995 and boasts a first-class clubhouse, a superb cantilevered main stand, a large covered terrace opposite and shallow open terracing at either end. As modern venues go, Wodson Park is one of the finest examples of the new breed of small town stadiums.

WARRINGTON TOWN
GROUND: Cantilever Park, Common Lane, Latchford, Warrington, Cheshire
CURRENT CAPACITY: 2,000
RECORD ATTENDANCE: 3,000 v. Halesowen Town (FA Vase) 1986
YEAR BUILT/OPENED: 1956
CURRENT LEAGUE: North West Counties League Division One
CLUB FOUNDED: 1948 as Stockton Heath FC
PREVIOUS GROUNDS: Stockton Lane; London Road

The club moved into their current ground in 1956 when the site was known as Loushers Lane. It has since been renamed Cantilever Park, after the truly incredible bridge that makes an unusual, but impressive backdrop to this venue. The current main stand was erected shortly after their arrival. The clubhouse was opened in 1960 and housed the dressing rooms and featured a veranda with seating accommodation. Stockton Heath changed their name to Warrington Town in 1961 to reflect their status as the leading club in the area. The club's best days came in the late 1980s and early

1990s when they reached the FA Vase final and gained promotion to the Northern Premier League. The promotion saw the club erect a sizeable covered terrace built opposite the existing main stand and the enclosing walls were improved. However, the late 1990s saw a fall from grace, although Cantilever Park remains a perfect venue for the club's current status.

WEALDSTONE
GROUND: Edgware Town FC
CURRENT CAPACITY: 5,000
RECORD ATTENDANCE: 13,504 v. Leytonstone (FA Amateur Cup) 05/03/49 at Lower Mead
YEAR BUILT/OPENED: Ground-shared since 1995
CURRENT LEAGUE: Ryman (Isthmian) League Division One (North)
CLUB FOUNDED: 1889
PREVIOUS GROUNDS: College Farm (1903–10); Belmont Road (1910–22); Lower Mead(1922–91); Watford FC (1991–93); Yeading FC (1993–95)

Wealdstone have been homeless since losing their Lower Mead ground in 1991. The club's massive success in the 1980's meant Lower Mead had become one of the best known of non-League grounds. However, six years after the club won the Alliance Premier League and FA Trophy double, Lower Mead was lying under a Tesco Superstore. The old ground was nothing special, but the old wooden stand had an interesting history, having previously given service at the ground of the now-defunct Summerstown FC. Since the loss of Lower Mead, the club have transferred across the pyramid from the Southern League feeder to the Ryman League and have had to work their way

Cantilever Park, Warrington Town

up from Division Three. It has been a long, hard road for the club with several ground-shares in the intervening years, most recently with Edgware Town, but support has remained strong. The club have now secured planning permission for a new stadium and leisure facility on the site of the former Prince Edward Playing Fields. The club now have to find financial backing for the project, which will bring about a long-awaited return to their own borough.

WELLINGBOROUGH TOWN
GROUND: Dog & Duck Ground, London Road, Wellingborough, Northamptonshire
CURRENT CAPACITY: 5,000
RECORD ATTENDANCE: 4,013 v. Kettering Town
YEAR BUILT/OPENED: 1901

CURRENT LEAGUE: Eagle Bitter United Counties League Premier Division
CLUB FOUNDED: 1867
PREVIOUS GROUNDS: Gas Works Ground

One of the oldest clubs in the country, Wellingborough Town have just celebrated 100 years at the Dog & Duck Ground. There are three major buildings around the ground. The first is a rather austere-looking clubhouse and dressing room complex opened in 1963 and situated behind the goal. On the far side is the large seated stand with a highly elevated roof. In recent years the nearly 40-year-old stand has begun to look slightly the worse for wear. However, the stand remains an impressively sized structure for the present status of the club and gives an indication of the club's one-time presence in the Southern League. The most historically interesting feature of the ground is adjacent to the stand – a small lean-to cover is attached to an elderly pavilion that was transported from Town's first home at the Gas Works Ground. At one time the ground boasted another sizeable stand but this was condemned and demolished some years ago. Adjacent to the Dog & Duck is the home of fellow United County Leaguers, Whitworths. Grave news was released during the summer of 2002 when it was announced that the 135 year old club had folded. Hopefully a swift re-formation may be possible in the near future and football will once again be staged at the Dog & Duck.

WELLING UNITED

GROUND: Park View Road, Welling, Kent

CURRENT CAPACITY: 5,500
RECORD ATTENDANCE: 4,100 v. Gillingham (FA Cup) 22/11/89
YEAR BUILT/OPENED: 1925
CURRENT LEAGUE: Dr Marten's (Southern) League Premier Division
CLUB FOUNDED: 1963
PREVIOUS GROUNDS: Butterfly Lane (1963–77)

The Park View ground has been in existence since at least 1925 and was home for many years to Bexley United, a powerful, well-supported, Southern League outfit. However from 1953 they were run as a professional club and by 1976 had incurred insurmountable debts and folded after completing the 1975/76 campaign. Welling United were an intermediate side until 1976 when, of ten applicants, they were successful in a bid to take over the tenancy of Park View

Dog & Duck Ground, Wellingborough Town

Road. In the interim, the ground had suffered an arson attack and vandalism, badly damaging the stand. The club have since improved the ground beyond all recognition. The stand was renovated and equipped with modern seating, and new enclosing walls were built to keep the vandals at bay. Modern turnstiles and extensive terracing were also erected. The most interesting development in recent years has been the ground's long deal with Erith and Belvedere. As part of the deal Erith have erected their own main stand, opposite Welling's, and also have their own social club. A unique arrangement indeed. After all the improvements at the ground, the club erected a sign on the grandstand that immodestly said 'Welcome to the San Siro'!

WELLS CITY
GROUND: The Athletic Ground, Rowden Road, Wells, Somerset
CURRENT CAPACITY: 2,000
RECORD ATTENDANCE: Not Known
YEAR BUILT/OPENED: Not Recorded
CURRENT LEAGUE: Somerset County League Premier Division
CLUB FOUNDED: 1919
PREVIOUS GROUNDS: Numerous pitches

A beautiful and ancient city, Wells boasts an equally attractive football ground. The exact date that Wells City moved to the Athletic Ground is not recorded, but it was certainly their home in the mid-1950s Western League heyday. The ground itself is not totally enclosed as its pitch forms part of the outfield for Wells Cricket Club. The large cover on the Alfred Street side of the ground appears to be a bit dark and dingy and always seems to be in shadow, making a good photograph hard to come

by. Since the cricket club disbanded in the late 1990s, the Somerset FA have earmarked the Rowden Road ground as a possible site for new County FA headquarters. Hopefully any such development will see the unusual main stand kept for future generations to enjoy; the club hopes that any such developments will result in promotion to the Western League within three seasons.

WEMBLEY
GROUND: Vale Farm, Watford Road, Sudbury, Wembley, Middlesex
CURRENT CAPACITY: 2,000
RECORD ATTENDANCE: 2,654 v. Wealdstone (FA Amateur Cup) 1952
YEAR BUILT/OPENED: 1928
CURRENT LEAGUE: Ryman (Isthmian) League Division One (North)
CLUB FOUNDED: 1946 merger of Sudbury Rangers and Sudbury Association
PREVIOUS GROUNDS: None

The Vale Farm ground was bought by the local council in 1928 and rented to the fledgling Wembley club in 1948, initially for only three years. After a longer lease was secured, the club began developing the enclosed ground. In 1955 the main stand was opened and doubled in length within two years. The lengthy, covered terrace was opened in 1956, replacing the existing modern stand. Five years later the clubhouse and floodlights were erected, although the latter were replaced in 1981. The ground remained unchanged until 1992 when a huge fire gutted the main stand. After the fire was dampened down, inspection of the covered terrace resulted in its condemnation. The double disaster nearly spelt the end for the club, but

Park View Road, Welling United

determination has seen the Vale Farm ground restored to operational order. The old terrace was re-roofed and a new stand opened, as well as a new turnstile block that utilized old British Rail ticket booths. Vale Farm is a triumph of determination over adversity.

WESTON-SUPER-MARE

GROUND: Woodspring Park, Winterstoke Road, Weston-super-Mare, Somerset
CURRENT CAPACITY: 2,000
RECORD ATTENDANCE: 2,623 v. Woking (FA Cup) 23/11/93
YEAR BUILT/OPENED: 1983
CURRENT LEAGUE: Dr Marten's (Southern) League Western Division
CLUB FOUNDED: 1899
PREVIOUS GROUNDS: Ashcombe Park; Milton Road; Great Ground; Langford Road

Considering Woodspring Park is less than 20 years old, it has not aged well. This may be due to the uninspiring design that lends a slightly down-at-heel appearance. However, when you consider that the club's sudden eviction from their old Langford Road ground in 1982 almost led to their extinction, then in reality any home is better than no home. The club were saved when the local council stepped in at the 11th hour, providing a plot of land off Winterstoke Road. An imposing clubhouse and dressing-room complex was erected along with a stand and covered terrace of basic breeze-block construction. The efforts made meant that the club could con-

The Athletic Ground, Wells City

tinue in the Western League. When the chance of promotion to the Southern League came in 1992, the provision of hard standing and additional cover meant the revitalized club had brought the highest-grade football ever witnessed in the town, a remarkable achievement by any standards.

WEYMOUTH

GROUND: Wessex Stadium, Radipole Lane, Weymouth, Dorset
CURRENT CAPACITY: 6,600
RECORD ATTENDANCE: 4,995 v. Manchester United (Ground Opener) 21/10/87
YEAR BUILT/OPENED: 1987
CURRENT LEAGUE: Dr Marten's (Southern) League Premier Division
CLUB FOUNDED: 1890

PREVIOUS GROUNDS: Lodmoor (1890–93); Westham (1893–97); Recreation Ground (1897–1987)

Although there is nothing essentially wrong with Weymouth's spacious Wessex Stadium, (which opened in August 1987, much to The Terras' undoubted chagrin) it will always compare less favourably with the far more aesthetically pleasing new ground of neighbours Dorchester Town. Weymouth had lost their 90-year-old Recreation Ground to a supermarket chain in early 1987. However, the local council fortunately made sure the club were well catered for by building a new stadium, costing £1 million, on the site of the old Weymouth Speedway Stadium in Radipole Lane. It is well up to Conference standard, with a large main stand and cov-

Vale Farm, Wembley

ered terracing all around the ground. The capacity was originally listed at 10,000, although a safety licence was obtained for a considerably more realistic 6,600. It will certainly not challenge the record gate at the Recreation Ground of 12,512 for the 1948 visit of Yeovil Town in the FA Cup. While the social, officials' and spectator facilities are second to none, the Wessex Stadium lacks any real focal point or character. But with a less co-operative council the club could well have been homeless, and the new ground was a more than welcome lifeline.

WHITBY TOWN
GROUND: Turnbull Ground, Upgang Lane, Whitby, North Yorkshire
CURRENT CAPACITY: 3,200
RECORD ATTENDANCE: 4,000 v. Scarborough (North Riding Cup) 18/04/65
YEAR BUILT/OPENED: 1929
CURRENT LEAGUE: Unibond (Northern Premier) League Premier Division
CLUB FOUNDED: 1926 merger of Whitby FC and Whitby Swifts
PREVIOUS GROUNDS: Upgang Lane; Stakesby Road

Many clubs represented the North Yorkshire coastal town before the 1926 merger of Whitehill Swifts and Whitby brought about the current Whitby Town club. The club's first ground was in Upgang Lane, next to the current ground and was shared with Whitby Cricket Club. In 1929 both clubs were served with eviction notices, although local shipbuilding magnate, Wilf Turnbull purchased much of the land and an additional field enabling both clubs to continue. While the new football ground was levelled and prepared, the club spent two seasons at an undeveloped ground in Stakesby Road. The new ground was opened in August 1929 and boasted a grandstand, which still remains, a covered enclosure, perimeter fencing and dressing rooms, all funded by the generous benefactor after whom the ground is named. The covered stand opposite the old stand was erected in 1951, although at a strangely obtuse angle to the pitch. The clubhouse was built in 1971 and floodlights arrived in March 1983. The continuing development of the Turnbull Ground carried on throughout the 1980s with new dressing rooms, turnstiles and new plastic seating for the grandstand. The club's drive, ambition and hard work were justly rewarded with a place in the Northern Premier League in 1997. A fine ground and a fine town, with quite possibly the best fish and chips in the country.

WHITLEY BAY
GROUND: Hillheads Park, Rink Way, Whitley Bay, Tyne & Wear
CURRENT CAPACITY: 4,500
RECORD ATTENDANCE: 7,301 v. Hendon (FA Amateur Cup) 1965
YEAR BUILT/OPENED: 1939
CURRENT LEAGUE: Albany Northern League Division One
CLUB FOUNDED: 1897 as Monkseaton
PREVIOUS GROUNDS: Uplands Ground

Hillheads Park has been home to Whitley Bay since just before World War Two, although the first version of the ground was radically different to the modern-day stadium. After the hostilities, with building materials in desperately short supply,

the club equipped the ground as best they could with wooden huts serving as changing rooms and spectator accommodation. In 1963 new changing rooms were erected and with volunteer labour from the players and supporter's club, the current brick-built main stand replaced the rickety wooden structure at the Ice Rink side. Developments continued throughout the 1960s, including a new clubhouse and floodlights. The second original stand stood until 1971, when it was condemned and demolished. A new dressing room block was built behind the main stand in 1982. Although the club lost their Northern Premier League place at the end of the 1999/2000 season and notwithstanding the odd bout of vandalism, Hillheads Park remains a fine venue. After some lean years the club battled through to win the final of the 2002 Carlsberg FA Vase, hopefully heralding a new era of optimism for The Bay.

WHITSTABLE TOWN
GROUND: Belmont Ground, Belmont, Whitstable, Kent
CURRENT CAPACITY: 2,000
RECORD ATTENDANCE: 2,500 v. Gravesend & Northfleet (FA Cup) 19/10/87
YEAR BUILT/OPENED: 1888
CURRENT LEAGUE: Go Travel Kent League
CLUB FOUNDED: 1885
PREVIOUS GROUNDS: Saddleston's Field; Westmeads

Yet another ground that is well past its centenary, having first been used for football by the defunct Whitstable club. That club split into two new clubs – Whitstable Town and Whitstable United – following

Turnbull Ground, Whitby Town

a dispute among officials. Town played on a couple of different pitches until returning to The Belmont in 1896. After four years the two clubs buried the hatchet and merged back into one club and again, after using two more sites, returned to The Belmont, this time for good, in 1909. The ground was requisitioned for the war effort in 1914 and the wooden stand was demolished and the timber used to repair bomb-damaged factories. On returning to the ground, the club set about rebuilding the ground with a new changing room hut and in 1922, a concrete stand. The Gasometer End terrace was covered in 1954 and little changed at The Belmont until 1972 when the new clubhouse was erected. Whitstable acquired their first set of floodlights as recently as 1989 and apart from keeping the paintwork

touched up, the Belmont Ground retains its mature and endearing look.

WHYTELEAFE
GROUND: Church Road, Whyteleafe, Surrey
CURRENT CAPACITY: 5,000
RECORD ATTENDANCE: 2,210 v. Chester City (FA Cup) 30/10/99
YEAR BUILT/OPENED: 1959
CURRENT LEAGUE: Ryman (Isthmian) League Division One (South)
CLUB FOUNDED: 1946
PREVIOUS GROUNDS: New Barn Lane

The club was formed after World War Two by several officials of the defunct Whyteleafe Albion club and entered the Caterham and Edenbridge League. As the club gained senior status on entering the

Hillheads Park, Whitley Bay

Surrey Senior League in 1958, they moved to their present home. The farmland off Church Road was returfed as a football pitch and existing farm buildings were converted into rudimentary changing rooms and a bar. A year later the ground was ready for use and it was stable until more improvements were needed on joining the Spartan League in 1975. The ground's first stand was built and a training pitch laid. Further developments came in 1981 in the shape of floodlights, new changing rooms and an extension to the clubhouse as the club rose to the Athenian League. The ground remained unchanged until the millennium when a new stand replaced the old one, part-financed by the record gate at Church Road for the FA Cup tie against then-Football League side, Chester City.

WILLINGTON
GROUND: Hall Lane, Willington, County Durham
CURRENT CAPACITY: 2,680
RECORD ATTENDANCE: 10,000 v. Bromley (FA Amateur Cup) 24/01/53
YEAR BUILT/OPENED: 1911
CURRENT LEAGUE: Albany Northern League Division Two
CLUB FOUNDED: 1906 as Willington Temperance
PREVIOUS GROUNDS: West End Ground

This club has fallen on hard times in recent years, but it has a proud history and a ground that oozes character. The club reached the Amateur Cup final in 1939, but lost to Amateur Cup kings Bishop Auckland at Roker Park. However,

Hall Lane, Willington

11 years later both clubs again reached the final, but this time Willington triumphed 4-0 in front of 88,000 at Wembley. Brilliant stuff. The club was originally formed out of a Temperance Club, common at the turn of the last century. The club have been members of the Northern League since 1911 and have taken the title on three occasions. Former managers include men of considerable reputation, such as Malcolm Allison and Alan Durban. The Hall Lane ground was relatively undeveloped until the mid-1950s, the club's glory years. A stand was erected with wooden bench-seating and a proud fascia board. Later still, in 1969, the clubhouse was erected, followed by new changing rooms. The original set of floodlights went up in 1973, to be replaced in 1992 by a set acquired from the former Vane Tempest Colliery. While the current team lan-guishes in Division Two of the Albany Northern League, it is likely that this historic ground will remain untouched. Good job too.

WINDSOR & ETON
GROUND: Stag Meadow, St Leonards Road, Windsor, Berkshire
CURRENT CAPACITY: 4,500
RECORD ATTENDANCE: 3,451 v. AFC Bournemouth (FA Cup) 12/12/83
YEAR BUILT/OPENED: 1912
CURRENT LEAGUE: Ryman (Isthmian) League Division One (South)
CLUB FOUNDED: 1892
PREVIOUS GROUNDS: Recreation Ground (1892–96); Ballon Meadow (1896–1912)

A leafy glade, and a church spire to the rear of the stand, Stag Meadow is every inch the sleepy home-counties ground.

The main stand, a standard pitched-roof design of its era, was erected in 1948 and has kept its good looks despite the insertion of the mandatory plastic seats. To the side and slightly back from the stand is the clubhouse and dressing-room block, housed in a frankly ugly building that is a fair blot on the landscape. On the opposite side is a substantial covered terrace, elongated in recent years. This stand's predecessor had the shortest of life spans, being blown down while the cement was still setting! Both ends have grassed banking dating from the mid-1970s as do the floodlights. The last work carried out on the ground came in the 1990s when flat, hard standing was laid to comply with the Isthmian League ground-grading requirements.

WINGATE & FINCHLEY

GROUND: Abrahams Stadium, Summers Lane, Finchley, London
CURRENT CAPACITY: 8,500
RECORD ATTENDANCE: 9,555 v. Bishop Auckland (FA Amateur Cup) 1950
YEAR BUILT/OPENED: 1930
CURRENT LEAGUE: Ryman (Isthmian) League Division One (North)
CLUB FOUNDED: 1991 merger on Wingate (1946) and Finchley (1874)
PREVIOUS GROUNDS: Long Lane; Green Man Field; Woodhouse Lane; Swan & Pyramids; Fallow Corner; Long Hill; Gun Meadow

The 1991 merger of two respected clubs saw the rejuvenation of the Summers Lane ground. Finchley, in existence since 1874, played on no less than eight different grounds until acquiring the ground in Summers Lane in 1929. The present stand was built a year later and in 1931 was adapted to provide a stand behind it for the adjacent rugby club. The two-sided stand is most unusual and is worth looking at from both sides. The rounded roof fascia is also most unusual and reminiscent of the old main stand at Mansfield Town's Field Mill ground. The 1960s was a good decade with the burgeoning supporter's club financing terracing, turnstiles and floodlights. The joining of forces with the predominantly Jewish Wingate club has seen steady improvements, with a new clubhouse bar and gymnasium opened and the pitch has been re-aligned closer to the main stand. The main stand has been painted and modernized and has never looked better.

WISBECH TOWN

GROUND: Fenland Park, Lerowe Road, Wisbech, Cambridgeshire
CURRENT CAPACITY: 3,800
RECORD ATTENDANCE: 8,004 v. Peterborough United (Midland League) 25/08/57
YEAR BUILT/OPENED: 1947
CURRENT LEAGUE: Jewson Eastern Counties League Premier Division
CLUB FOUNDED: 1920
PREVIOUS GROUNDS: Wisbech Park; Waisoken Rectory; Harecroft Road

Interestingly, in his autobiography former England International, Les Ferdinand, described Fenland Park as the most intimidating venue that he ever played at as a footballer. I can understand that sentiment, with its ample covered end terraces and its infamous dark, brooding cowshed, which was originally a farmyard barn. Packed full with hostile marauding Fenmen, I can imagine Ferdinand's reticence. Although it is only just over 50 years old,

Stag Meadow, Windsor & Eton

Fenland Park is one of those great venues that appears to be far older than it really is. The ground's original main stand was a timber affair that followed the club from their previous home at Harecroft Road. In the late 1980s this stand was condemned, demolished and replaced by a brand-new seated stand in late 1990. The club boasted such a fine ground with extensive cover, that, unusually, no improvements were required when Wisbech gained promotion back to the Southern League in 1997. However, their return to a higher grade was somewhat brief, ending in relegation back to the Eastern Counties League at the end of the 2001/02 campaign. On a historical note, the club's first ground at Wisbech Park is still used for local football.

WITHAM TOWN
GROUND: Spa Road, Witham, Essex
CURRENT CAPACITY: 2,500
RECORD ATTENDANCE: 800 v. Billericay Town (Essex Senior League) 1976
YEAR BUILT/OPENED: 1975
CURRENT LEAGUE: Ryman (Isthmian) League Division Two
CLUB FOUNDED: 1948
PREVIOUS GROUNDS: Crittall Athletic FC

The club were re-formed, after a long absence, in 1948 and played at Crittall Athletic's ground for many years. In 1964 the club began the hunt for a ground of their own. A suitable site was eventually found after an 11-year search when a field in Spa Road was made available to the club. The club progressed through

Abrahams Stadium, Wingate & Finchley

the Essex Senior League, gaining promotion to the Isthmian League in 1987. It has to be said that the current set-up is a little dull. The first building you see following the long, winding approach road is the excellent clubhouse. On through the turnstiles, the pitch surround incorporates an attractive wrought-iron gate. The only covered accommodation is on the far side and is a long, low-roofed stand with a section of seating. The rest of the ground is flat, hard standing, although a covered area behind one goal is on the agenda.

WITTON ALBION
GROUND: Wincham Park, Chapel Street, Wincham, Northwich, Cheshire
CURRENT CAPACITY: 4,500
RECORD ATTENDANCE: 3,940 v.

Kidderminster Harriers (FA Trophy) 13/04/91
YEAR BUILT/OPENED: 1989
CURRENT LEAGUE: Unibond (Northern Premier) League Division One
CLUB FOUNDED: 1887
PREVIOUS GROUNDS: Vicarage Field; Penny Lane; Central Ground

Witton Albion's home since 1989, Wincham Park on the outskirts of Northwich, can at best be described as functional. Unfortunately it does look like dozens of other grounds built in recent years and therefore has no individuality or character. It is the very antithesis of their much-missed Central Ground, a 10,000 capacity venue that was full of history and was ruthlessly demolished for a retail development. Wincham

275

Fenland Park, Wisbech Town

Park, or to give it its hideous sponsored name, 'The Bargain Booze Stadium', has everything a modern ground requires – ample seating, covered accommodation on all four sides, floodlights and plush social facilities. However a pretty unique feature is the Witton Albion Football Museum opened at the north end of the ground in May 2002. It houses a vast collection of Albion memorabilia, covering the club's hundred plus years of existence, lovingly displayed in purpose-built cabinets and is a real treat for fans of football history and development. Ironically Northwich Victoria's proposed new stadium is adjacent to Wincham Park, so bitter rivals could be grudging neighbours. Rumours of a merger between the two clubs continue to surface periodically.

WIVENHOE TOWN
GROUND: Broad Lane, Elmstead Road, Wivenhoe, Essex
CURRENT CAPACITY: 3,000
RECORD ATTENDANCE: 1,912 v. Runcorn (FA Trophy) 1990
YEAR BUILT/OPENED: 1978
CURRENT LEAGUE: Ryman (Isthmian) League Division One (North)
CLUB FOUNDED: 1925 as Wivenhoe Rangers
PREVIOUS GROUNDS: Spion Kop; Broomfield; Watchman's Meadow; Vine Farm; King George V Playing Field

In a rural and remote part of Essex, Wivenhoe's impressive home was a carrot field before the club bought the site for £2,500 in 1978. The clubhouse dates from their Essex Senior League days

Spa Road, Witham Town

and the first covered stand was erected for their promotion to the Isthmian League in 1986. The club was heavily backed financially and made it to the Premier Division at an impressive speed. In the rise to the top echelon, both ends of the Broad Lane ground were terraced and covered and a new main stand was erected opposite the older stand. The centre section was built and had seats installed, but while the end sections had the framework erected, the money ran out and the building work was never finished. The club managed to avoid bankruptcy, but tumbled back down the divisions. However, despite the hardship of recent years, the club have one of the finest venues in the county.

WOKING

GROUND: Kingsfield Stadium, Kingfield, Woking, Surrey
CURRENT CAPACITY: 6,000
RECORD ATTENDANCE: 6,000 v. Swansea 19/12/78 and Coventry 07/01/97 (both FA Cup)
YEAR BUILT/OPENED: 1922
CURRENT LEAGUE: Nationwide Football Conference
CLUB FOUNDED: 1889
PREVIOUS GROUNDS: Brewery Road; Pembroke Road; Hobb's Meadow

Kingsfield has an interesting mix of the old and new, especially since the opening in 1997 of the new Kingsfield End stand, which dwarfs any structure at the ground. The ground was opened in 1922 as was the existing main stand. There are two

Wincham Park, Witton Albion

additional stands on this side of the ground, the elder being erected in 1930. Little changed at the ground until the 1960s when floodlights and a new clubhouse were erected. In recent years the club have graced the highest reaches of the non-League game and the side opposite the stands has a modern pitch-length sweep of uncovered terracing. The carpark end is covered and has recently acquired seating. It is a sad fact of progress that the collection of three old stands will eventually be replaced, but until then they give an insight into the complete history of the ground. Over the road from Woking's ground is the home of Combined Counties League side Westfield.

WOKINGHAM TOWN
GROUND: Windsor & Eton FC
CURRENT CAPACITY: 4,500

RECORD ATTENDANCE: 155 v Windsor & Eton (League) 23/12/00
YEAR BUILT/OPENED: Ground-shared since 1999
CURRENT LEAGUE: Ryman (Isthmian) League Division Two
CLUB FOUNDED: 1875
PREVIOUS GROUNDS: Oxford Road; Wallington Road; Langborough Road; Finchampstead Road

After 93 years the last game was played at Wokingham Town's ageing, but endearing, Finchampstead Road ground on 1 May 1999. Crippling debts had forced the club to sell up and sign an initial three-season ground-sharing deal with Windsor & Eton. The old ground was always hemmed in by the railway line but this did not stop the erection in recent years of a new stand with the requisite plastic seating. This was in stark contrast to the small

Broad Lane, Wivenhoe Town

stand opposite that had stood defiantly since 1939, until battered into submission by the demolition team 60 years later. It had a brick base and pitched roof, with wooden tip-up seats. The clubhouse had an overhanging roof to provide extra cover, and there was also additional uncovered terracing. The record attendance at the ground was 3,473 for the Amateur Cup visit of Norton Woodseats in 1958. The prospect of the club ever returning to the town is looking remote, with little help from the council and opposition from various residents' groups.

WORCESTER CITY
GROUND: St George's Lane, Barbourne, Worcester, Worcestershire
CURRENT CAPACITY: 3,443

RECORD ATTENDANCE: 17,042 v. Sheffield United (FA Cup) 24/01/59
YEAR BUILT/OPENED: 1905
CURRENT LEAGUE: Dr Marten's (Southern) League Premier Division
CLUB FOUNDED: 1902 merger of Berwick Rangers and Worcester Rovers
PREVIOUS GROUNDS: Severn Terrace; Thorneloe; Flagge Meadow

Few grounds have been savaged so brutally by ground-grading requirements in recent years than Worcester City's St George's Lane Stadium. Home since October 1905, the ground now has a limited lifespan as the club actively search for a replacement site. The magnificent wooden Brookside Stand, erected in 1929, was condemned and eventually demolished in 1998, spelling an effective

Kingsfield Stadium, Woking

death knell for the ground. Since its demolition, the covered terrace known as the 'Cowshed' and built in 1906, sits awkwardly in one corner. The main stand, called the New Stand, something of a misnomer seeing as it was built in 1963, remains the ground's most useful building and was solely financed by the supporters' club. The present social club dates from 1972. Success in the late 1970s saw further improvements, including new terracing and floodlights. The future of St George's Lane is awaiting the outcome of planning permission sought by B&Q to build another giant warehouse store on the ground. Subject to approval, the DIY firm will part-fund the construction of a new stadium for Worcester City at Nunnery Wood.

WORKINGTON
GROUND: Borough Park, Workington, Cumbria

CURRENT CAPACITY: 2,500
RECORD ATTENDANCE: 21,000 v. Manchester United (FA Cup) 04/01/58
YEAR BUILT/OPENED: 1937
CURRENT LEAGUE: Unibond (Northern Premier) League Division One
CLUB FOUNDED: 1921 re-formation of a club formed in 1884
PREVIOUS GROUNDS: Lonsdale Park (1921–37 and 1986); Ellis Sports Ground (1937)

Borough Park is a real throwback to yesteryear and is much the same as it was during the club's lengthy spell in the Football League between 1951 and 1977. The club initially played at Lonsdale Park, the stadium adjacent to Borough Park, which is still in existence, albeit in a run-down state, for greyhound racing. For the 1937/38 season Workington moved to a new ground with tremendous assistance from the Borough Council, from where the ground takes its name. However the new ground was not quite ready and the first matches of the campaign were played on the Ellis Sports Ground. Interestingly this ground is still in use for sport by Workington RUFC. The magnificent brick-built main stand was opened in September 1937 and after the war the ash banking was replaced by concrete terracing and extensively covered to give a capacity of 20,000. The club also bought two railway carriages for use as refreshment huts. The floodlights, with unusually squat pylons, were erected in 1957. Twenty years later the club lost their League status in favour of Wimbledon and the Cumbrians begun a long period of struggle. Borough Park has essentially remained unchanged except for the 1986 closure of the main stand. It was deemed unsafe for spectators, so rather than lose all the facilities under the stand, the club simply 'beheaded' the stand and put a roof where the seating was once located. This meant that for five games in 1986/87, the Reds once again used the ancient Lonsdale Park for home games. A visit to Borough Park is a real nostalgia trip and this remote but beguiling football outpost remains a firm favourite for enthusiasts.

WORKSOP TOWN
GROUND: Babbage Way, off Sandy Lane, Worksop, Nottinghamshire
CURRENT CAPACITY: 3,000
RECORD ATTENDANCE: 1,503 v. Sheffield United (Friendly)
YEAR BUILT/OPENED: 1992
CURRENT LEAGUE: Unibond (Northern Premier) League Premier Division
CLUB FOUNDED: 1861
PREVIOUS GROUNDS: Netherton Road; Bridge Meadow; Central Avenue; Gainsborough Trinity FC

Worksop Town sold their Central Avenue ground in 1989, with plans for a new ground at only an embryonic stage. Within weeks the old stadium, home since 1893, had been levelled and tarmacked and was in use as a car park. The old ground was causing problems, as it shared one side with Worksop Cricket Club. The Northern Premier League's insistence on fully enclosed grounds meant Central Avenue's days were numbered. However, The Tigers had not planned for problems with the proposed new ground at Claylands Avenue. The application was turned down due to the lack of access and when plans were resubmitted with an access road replacing one side of the ground, the club were effectively placing one old three-sided ground with a brand-new three-sided ground. The plans were unsurprisingly withdrawn and Worksop began a three-season sojourn at Gainsborough Trinity's Northolme ground. The Tigers returned to the borough in 1992 when the local council provided a playing field site off Sandy Lane. The ground now has a clubhouse and grandstand and three remarkably narrow covered terraces. The current ground, albeit relatively modest, represents salvation for The Tigers who faced the real threat of extinction during their homeless years.

WORSBOROUGH BRIDGE MINERS WELFARE & ATHLETIC
GROUND: Park Road, Worsborough Bridge, Barnsley, South Yorkshire
CURRENT CAPACITY: 2,000
RECORD ATTENDANCE: 1,603 v. Blyth Spartans (FA Amateur Cup) 1971
YEAR BUILT/OPENED: 1947
CURRENT LEAGUE: Northern Counties East League Division One

Borough Park, Workington

CLUB FOUNDED: 1947 re-formation of a club formed in 1923
PREVIOUS GROUNDS: None

This club must surely have the longest name in senior football and possess a picturesque little ground. A fine view of this ground can be seen from the bridge over the River Dove on the main road through the village. The river flows down one side of the ground and opposite is the changing rooms, Welfare Hall and the main stand. The stand is given a little bit of individuality with a name board and unusual diamond-shaped holes on the roof support. Interestingly this is one of a very few grounds that hosts a miners welfare team but is not actually owned by the welfare. Instead Park Road was brought by the Athletic club in 1953 but leased to the Miners Welfare since 1959. There was

already grass banking on one side and in 1970 the main stand was cut into the bank. Floodlights came as recently as 1993 but the club will be hampered on a quest for higher-grade football by the sharing of the far end with the cricket club. Certainly the Northern Premier League would frown upon a three-sided ground. Park Road, however, is a pretty little venue and the record gate remains at the official figure of 1,603 for an Amateur Cup tie with Blyth Spartans although locals will tell you the true figure was nearer 2,500.

WORTHING

GROUND: Woodside Road, Worthing, West Sussex
CURRENT CAPACITY: 4,500
RECORD ATTENDANCE: 4,500 v. Depot Battalion Royal Engineers (FA Amateur

Park Road, Worsborough Bridge Miners Welfare & Athletic

Cup) 1908
YEAR BUILT/OPENED: 1889
CURRENT LEAGUE: Ryman (Isthmian)
League Division One (South)
CLUB FOUNDED: 1886
PREVIOUS GROUNDS: Homefield Park;
Beach House Park

Although Woodside Road has a modern outlook it has been home to Worthing since 1889. However, the original pitch was at right angles to the current orientation. The impressive brick-built main stand was erected in 1986 and replaced the burned-out shell of the old stand, gutted by fire just a fortnight before the Valley Parade Fire Disaster. Opposite the main stand is a steep bank with a modest cover dating from the mid-1970s. Floodlights came to Woodside Road in 1976 although the bulbs have since been upgraded. The ground's best feature, however, remains the main stand, which houses a boardroom and hospitality suite. The clubhouse is also well appointed and the supporters' club remains active having, in the past, been responsible for the volunteer labour that provided much of the terracing around the ground. Woodside Road remains a blueprint for potential Ryman League clubs.

Woodside Road, Worthing

Y

YEADING

GROUND: The Warren, Beaconsfield Road, Hayes, Middlesex
CURRENT CAPACITY: 3,000
RECORD ATTENDANCE: 3,200 v. Tottenham Hotspur (Floodlight Opener) 1991
YEAR BUILT/OPENED: 1984
CURRENT LEAGUE: Ryman (Isthmian) League Division One (North)
CLUB FOUNDED: 1961
PREVIOUS GROUNDS: Brookside Recreation Ground; Warren Park

As usual, the local council hindered the progress of Yeading in the late 1970s by dragging their heels in finding the club a suitable site for a new ground. The progressively minded club first applied for a new ground in 1978 but it would be six years before a site had been located, planning permission granted, and the new ground built. The ground was eventually opened in September 1984 and has developed into the ideal Ryman League venue. It has a spectacular two-storey clubhouse and a functional seated stand. There is another stand under the boardroom that is known as the Willie Barrett stand after a club stalwart. A rise up the Ryman League divisions saw a sizeable covered stand erected behind the goal. The floodlights were erected in 1991 and the match arranged to celebrate their inauguration remains The Warren's record attendance. Nowadays the club gain welcome

The Warren, Yeading

revenue by hosting QPR's reserve team. While The Warren has developed into a splendid arena, its progress has been mirrored by the demise and eventual demolition of neighbours Southall's Western Road ground.

YEOVIL TOWN
GROUND: Huish Park, Lufton Way, Yeovil, Somerset
CURRENT CAPACITY: 8,720
RECORD ATTENDANCE: 8,868 v. Rushden & Diamonds (Conference) 21/04/2001
YEAR BUILT/OPENED: 1990
CURRENT LEAGUE: Nationwide Football Conference
CLUB FOUNDED: 1897
PREVIOUS GROUNDS: Pen Mill (1895-1921), The Huish (1921-90)

Many tormented Football League sides shed no tears when the old Huish ground, with its horrendous slope, was sold to Bartlett Construction in 1990. The classic old ground, scene of many an FA Cup giantkilling, now lies under a Tesco's superstore, but The Glovers now boast a state-of-the-art stadium on the outskirts of the Somerset town. From the outside, the ground looks somewhat unprepossessing, but once inside the spectator can appreciate the size and practicality of the facility. Both sides of the ground are essentially identical, save for a few fixtures and fittings, such as the press box on one side, and for a time both open-end terraces were carbon copies of each other. However, in the summer of 2001 the symmetry was changed forever when the terrace was covered with considerable monetary assistance from the

Huish Park, Yeovil Town

Supporter's Club. The new ground has stretched the club financially over the last decade, as the total building costs far out-reached original estimates, but that said, the club now possess the best ground in non-League football and indeed many Football League clubs have cast an envious glance towards the Somerset town.

BIBLIOGRAPHY

The author readily acknowledges that without the books and publications listed below this volume would have been less interesting and less historically accurate. I heartily recommend all of the following for further reading.

The History Of Non-League Football Grounds by Kerry Miller (Paper Plane 1996)

The Football Grounds of Britain by Simon Inglis (Collins Willow 1983,1987,1996)

Official Centenary History of the Southern League by Leigh Edwards (Paper Plane 1993)

Non-League Directory by Tony Williams (Various Editions)

Groundtastic – The Football Grounds Magazine by Paul Claydon & Vince Taylor (Various Editions)

Northern Goalfields by Brian Hunt (The Northern League 1989)

Gone But Not Forgotten by Dave Twydell (Volumes 1 -20, Yore Publications 1992-present)

Rejected FC by Dave Twydell (Volumes 1,2 & 3, Yore Publications 1992 & 1995)

Denied FC by Dave Twydell (Yore Publications 2001)

Non-League by Bob Barton (Tyneside Free Press 1985)

A Pictorial Guide to The Jewson Eastern League by Paul Claydon & Vince Taylor (Groundtastic 1996)

Way Out West by Paul Claydon and Vince Taylor (Groundtastic 2000)

A Guide to the United Counties League by Paul Claydon & Vince Taylor (Groundtastic 2001)

Non-League Football Grounds of Kent by Mike Floate (Newlands 1995)

Non-League Football Grounds of Essex and East London by Peter Miles (Newlands 1996)

Non-League Football Grounds of the West Midlands by Colin Peel (Newlands 1996)

Non-League Football Grounds of Hertfordshire by Peter Miles (Newlands 1997)

Non-League Football Grounds of Dorset by Tim Lancaster (Newlands 1998)

Echoes Across Crown Meadow by Mike Pearce (1997)

Cressing Road – A 75 year History by Jon Weaver (Groundtastic 1998)

Wheel 'Em In – The Official History of Chelmsford City by Steve Garner (2001)

The History of Guiseley AFC by GL Wood (1994)

Gravesend & Northfleet, Golden Jubilee Yearbook by Paul Harrison (1996)

The History of Harlow Town by Colin Barratt (1998)

The History of Tiverton Town by Kerry Miller (1995)

The History of Walton & Hersham by Kerry Miller (1997)

South Shields – The Football League Years by George Thompson (Yore Publications 2000)

The Magpies – 100 Years of Penzance AFC by Greg Nicholas (1998)

The Kings Of Amateur Soccer by Chris Foote-Wood (1985)

An Intention To Play and The Journey From Tite's Field by Steve King (1992 and 1999)

Wheel 'Em In – The History of Bungay Town by Terry Reeve (1985)

Official History of Diss Town by Gary Enderby (1995)

Newmarket Town 1877–1977 by EJ Wybrew (Jomyra Press 1992)

History of Saffron Walden Town 1872–1980 by Paul Daw (1980)

Arlesey Town – The First Hundred Years by Malcolm Skillings & Tony Smith (1991)